DIMENSIONS OF FORGIVENESS

Psychological Research & Theological Perspectives

LAWS OF LIFE SYMPOSIA SERIES
VOLUME I, DIMENSIONS OF FORGIVENESS

from

A JOURNEY TO HOPE:

*A Research Workshop
to Launch the John Templeton Foundation's Program
to Encourage the Scientific Study of Forgiveness*

Hope College
Holland, Michigan
October 13, 1997

DIMENSIONS *of* FORGIVENESS

✦

Psychological Research &
Theological Perspectives

Edited by
Everett L. Worthington, Jr.

TEMPLETON FOUNDATION PRESS
PHILADELPHIA & LONDON

Templeton Foundation Press
Five Radnor Corporate Center, Suite 120
100 Matsonford Road
Radnor, Pennsylvania 19087

Printed in the United States of America

Library of Congress Cataloging-in-Publication Data

Dimensions of forgiveness : psychological research and theological
perspectives / edited by Everett L. Worthington.
    p.   cm. (Laws of life symposia series : v. 1)
    "A Journey to hope: a research workshop to launch the John
Templeton Foundation's program to encourage the scientific study of
forgiveness, Hope College, Holland, Michigan, October 13, 1997"—
    Includes bibliographical references and index.
    ISBN 1-890151-21-1 (hardcover : alk. paper)
    ISBN 1-890151-22-X (pbk. : alk. paper)
    1. Forgiveness — Congresses   2. Forgiveness — Religious
aspects — Congresses. I. Worthington, Everett L., 1946–   II. Series.
BF637.F67 D53   1998
155.2 — ddc21   98-37444
                                                         CIP

ISBN 1-890151-21-1 (hardcover)
ISBN 1-890151-22-X (paperback)

Designed by Gopa Design

Reason to rule, mercy to forgive:
The first is law, the last prerogative.

—John Dryden,
"The Hind and the Panther" (1687)

✦ Contents ✦

PART IV. FORGIVENESS IN PUBLISHED RESEARCH

PART V. FORGIVENESS IN FUTURE RESEARCH

✦ Preface ✦

THIS VOLUME ON FORGIVENESS is the first in a projected series of collected symposia presentations on research into the scientific foundations of effective living—how positive mindsets and virtues enhance the lives of individuals and, ultimately, the well-being of society. Future volumes in this *Laws of Life Symposia Series* will focus on optimism and hope, wisdom, and other life-changing positive states as viewed from various research perspectives.

This series of investigations begins with an exploration of the profound value of the multiple dimensions of forgiveness in our lives. In October, 1997, the John Templeton Foundation invited more than forty scholars to participate in a conference on the scientific study of forgiveness, entitled "A Journey to Hope: A Research Workshop to Launch the John Templeton Foundation's Program to Encourage the Scientific Study of Forgiveness," held at Hope College in Holland, Michigan.

Following the conference, more than one hundred researchers submitted proposals in response to a Request for Proposals. Sixty proposals were approved for funding, and twenty-nine have been guaranteed funding through the Campaign for Forgiveness Research. The Templeton Foundation's grant program is expected to initiate forgiveness research by both established and developing scholars, as well as to assist those researchers who are already embarked on such projects in expanding their investigations.

The speakers were asked to reflect on the present and future status of research into forgiveness from the perspectives of their particular interests. The individual articles were drafted from the presentations and circulated among all of the contributing authors, who then revised their work based on the feedback they received. This provided a rigorous peer review of each chapter.

All authors gratefully acknowledge the work of their colleagues, who have contributed to our collective thinking about this topic; however, all authors remain solely responsible for what they have written.

I commend this volume to those investigating forgiveness, not only to provide scholars with a sound research foundation, but also to provide the general knowledge and tools that can touch the lives and spirits of us all—at *our* foundation.

As Dryden said in the epigraph that begins this book, to forgive is our "prerogative." Indeed, it is one of the most life-affirming choices we can make.

Everett L. Worthington, Jr.

✦ Acknowledgments ✦

T HIS BOOK GREW from a conference of research scientists and theologians who came together for "A Journey to Hope" to share their ideas with one another. Of the forty participants, a handful were privileged to present their views on forgiveness and to receive the exciting reactions, thoughts, and ideas of the other distinguished participants. The majority of the contributors to this volume delivered their thought-provoking papers at this gathering. Following the presentations, the spirited conversations among presenters and nonpresenters alike enriched all who attended.

Many people collaborated to bring this book to fruition. My thanks go especially to Sir John Templeton, who generously supported this initiative with funding through the John Templeton Foundation. John M. Templeton, Jr. and Charles L. Harper, Jr. proposed the meeting and invited me to plan it. David Myers hosted the conference at, as he likes to say, "a place called Hope." Karyl Wittlinger of the John Templeton Foundation collaborated most helpfully with staff members at David Larson's National Institute for Healthcare Research (NIHR) to arrange the conference. Michael McCullough of NIHR (and a contributor to this volume) served as conference manager; his vision and handiwork made a substantial contribution to the day's success.

Dr. Harper believed that the proceedings should be written as chapters and recorded in a scholarly volume for the benefit of many current and future students of the exciting new field of forgiveness research. I was delighted to accept when he invited me to serve as the book's editor. Working with the contributors has been both enjoyable and edifying;

all authors met their deadlines and submitted critiques of their colleagues' work with thoughtfulness and professionalism. Pamela Bond of the Templeton Foundation Press has done a great deal of commendable work to transform the manuscripts into a coherent, attractive, readable book, and she deserves much of the credit for the quality of this volume.

The scientific study of forgiveness is only just beginning. I am indebted to the several pioneer researchers whose contributions are recorded in this work for blazing the trail. I also remain especially grateful for the foresight—and insight—of our generous benefactor, Sir John Templeton, through whose visionary ideas and generosity we have been stimulated to advance theology through the adventure of science using the "humble approach." This approach has enabled us to discover more about the psychological and theological dimensions of forgiveness.

The interdisciplinary enterprise presented in this volume is the mechanism by which we are exploring new possibilities for human reconciliation in many areas of life.

DIMENSIONS OF FORGIVENESS

Psychological Research & Theological Perspectives

✦ Introduction ✦

FOR THOUSANDS OF YEARS, people have practiced and studied forgiveness, both within religious and philosophical systems and as
part of their personal lives. However, the scientific study of forgiveness began only recently: Before 1985, only five studies investigating
forgiveness had been identified. In the thirteen years since then, more
than fifty-five scientific studies have been conducted to study forgiveness and to help people learn how to forgive,* as shown in the graph:

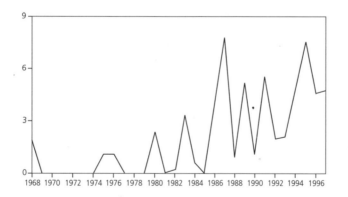

Figure 1
Graph showing the growth of scientific studies on forgiveness by year, 1968 to 1996.

What stimulus triggered this surging scientific interest in forgiveness?
Reflection on this subject might have been stimulated by the fall of
communism, which could have prompted people to reflect on how to

---

*For a summary of many of these studies, see McCullough, Exline, and Baumeister (Chapter 8).

forgive long-time enemies. It might have been spurred by the need to deal with increased racial tensions in communities and violent conflicts within nations—South Africa, Northern Ireland, Rwanda, the United States, and elsewhere. It might have been ignited by the budding communitarianism movement signaled by published works (e.g., Bellah, Madsen, Sullivan, Swidler, & Tipton, 1985; Etzioni, 1983, 1984), as well as a growing postmodern philosophy (Gergen, 1992).

While these and other factors have contributed to a zeitgeist that permits reflection on forgiveness, a simpler impetus may have been at work. *Forgive and Forget: Healing the Hurts We Don't Deserve*, published in 1984 by Lewis Smedes (who contributed Chapter 10 to this volume), has sold well in the United States and may have stimulated both the general public and practitioners of the helping professions to initiate programs to help us learn the value of forgiveness, as well as how to forgive.

The study of forgiveness has followed the example of many clinical research models. Beginning largely in the therapeutic realm, it spread to researchers who created and studied clinical protocols and then branched out into the basic scientific realm. Two notable exceptions to this pattern have been basic research by Enright (who contributed Chapter 6 to this book) on the development of reasoning about forgiveness, which he has shown to be similar across several cultures, and some of the social psychological research on topics related to forgiveness. For example, from the 1960s and early 1970s, research programs by numerous social psychologists have investigated revenge, blame, apologies, confession, and accounts of transgressions. Thus, the foundation for an integrated basic-applied scientific research effort—albeit one that is still emerging—has been laid.

Besides the growth in research, there is evidence that forgiveness is an especially meaningful topic today—both within the scientific community and in the larger world community:

✦ *The Journal of Family Therapy* recently published a special issue on forgiveness in family therapy (Vol. 20 [1998], No. 1).

✦ *MARRIAGE AND FAMILY: A Christian Journal* has collected articles for two special issues on forgiveness in the family (Vol. 2 [1999], Nos. 2 and 3).

✦ McCullough, Pargament, and Thoresen (who contributed to Chapters 8, 3, and 7, respectively, to this book) are collecting chapters for an edited book on forgiveness written by psychologists for Guilford Press (New York); it is expected to be published in August, 1999.

✦ Enright founded the International Forgiveness Institute (IFI), which has created a network of scientists, healing practitioners, and people within the general population who can share current information about forgiveness.

✦ Prime-time television—the newsmagazine *20/20*—featured appearances by DiBlasio, Enright, and Hargrave in a twenty-minute segment on forgiveness that originally aired on January 3, 1997.

✦ *The Chronicle of Higher Education* has also featured forgiveness (1998, July 17).

✦ Forgiveness has been relevant within countries plagued by strife. The Truth and Reconciliation Commission of South Africa has provided a focus for world attention on righting the wrongs of the apartheid era. Numerous stories of brutality and harm have been confessed in public hearings, and many have been forgiven by the victims' families, as well as by the victims themselves. And, even as the "Troubles" continue in Northern Ireland, the restoration of peace has brought about examples of forgiveness.

Although forgiveness is receiving attention within scientific journals and the media, the need for further investigation in this area seems to be outpacing the research being done. Throughout the world, hostility among people and perpetration of evil continues, and the need for forgiveness for political abuses is high. In the United States, violence seems to continue to rise as well. And in our homes, the conflict and hurtfulness between partners that often occur before the dissolution of a marriage—at current rates, almost half of the couples who marry can expect to divorce—argue for increased knowledge about how to repair such personal damage, for ourselves and for the most vulnerable victims, our children.

With interest and effort burgeoning, it is timely to examine the scientific research into forgiveness that can both inform and invite further scholarly dialog on the topic. The articles in this volume derived from the symposium presentations provide views on the role of forgiveness from different perspectives: *religion* (Marty considers Christianity in Chapter 1; Dorff reflects on Judaism in Chapter 2); *basic social processes* (Pargament and Rye examine the psychology of religion in Chapter 3; Baumeister, Exline, and Sommer investigate a social psychological point of view in Chapter 4); and *interventions* (Worthington explores his Pyramid Model in Chapter 5; Enright and Coyle explain Enright's process model in Chapter 6; Thoresen, Luskin, and Harris set forth general guidelines for conducting interventions in Chapter 7).

In addition to reviewing some of the directions in which research on forgiveness is heading, it is appropriate to consider the *published research*, and McCullough, Exline, and Baumeister provide an indexed collection of annotated research articles in Chapter 8. An earlier version of this annotated bibliography, less up to date and less focused specifically on forgiveness, was available on the John Templeton Foundation website (http://www.templeton.org, Grant Opportunities, Forgiveness RFP [1997]) to inform researchers in the field of extant empirical studies. The annotated bibliography in this volume includes several research studies that were not contained in the web version.

The symposium presentations on current topics, a review of the literature, and an analysis of *future research* provide a foundation for investigators who wish to study forgiveness scientifically. To round out the book, I provide a discussion in Chapter 9 that suggests an ambitious matrix of studies needed to create a vital science of forgiveness. We need to determine the psychological, social, and even physical mechanisms of forgiveness; study different levels (event, relationship, and personality) of forgiveness predictors; discern the social processes that occur in forgiveness within ongoing relationships; investigate the correlates and sequelae of divine forgiveness; and determine the best methods of intervening to promote forgiveness in the lives of individuals, dyads, families, communities, racial and ethnic groups, and countries.

The book closes with the stirring account in Chapter 10 by Smedes, who sets forgiveness into the larger context of reconciliation and hope. He not only describes the "stations" along the "journey" to hope (estrangement, forgiveness, reconciliation, hope), but also poignantly discusses the limitations of and quandaries in forgiving that continue to haunt us as individuals and societies. This chapter will, I hope, motivate researchers to carry out their studies with clear thinking and energy fueled by zeal, passion, and compassion.

REFERENCES

Bellah, R.N., Madsen, R., Sullivan, W.M., Swidler, A., & Tipton, S.M. (1985). *Habits of the heart: Individualism and commitment in American life*. New York: Harper & Row.

Etzioni, A. (1983). *An immodest agenda: Rebuilding America before the twenty-first century*. New York: McGraw-Hill.

Etzioni, A. (1984). *Capital corruption: The new attack on American democracy*. New Brunswick, NJ: Transaction Books.

Gergen, K. (1992). *The saturated self: Dilemmas of identity in contemporary life*. New York: Basic Books.

McCullough, M..E., Exline, J.J., & Baumeister, R.F. (1998). An annotated bibliography of forgiveness and related concepts. In E.L. Worthington, Jr. (Ed.), *Dimensions of forgiveness: Psychological research & theological perspectives* (pp. 193–317). Philadelphia, PA: Templeton Foundation Press.

Smedes, L.B. (1984). *Forgive and forget: Healing the hurts we don't deserve*. New York: Harper & Row.

PART I

✦

Forgiveness in Religion

CHAPTER I

The Ethos of Christian Forgiveness

Martin E. Marty[1]

ON THE USES OF CHRISTIAN HISTORY

"TELL ME, DADDY. What is the use of history?" the boy asked his father. Marc Bloch, one of the great French historians of the century, remembered his son's question years later when he was in a concentration camp during World War II. There, without library resources, he wrote a classic book-length response, *The Historian's Craft* (Bloch, 1964, p. 3).

The boy's query deserves to be recalled whenever an historian is asked to help provide a framework for an inquiry—in this case, for a scientific study of forgiveness. Not everyone who reads this collection of essays may think of himself or herself as an historian or as someone interested in history. Yet we all carry personal histories in our genes and memories. We also express cultural history along with it: Every word we speak, every phrase we repeat, is rooted in the earlier experience of a people. While it is not necessary to be self-conscious about this past at all times, there are occasions, such as now, when it is both valid and valuable.

Forgiveness has a history. Much of that history derives from Hebrew roots and Scriptures. Christians have adopted those roots and grafted on some nuances from the New Testament and myriad later Christian references. "Forgiveness" is one of those words—like "vocation," "covenant," and "stewardship"—that belongs to the culture of life in the sanctuary or is from a source in sacred Scriptures.

"What is the use of Christian history?" "Of Jewish history?" "Of any other source of history?," a practical generation asks. Historian G.J. Renier provided a clue in *History: Its Purpose and Meaning* (Renier, 1950, p. 26). While most of us are not historians in a formal or disciplined sense, and while most of what most historians do most of the time may seem to be of no immediate concern to us, there are moments when historians are consulted. Those moments, Renier says, match the human experience of "stopping to think." We make personal decisions based on personal memories. We make decisions in the contexts of culture when we are in crisis or when we want to delve deeply into a subject. This is one of those occasions.

"What is the use of Christian history" inside a pluralist culture, wherein millions of people are not Christians and many of them do not want to be? What is more, many in vestigially Christian cultures, and even in communions, may have short memories or never have heard many details about religious elements of the past; the details are said to be fading progressively from mind and view. Why bother with the longer story if the Christian tradition is fading for so many?

One answer could be that that tradition is being revivified for millions of others, and we have to understand them. Another would be that we have to comprehend something of a legacy even as it fades, as such lore helps to explain *us*. Here, one thinks of an instance related by Jaroslav Pelikan, historian of the Christian tradition, about Jerome Robbins, the great choreographer who died this year (1998) at the age of 79. When he was called to help produce *Fiddler on the Roof*, Robbins was informed that the show had to do with an aspect of the Jewish tradition that was receding and disappearing. He then insisted that he had to learn that tradition if he was to deal with it at all. So it is with our present inquiry, as we choreograph "scientific" studies of the effects of forgiveness.

To these reasons we might add that in a society where more than eighty percent of the polled public identifies with God in and through belief in Jesus Christ, the inherited associations of words such as "forgiveness" with God and with Christ need exploration. Scientific students of forgiveness will know more of what they are pursuing if they have some notion of religious (in this case, Christian) connections and sources.

In the Christian vocabulary, the concept of forgiveness, although often thought of in cognate terminological guises such as "justification," "redemption," "atonement," and "reconciliation," is certainly central. (Some contributors to this volume draw considerable distinctions between "forgiveness" and "reconciliation." In the New Testament, while each has its nuances, forgiveness always leads to reconciliation, and reconciliation results from mutual experiences of forgiveness. They cannot, finally, be separated.)

One hesitates to condense into digests and single concepts the almost infinitely complex religious traditions, especially someone else's. Yet if some say Buddhism = suffering, Islam = submission, Judaism = *Shema Israel*, then a good candidate in the present case (although, as we shall see, Christians will not want or dare to adopt an exclusive attitude about their point of view) might well be Christianity = forgiveness. One is called to the Christian community or church to experience forgiveness from God and a consequent awareness and reality of a "new creation" or "the new being." The consequence of this experience is that the divine version somehow inspires forgiveness among humans.

The preceding paragraph demands cautionary reminders. The "equal signs" model presented is an oversimplified one; actually, other attributes can be included to the right of each sign. Islam, Judaism, Buddhism, and other faiths discuss and teach "suffering," and most religions teach obedience to the will of God—Islam does not have a monopoly on "submission." Likewise, Christians are taught to be obedient to the God of Israel. And forgiveness is a tenet spread through many religions; indeed, it does not even demand a religious context in the first place.

The "equal signs" model suggests that how one picks up the first beat or puts down the tapping foot determines much of what follows. For Christians, the concept of divine forgiveness, mediated through humans, is one form of the love that should characterize the full life in the community and beyond.

So, Christians learn from others, including social scientists (as in the present venture), because they do not believe that they alone experience human—or, for that matter, necessarily divine—forgiveness. One respondent to an interviewer several decades ago, after having set forth the themes of his faith tradition, was asked whether his fellow believers thought that theirs was the only true faith. He answered something like "Yes, but they don't believe they are the only ones who have it" (Rosten, 1975, p. 165). So many might answer, in some phrasing or other, in the present instance—although I have not been authorized to speak for all Christians and certainly lack the credentials for doing so.

It may be appropriate to illustrate from my own confession within Christianity—Lutheranism—the centrality of forgiveness. Lutheranism is one among many denominations that claims to put forgiveness at or near the center. For fifty years, I have reflected on a very small book on this point, *Our Calling*, written in 1909 by a Swedish Lutheran bishop, Einar Billing. He noted that Martin Luther's own thoughts do not lie alongside each other like pearls on a string, but that they all, "as tightly as the petals of a rosebud, adhere to a common center, and radiate out like the rays of the sun from *one* glowing core, namely, the gospel of the forgiveness of sins." Billing went on, "Never believe that you have a correct understanding of a thought of Luther before you have succeeded in reducing it to a simple corollary of the thought of the forgiveness of sins" (Billing, 1947, p. 7).

The same might be said of the apostle Paul, author of so much of the New Testament; or Saint Augustine, who had much to do with the shaping of the West; or medieval Catholicism, with its intricate system of sacraments, especially penance; or most Protestant Reformation-era movements; or modern evangelicalism. Many of these surround the experience and idea of forgiveness with supportive and corollary notions. Those who make so much of forgiveness at the center of faith, however, also are aware of risks that go with this theological and practical theme. Thus, Billing himself noted that "if there be a weakening at this all-important point" whence discipline and ethics issue from forgiveness, "there will be a slackening all along the line." He then added a cultural judgment: "Slackness is the hereditary sin of Lutheranism, and with the exception of Greek Catholicism, there is nothing more slack than slack Lutheranism" (Billing, 1947, p. 35). Representatives of other traditions might want to challenge Billing by citing their own lineage as competitors in the "slackness" competition.

A modern Lutheran, Dietrich Bonhoeffer, who made so much of divine and human forgiveness all the way to his end in a concentration camp, worried about what he called "cheap grace," but that did not deter him from speaking of grace expressed through forgiveness (Bonhoeffer, 1948, p. 38). A modern Anglican, poet W. H. Auden, provided a dramatic illustration of the risks that go with forgiveness, risks that need to be assessed by those who measure forgiveness in personal life and culture using the instruments of social and other science. In *For the Time Being: A Christmas Oratorio*, Auden gives voice to King Herod after the visit of the Magi, the wise men who announced that grace and forgiveness had entered the world and Herod's realm with the birth of the child Jesus:

> Today, apparently, judging by the trio who came to see me this morning with an ecstatic grin on their scholarly faces, the job [of undercutting authority, discipline, and standards] has been done. "God has been born," they cried, "we have seen him ourselves. The World is saved. Nothing else matters."
>
> One needn't be much of a psychologist to realize that if this rumour is not stamped out now, in a few years it is capable of diseasing the whole Empire, and one doesn't have to be a prophet to predict the consequences if it should....
>
> Justice will be replaced by Pity as the cardinal human virtue, and all fear of retribution will vanish. Every corner-boy will congratulate himself: "I'm such a sinner that God had to come down in person to save me. I must be a devil of a fellow." Every crook will argue: "I like committing crime. God likes forgiving them. Really the world is admirably arranged" (Auden, 1976, pp. 303–04).

Say what one will, forgiveness survives as a guiding principle in our lives. It remains an honored theme in culture, an element that can be the subject of what Catholic theologian Karl Rahner called the "selective retrieval" that must occur whenever people want to plumb a complex tradition.[2] Here the mode of retrieving is historical.

Using British philosopher Michael Oakeshott's distinction of various "modes" ("arrests in human experience") and R.G. Collingwood's elaboration of them, we are restricted as historians to a method that confines itself to viewing the world *sub specie praeteritorum*.[3] This means that the differentia in question in this discipline is "the attempt to organize the whole world of experience in the form of the past."

People in the act of being religious may reflect on stories that come from the past, but by that act they are not being historians. Collingwood called theirs "the practical mode" and saw it pursued "*sub specie voluntatis*. In that case, the world is seen as a system of acts, each modifying 'what is' so as to bring it into harmony with what ought to be." For example, the religious impulse is not to be content with a review of the past, but would change someone or other from being "unforgiven and unforgiving" to being "forgiven and forgiving."

Those in the present study who pursue the subject of forgiveness scientifically will, in the views of Oakeshott and Collingwood, do so in another mode that commits them to other methods. (No one is "pure" in respect to modes; as full human beings, we work with numerous "arrests in experience," and we could not avoid doing so if we tried. But in respect to the refinement of disciplines and the definition of qualifications, we do not find ideas from one mode traveling well to another.)

So for the moment we concentrate on the observation that "science is the world *sub specie quantitatis*: Its differentia is the attempt to organize the world of experience as a system of measure" (Oakeshott, 1933, p. 163). The scientific community in this study includes some that measure brain waves and blood systems in chimpanzees. Others concentrate on appraising the physical health of the stressed-out unforgiving. Still others count the numbers of people who adhere to this or that religious system that stresses forgiveness or does not. Their colleagues may measure the psychological effects of forgiveness and reconciliation. In many accounts of what used to be called "the warfare of science and theology," these inquiries would have represented a threat to Christian faith and community. Now only certain conservative Christians would perceive them that way. Today there is a tendency to welcome insight—whatever its source—and to do a critical analysis when the returns are in, rather than to discourage it before the outset of scientific inquiry.

We who as historians are confined to the *sub specie praeteritorum* mode and the methods that go with it can appreciate the scientific modalities. They bring forth data that becomes part of the historian's story. But when historians make religious proposals, which as human beings they have a right—and perhaps an obligation—to do, they are mixing categories, stepping out of their mode, and asking history to do what it cannot do. We concentrate on exploring the past, finding it potentially "useful" in its own contexts and as one among numerous "arrests in human experience."

A QUATRITARIAN ORGANIZATION
OF THE CHRISTIAN REALITY

In what follows, I shall speak regularly of forgiveness in the Christian tradition, not so much as a doctrine, although countless have crystallized it as such, but as an *ethos*. Here it is used in the dictionary senses that go back to the Greeks, and especially to Aristotle, for whom the word "ethos" correlates with our word "character." Thus, in the dictionary, ethos is the "disposition, character, or fundamental values peculiar to a specific person, people, culture, or movement."[4] This ethos is apparent in the context of a quaternity of testimonies, experiences, or realities. Three of them match the "persons" of the Divine Trinity, and the fourth is the human creature, especially viewed *sub specie voluntatis* or *moris* or *fidelis*, which means in the context of the will or morals or faith. Within the context of the Christian community, the human individual (or the community itself) is not so much an agent as a respondent or transmitter of divine activity.

The concept of forgiveness in Christian creed issues first from the ethos of God, the "Father" (and "Mother," if one wills), as portrayed in the Hebrew Scriptures, the New Testament, and subsequent Christian writings. The second context relates to the ethos of Jesus Christ, the "Son," the rabbi from Nazareth who is considered the exalted Lord—in creedal terms, the Second Person of the Trinity. The third connects the theme of forgiveness to the "Holy Spirit," the Third Person of the Trinity, and thus to the holy Christian church. Finally, the human agent, the "anthropological" theme in theology and Christian practice, follows.

This is not the moment to review all aspects of Trinitarian thought or to defend the choice of the term in the face of those who remind us of the obvious: Although the concept is anticipated (e.g., in narratives such as Matthew 28:19), the word "Trinity" does not appear in the Scriptures. The word is a later invention. The Greek philosophical framework made it more nearly comprehensible to the believing community and those around it long ago, when "person" meant something different from what it means today. In earlier Christianity, the Greek word *hypostasis*, which means "substance," came to also mean "individual reality"; as such, it came to be applied to Jesus as an "individual reality" or "person" in the Divine Trinity. This usage caused confusion then as it does now because "person" is simply identified with the human person and personality. We are further reminded that not all parts of the Christian community use explicit creeds or ever use the term "Trinity." Add to this the understanding that even the greatest contributors to Christian thought spoke of it as a mystery, for which or for whom no concept or word, including "Trinity," was worth much more than saying nothing at all.

Why should Christians think "Trinitarianly"? The best answer is that most *do* think thus, although often reflexively, unself-consciously, and without thinking of such approaches as formulas. Here we stress this approach because, in short compass, we are able to give some balance to main Christian themes as they interrelate. It is also quite possible that if all the relevant sciences are brought to bear on the subject, they are likely to come up with humanistic or secular analogs to what the Christian stresses under various Trinitarian categories.

Those who are uneasy with the term and tradition of the Trinity, which they are free to be even though the encyclopedias and dictionaries of religion almost always describe it as the basic teaching or doctrine of Christianity, might think of it here as a way of organizing the Christian tradition and present reality.

What such an approach does is ensure that talk about human forgiveness in this tradition is always connected with the divine authorization and experiences connected with it. The Christian faith is theocentric, but in a peculiar way; it has a distinctive ethos that sets it apart from, say, Judaism or Islam, which are also theocentric and monotheistic. Describing those in the secular culture of the 1960s that wanted to claim the mantle of the prophetic, novelist Saul Bellow is reported to have said that being a prophet is nice work if you can get it—but sooner or later you have to say the word "God." In respect to the theme of forgiveness, the Christian tradition says "God" sooner—virtually at once.

Trinitarian Forgiveness Themes and God as "Abba"

What does forgiveness mean when it is connected with the one Jesus called "Abba" (Father)? What is the ethos of this God and hence of forgiveness issuing from this Holy One? The Christian tradition, by adopting—some would say seizing—the canon of the Hebrew Scriptures and choosing or claiming it as its own, took over all that these Scriptures (what Christians came to call "the Old Testament") had said about a forgiving God. We leave to Elliot Dorff (see Chapter 2) an explanation from inside Judaism of what this means to Jews in their reading of the Scriptures. Here, let it be said that the witness is thus consistent. As Israel experiences the Holy One, this God does not "remember" iniquities, but chooses out of *chesed*, steadfast love, to forgive the individual and the community. In Exodus 34, Yahweh appears to Moses on Mount Sinai and discloses the divine ethos as "abounding in steadfast love and faithfulness, keeping steadfast love for the thousandth generation, forgiving iniquity and transgression and sin" (Exod. 34:6–7, New Revised Standard Version [NRSV; cited hereafter]). Henceforth, biblical characters make their appeal to the divine character as forgiving.

In Jewish eyes, Christians misrepresented the Jewish ethos of this God, and hence of forgiveness, whenever they claimed that Jews confined God to being the lawgiver and judge, and whose fuller ethos was realized only when God was seen "in Christ." But whatever wrenching and distortion occurred, as it must when a canon is thus taken over into a somehow different faith or what Martin Buber would call "type of faith,"[5] the consistent theme of a God who does not remember, who forgets iniquity, wants to forgive, and is, in fact, forgiving, is taken over into earliest and consequent Christian witness.

In contemporary studies, most Christian scholars have tended to move from themes of exclusivity. God, as witnessed to in the Hebrew Scriptures, forgives Jews. There is less impulse than before, except in groups with fundamentalist tendencies, to try to claim a monopoly on forgiveness, including divine forgiveness. Christians know that other fellow monotheists, Jews and Muslims in particular, are confused or offended by witness to a divine Trinity or to the idea that God can be incarnate in Jesus. This is not the place to address such issues, except to say that the forgiveness Christians claim and experience *through* Jesus is the same as forgiveness from God as revealed in the Hebrew Scriptures. There may be new modes of expressing it and new means of access to the divine forgiving grace, but God is God and divine forgiveness is divine forgiveness.

Søren Kierkegaard somewhere said that for this God to be creator of the cosmos out of the chaos was easy; the difficult, and even most miraculous achievement lay in the fact that this Holy One could forgive the sinner and make a new creation out of the fallen old one by that act. It is this mysterious and miraculous activity and ethos that is central to all Christian activities: confession, prayer, preaching, the sacramental acts, and the works of justice and mercy that are to issue from the community and into and through individual lives.

The reason we choose or are obliged to see the Christian tradition behind forgiveness as Trinitarian and not "merely" theistic has to do with the impulse it gives us to find in God's self a paradigm and enabler of human actions connected with forgiving. In a book-length elaboration of the Trinitarian theme, into whose ramifications and implications we need not follow the author in every detail, L. Gregory Jones, in his book *Embodying Forgiveness,* said

> that the overarching context of a Christian account of forgiveness is the God who lives in trinitarian relations of peaceable, self-giving communion and thereby is willing to bear the cost of forgiveness in order to restore humanity to that communion in God's eschatological Kingdom. That is, in the face of human sin and evil, God's love moves toward reconciliation by means of costly forgiveness. In response, human beings are called to become holy by embodying that forgiveness through specific habits and practices that seek to remember the past truthfully, to repair the brokenness, to heal divisions, and to reconcile and renew relationships (Jones, 1995, p.xii).[6]

"Relationships" is the key word here, for Trinitarian thinking as it derives from biblical witness sees the three "persons" of the one God in dynamic "internal" relationships of self-giving, self-receiving, and perpetual externally expressed love.

Trinitarian Forgiveness Themes and God in Jesus Christ

Consistently, Jesus of Nazareth, as depicted in what some scholars call "memory-impressions" of disciples and their contemporaries and what Christians see as divinely inspired messages called *Gospels*, witnesses to this "Abba." In such stories and testimony, Jesus connects forgiveness with God. But he is also seen offending those who were sincere and devoted in their thinking that the ability and authority to forgive belongs to God alone.

Rather than treat all this doctrinally, most Christians have relied on the stories in the New Testament Gospels to inspire, regulate, measure, and recall what forgiveness was, is, and is to be in their community and in their lives. To detail all of the references to forgiveness in connection with the ethos of Jesus in the Gospels would require a book unto itself. But the whole subject will not make sense without reference to some of the sayings and stories that serve both as paradigms and determiners of parameters in Christian witness and impulse.

A decisive scene occurs in Matthew 9:2–8, where Jesus faces a paralyzed person brought for healing and utters, "Take heart, son! Your sins are forgiven." Some scribes called this blasphemy, but Jesus says of himself that "the Son of Man has authority on earth to forgive sins" *and* uses that authority to heal. Here and elsewhere, Jesus claims for himself what had been God's privilege and prerogative alone — to forgive sins. So the crowds, or most people within them, are pictured as subsequently recognizing this authority and divine connection or manifestation, however offensive it might be in the eyes of others around him and them.

This theme of forgiveness courses through the many snapshots of Jesus in action or word. The parable of the great debtor is typical (Matt. 18:21–35). A forgiven debtor, relieved of a vast amount of obligation, turns around and refuses to forgive another who owes him little and is condemned because the "other" is a brother and the two share the same forgiving God as Father. The condemnation is not a capricious statement, but something that naturally flows from the debtor's misunderstanding or ignorance of the ethos of God as witnessed to and revealed by Jesus.

Similarly, in what is probably the best known parable, that of the prodigal son, the father in the story has been waiting to let loose with the dynamics of forgiveness and shows this to be the case as the son returns. The elder brother, who had stayed home and never strayed, is portrayed alongside the "unmerciful servant" of the story in Matthew 18 as one who is so preoccupied with other ways of looking at reality that he cannot forgive or enjoy forgiveness and reconciliation (Luke 15:11–32).

Another familiar story is that of a woman "taken in adultery," a narrative that is not present in the most recognized ancient texts and is therefore reduced to a small italicized statement in most new translations. But it is still "canonical" in that it parallels the paradigmatic canonical gospel cases in the way it represents Jesus and the manner in which it sticks in the Christian mind. Jesus unhesitatingly and without qualification forgives her and challenges only the "sinless" ones — thus ruling out everyone — to cast the first stone.

The Sermon on the Mount frames sayings of Jesus as calling for forgiveness and commanding that disciples should not judge others (Matt. 5–7; see specifically Matt. 5:21–26, 6:9–15, 7:1–5,). In the Lord's Prayer (Matt. 6:9–13), the mirror, impulse, and instrument for prayer by the community, forgiving is the *only* human action; the rest of the prayer calls for God to act apart from human participation. On the cross, Jesus does what anti-Semitic Christians never do: He "forgives" those among the Jews, the Romans, and others, even though they are killing him. Dozens of stories about Jesus and scores of his sayings in the Gospels consistently match this sample.

In a pluralist society, Jews can find Jesus—not the rabbi, but the Second Person of the Trinity (and hence disruptive to their monotheism)—to be the remembered agent who inspires the anti-Semitism of the ages. He is thus and will remain "offensive" and "scandalous." Christians will protest, explaining that the problem lies in what believers through centuries have made, by way of misinterpretations, of the Jesus of gospel stories. But the negative image remains in most Jewish eyes and minds.

Muslims locate Jesus among the prophets and are equally offended when told by believers in Jesus that, as Christians, they see him as divine—but in ways that do not violate monotheism. Millions of others do not share the faith in Jesus the forgiver, the Jesus that Christians find normative and consuming in his power to attract and serve as a motivator and a model for action. But they may recognize in sensitive and forgiving Christian neighbors the positive effects of a faith they do not share. And Christians in turn, when they are sensitive to the different commitments they make to their neighbors who do not share their faith, are called to deal with all others, even as they are to relate to fellow members of their community—which means as forgivers.

The "scientific study of forgiveness" will measure some of the ways this ethos of forgiveness in Christ offends and inspires Jews, Muslims, and others and where it is visible in the actions of the Christian community. It is possible that findings of such measurement and assessment can help Christians gain a better name among the minorities in our culture whom they may have offended and among whom they may still have a bad name. Or, if such findings indicate that Christians have a long way to go, they will have a charter for reform and revision. Throughout, it will be important to be very clear about the terms in questionnaires and studies; the terms themselves have often been confusing and have led to unnecessary misunderstandings and polemics.

Coda: Many of the sayings of Jesus in the Gospels and many of the writings of Paul are so concerned with the actions of the members of the believing community toward one another that they can breed a sense of exclusiveness. That is, they seem to have little regard for forgiving others who are not part of the company of believers. But there is no logical or theological contradiction in taking the commands to forgive to others beyond the believing community. Divine forgiveness may well be the model for forgiveness by Christians, but most theologies also see God acting where God is not explicitly recognized. One might say that "humanistic forgiveness" is always a plus in human relations. Humans can also model the forgiveness ethos to others without invoking the divine or consciously imitating it.

Trinitarian Forgiveness Themes and the Holy Spirit
Within the Christian Community

Speaking of "the believing community" leads to witnessing to the Third Person of the Trinity, the Holy Spirit. The Apostles' Creed, one of the most ancient and certainly the most widely used of all Christian creeds in the Western churches, connects Spirit and forgiveness in community: "I believe in the Holy Spirit, the holy Catholic church, the communion of saints, the forgiveness of sins." Forgiveness in the Hebrew Scriptures occurred within and affected the whole community—the *Qelal Yahweh*, the congregation of Yahweh. Christians took over that concept in the *ekklesia*, the "called out" community of the forgiven and forgivers. Thus, in ways hard to recall in the modern world, where purely individualistic expression of Christianity is so common, the New Testament words about forgiveness were perceived as issuing from, in, and to the believing community. Thus, the community's distinguishing character was derived from the ethos of God, of God in Christ, and of God the Holy Spirit.

In John 20:22–23, for example, Jesus is depicted thus: "When he had said this, he breathed on them and said to them, 'Receive the Holy Spirit. If you forgive the sins of any, they are forgiven them; if you retain the sins of any, they are retained.'"

Texts in the synoptic Gospels, especially Matthew 18, give glimpses of the earliest Christian community as a context in which the dynamics of forgiveness begin to be routinized in authority patterns. Speaking of forgiveness, Jesus is heard saying, "Truly I tell you, whatever you [plural] bind on earth will be bound in heaven. And whatever you [plural] loose on earth will be loosed in heaven" (Matt. 18:18). The holy, later called sacramental, acts that are almost universal in the Christian church, especially baptism and the Lord's Supper (called variously Holy Communion, the Eucharist, or Mass), connect with and are portrayed in the texts as instrumental in the act of forgiving sins.

Why should Jesus be baptized, John the Baptist asks, as he is in no need of forgiveness? The connecting of baptism with forgiveness is made clear in Matthew 3:13–15. John has been baptizing people after calling them to repentance and confession of their sins. So when Jesus presented himself, John said, "I need to be baptized by you, and do you come to me?" The gospel writer pictures this puzzlement of John the Baptist because Jesus had no need of repentance or confession, and thus of forgiveness. Jesus simply said, "Let it [the baptism] be so now; for it is proper for us in this way to fulfill all righteousness."

In the letters of Paul, as in Romans 6:1–4, the apostle associated sin with life before or apart from baptism. Baptism identifies the sinner with Christ; after baptism or in connection with it, the believer walks "in newness of life," the forgiven life.

Jesus also asked the disciples to continue to share the eucharistic meal into the future "for the forgiveness of sins" (Matt. 26:26–28). In Matthew 16:19, Jesus, when speaking to the disciples, said to Peter that he was giving him "the keys of the kingdom," so that "whatever you bind on earth will be bound in heaven, and whatever you loose on earth will be loosed in heaven." Catholic Christianity identified this act and word with the authority given to Peter and through him to the apostles and their successors. If they forgave a penitent, the penitent would be forgiven; but if they did not extend forgiveness, the penitent would be "bound" and thus excluded from heaven. This understanding naturally led to abuses in the church of the Middle Ages, which came to be tied to empire and civil authority and was an instrument for garnering and holding church power.

The scientific study of forgiveness will have to pursue the ways it connected for centuries and still may connect with patterns of authority and often of dominance. In such cases, ecclesiastical strictures and instrumentalities all but obscured the simpler acts of forgiveness within the community and among the individuals who made it up. All of them were supposed to forgive and be forgiven by one another and be given grace so they could accept forgiving and forgiveness as gifts.

It will not be difficult to measure through history many of the effects of confession, penance, and other measures and agencies; to count the numbers of confessors in some circumstances; and to weigh the significance of church action. The psychologists, and especially social psychologists, in our scholarly company can view *sub specie quantitatis* some dimensions of the ethos exemplified in the community of forgiveness "under the Holy Spirit" and thus the divine ethos exemplified in "the

holy Catholic church" in its myriad expressions. They will do this by
close-up study of congregations and other communities that are torn
by conflict or have come to reconciliation. Or they can engage in ethno-
graphic and biographical witness, wherein is revealed the understanding of the unforgiven versus the forgiven, the unforgiving against the
forgiving, in matched contexts.

All of these realizations in contemporary life appear against the background of controversies over historic reform movements in the church
that challenged the hegemony of authorities as forgivers or withholders
of forgiveness.

Reference to the community of forgiving and forgiveness will help
scientific scholars study a most problematic element in the Christian
legacy. I refer to the reality of collective guilt, the injunctions to engage
in communal repentance and return, and the potential realization of
communal forgiveness as it affects individuals. Here, Christian history
will help inform discussions of forgiveness in respect to experiences
such as the legacy of slavery, the placement of Native Americans on
reservations, the tragedy of the Holocaust and Christian guilt, and other
troublesome events.

Quatritarian Forgiveness Themes and
the Ethos of the Believer Who Embodies Forgiveness

Jones, who went into Trinitarian implications more than we can here,
set forth his argument in *Embodying Forgiveness* (Jones, 1995). With that
title, he picked up the most ancient of Christian themes, one that courses
through the scriptural canon and the life of the community through the
ages. Let me quote him once more as he sets forth his program, one with
which I concur as an accurate representation of a major, if not the normative, expression of this aspect of "the phenomenology of forgiveness"
(my phrase):

> Most fundamentally. . .forgiveness is not so much a word spoken,
> an action performed, or a feeling felt as it is an embodied way of
> life in an ever-deepening friendship with the Triune God and with
> others. As such, a Christian account of forgiveness ought not simply

or even primarily be focused on the absolution of guilt; rather, it ought to be focused on the reconciliation of brokenness, the restoration of communion—with God, with one another, and with the whole Creation. Indeed, because of the pervasiveness of sin and evil, Christian forgiveness must be at once an expression of a commitment to a way of life, the cruciform life of holiness in which we seek to "unlearn" sin and learn the ways of God, and a means of seeking reconciliation in the midst of particular sins, specific instances of brokenness.

Further. . .forgiveness must be embodied in specific habits and practices of Christian life. . . .Learning to embody forgiveness involves our commitment to the cultivation of specific habits and practices of the Church. . . .Indeed, just as Aristotle emphasized the importance of learning a "craft" for learning how to live, so there is a craft of forgiveness that Christians are called to learn from one another, and particularly from exemplars, as we seek to become holy people (Jones, 1995, p. xii).

Jones aspires, as I would in a longer essay, to "provide a theological analysis" (mine would be historical) that is at the same time "social, political, philosophical, cultural, and psychological," a fivefold charter for the scientific study of forgiveness. I contend that there is a distortion in his treatment, what looks to be a false polarization. He poses theology against therapy, inventing a therapeutic mindset, or *habitus*, that must oppose the evangelical reality and divine activity. Such a polemic is unnecessary, even if it helps him define the theological case. In biblical contexts, forgiveness by God or God's human instruments almost always is shown in transactions that we would call therapeutic, with therapeutic effect.

The discussion by Lewis Smedes (see Chapter 10) may lead some readers to scratch their heads and wonder where Jones got his negative interpretation or why he felt called to offer it. The theological theme has an independent integrity and can stand association with all manner of practical corollaries—and our scientific studies of forgiveness should bear that out. Having said all that, it should be noted that Jones's exploration is one of the most expansive and searching considerations of the

Trinitarian theme in forgiveness and the relational theme within the Trinity.

We can conclude by pointing in several directions, using the word "measure."

Socially, one measures the ethos of the believer as he or she relates to the neighbor, the other. The question is, What difference does forgiveness or nonforgiveness make in social relations?

Politically, the scientist appraises and measures the implications for the *polis* (the human city) of the presence of a community within that claims to be made up of individuals who embody forgiveness and engage in practices of reconciliation. What difference does forgiveness or nonforgiveness make in political relations in a violent and often unforgiving, irreconcilable world?

Philosophically, one measures the logic and ideal expressions that explicate the ethos and actions, behaviors and practices, of individuals and asks, What difference does forgiveness or nonforgiveness make in the context of human systems and ideas about them?

Culturally, the observer measures the images and symbols, the artifacts and gestures, through which forgiveness is enacted—whether by "fine" artists who leave great cultural deposits or the ordinary people who are most expressive of an ethos.

Psychologically, we measure the effects on the human psyche when individuals, whether in Christian community or not, withhold forgiveness, shroud their other emotions in anger, and live lives of alienation. *Or*, on the other hand, we measure the effects when they embody forgiveness and experience freedom and release—freedom being the consistent corollary and outcome of both forgiving and being forgiven. This part of our scientific probe would lead into the "therapeutic" dimensions that Jones mistrusted and that Smedes, to my taste, connects so well with the Trinitarian ethos and habitus.

All kinds of corollary themes and arguments can issue from such inquiries and accents. Notable among them will be the scientific study, based in philosophical inquiry, of whether Jesus and Aristotle can easily mix and what the effects of such mixing are and would be. That is, to frame the question of ethos another way, Is forgiving one of the virtues? Is it the *core* virtue? Or does developing the habits of forgiving

complicate biblical understandings of forgiveness as an often spontaneous, surprisingly eruptive grace? Psychologists and sociologists will
have good reason to explore all of that, knowing that they tread on theologians' soil as they pose the alternatives.

Other themes that used to be called part of the doctrine of man, and
today are best called anthropological, will also emerge in scientific study
and will connect with the Trinitarian ethos. Is the human good or bad?
Is human nature neutral? Are humans "born good," or are they descended
from particularly vicious and violent simian strains? What are the effects,
in practice, of efforts to embody the results of baptism as participation
in "a new creation" and of seeing the believer as "a new creature," forgiven and forgiving? How does the Christian community measurably
seek to effect ways that cause believers to hold grudges, as Christian
communities often do, or conversely to issue forgiveness in freedom,
because it is so crucial?

These and other corollaries of forgiveness will emerge in the dialec-
tic among scientists as they pursue their work *sub specie quantitatis*; in the
face of ancient Scriptures and the experience and testimony of Christian as well as other believing communities through the ages; and by
studying those who embody and represent these traditions and their
variations or replacements in our own time.

NOTES

1. Everett Worthington, Lewis Smedes, Kenneth Pargament, and Robert
Enright made especially helpful suggestions after reading an earlier draft of this
chapter, and I thank them.

2. This reference is from the massive works of Karl Rahner, which R. Scott
Appleby and I used frequently during a six-year effort to define fundamentalism.

3. For further elaboration and references to the works of Oakeshott and
Collingwood, see Marty, 1996, pp. 31–35.

4. See *The American Heritage dictionary of the English language* (3rd ed.).
Boston: Houghton Mifflin, 1992:631.

5. See a development of this in Buber, 1951.

6. This is the most well-executed and extensive book to connect forgiveness and the Trinity in recent years. However, I do not think that Jones has read Lewis Smedes contextually, and his critique of Smedes (pp. 48–53) seems gratuitous.

REFERENCES

Auden, W.H. (1976). *Collected poems* (E. Mendelson, Ed.). New York: Random House.

Billing, E. (1947). *Our calling* (C. Bergendoff, Trans). Rock Island, IL: Augustana Book Concern.

Bloch, M. (1964). *The historian's craft* (P. Putnam, Trans.). New York: Vintage.

Bonhoeffer, D. (1948). *The cost of discipleship*. London: SCM Press.

Buber, M. (1951). *Two types of faith* (N.P. Goldhawk, Trans.). New York: Macmillan.

Dorff, E.M. (1998). The elements of forgiveness: A Jewish approach. In E.L. Worthington, Jr. (Ed.), *Dimensions of forgiveness: Psychological research and theological perspectives* (pp. 29–55). Philadelphia, PA: Templeton Foundation Press.

Jones, L.G. (1995). *Embodying forgiveness: A theological analysis*. Grand Rapids, MI: William B. Eerdmans.

Marty, M.E. (1996). The modes of being, doing, teaching, and discovering. *Criterion, 35*, 31–35.

Oakeshott, M. (1933). *Experience and its modes*. Cambridge: Cambridge University Press.

Renier, G.J. (1950). *History: Its purpose and meaning*. Boston: Beacon.

Rosten, L. (1975). *Religions of America: Ferment and faith in an age of crisis*. New York: Simon and Schuster.

CHAPTER 2

The Elements of Forgiveness:
A Jewish Approach

Elliot N. Dorff

FOR SIXTEEN YEARS, I spent part of my summers as the Rabbi-in-Residence at Camp Ramah in California, a camp affiliated with the Conservative Movement in Judaism. In addition to teaching staff classes, I made it a point to get involved in as many camp activities as possible.

One summer, there was an immense feud between two bunks of twelve-year-old boys. The counselors, the division head, and even the camp psychologist tried to bring some peace, but to no avail. As a last resort, they asked me to do what I could.

GOD'S ROLE IN FORGIVENESS:
THE GUIDANCE OF THE PRAYER BOOK

When I met with both groups of boys together, I handed out prayer books. I could see the boys' eyes roll and their eyebrows lift: Here was the rabbi doing his thing again!

I had them look at a section of the weekday Amidah, which, together with the Shema and its attached blessings, constitutes the core of the morning synagogue service. The Amidah is built on nineteen blessings of God together with accompanying paragraphs that expand on the themes of those blessings. The first three paragraphs identify and describe the parties to the prayers as well as their primary relationships: The people praying are the descendants of Abraham, for whom God was a shield; the prayer is to God, who is the source of power, even to the point of resurrecting the dead in the future; and just as God was manifest in the past and will be in the future, so too is God manifest in the present and is experienced as "holy"—that is, as wholly Other.

Immediately after identifying the parties to Jewish prayer, the Amidah turns to these three blessings, the fourth, fifth, and sixth of the Amidah:

> You graciously give human beings knowledge and teach people understanding. Graciously grant us of Your knowledge, discernment, and wisdom. Blessed are You, Lord, who graciously grants knowledge.
>
> Return us, our Father, to Your Torah, and bring us close, Our Sovereign, to Your worship. And bring us back in complete return (*teshuvah*) to You. Blessed are You, Lord, who wants return.
>
> Forgive us, our Father, for we have missed the mark; have compassion on us, Our Sovereign, for we have transgressed, for You show compassion and forgive. Blessed are You, Lord, compassionate One who forgives often.

After the Amidah identifies who we are and who God is, the fourth blessing articulates our gratitude for what we are first aware of—namely, that we know things. Specifically, we have, as the prayer says, *de'ah* (information), *binah* (the ability to distinguish the difference between things [analytical knowledge]), and *haskel* (the wisdom gained from experience). We thank God immediately for such forms of knowledge because, à la Descartes, our realization that we possess knowledge is one of the first and most fundamental things we recognize about ourselves, and, probably, also because our knowledge distinguishes us from the other animals and is the source of our free will.

In the very next blessing, though, we ask God to help us return to Him. That is, as soon as we think about what we know about ourselves, we recognize that we make mistakes and even deliberately sin. We have hope that God will indeed help us to return to Him because we know God to be, as the prayer says, One who desires human return. (I am tempted to use the word repentance here, as the English language would have me do; but, as I shall develop further, that would invoke Christian understandings of the process, and I want to adhere carefully to both the words and the substance of Judaism's description of a return to God.)

Finally, in the sixth blessing, having invoked God's aid in helping us return to Him, we ask God for forgiveness. We do this because God is not only One who wants our return, but also One who is known to be compassionate and forgiving when we take steps to return.

OBSTACLES TO ASKING FOR FORGIVENESS

After studying these paragraphs with the two bunks of boys (twenty-four of them altogether), I asked them, first, why they thought that the prayer book asks God to help us return to Him. I suggested that instead of thinking about offending God, which may be difficult to fathom, they should think about parallel situations in human relationships. When I posed the question in this way, the boys were amazingly forthcoming and astute in identifying the factors that make it hard to ask for forgiveness. I shall rephrase, summarize, and add to that discussion here; but I continue to be impressed by how much of this list they themselves articulated. Specifically, then, to ask for forgiveness is hard because you must:

1. Give up your self-image of being morally innocent, together with any defenses that you may have established to reinforce that self-image. This step is very hard on the ego.

2. Give up any moral claims to the effect that you were in the right after all. This step requires you to relinquish your superior moral position in the argument, thus dramatically diminishing your status and power in the relationship with the person you have wronged.

3. Acknowledge that you have done wrong. That is, asking for forgiveness not only requires that you abandon the general, positive view that

you have of yourself, but that you also accept a negative evaluation of what you did.

4. Articulate that admission to the wronged party. It is not enough to realize in your own mind that you have done something wrong to another; you must admit that openly to the injured party. This step can be humiliating.

5. Trust the other person to be both willing and able to overcome the many impediments to forgiveness, delineated below, so that he or she can and will respond favorably to your request for forgiveness. If, however, forgiveness is denied, the refusal only serves to compound the humiliation you already feel. Moreover, in the face of refusal, you wonder whether you should have admitted the wrong in the first place, for now you have lost your edge in the argument. Inevitably, you also feel angry that your willingness to humble yourself to seek forgiveness was not met by a reciprocal willingness on the part of the wronged party to take steps to repair the relationship. Indeed, you may feel that now you are the wronged party.

These factors in human interactions, as I pointed out to the two groups of boys, amply explain why the prayer book begins by asking God to be willing to forgive. Only if God—and, by extension, people—are *open* to the possibility of forgiveness can it ever happen. Given the numerous and difficult obstacles to such openness, as described above, one can understand why the prayer book first has us ask God to be open to our return. Otherwise, no request for forgiveness can be heard, let alone granted. And if it is hard to ask forgiveness from God, who, after all, is known to desire our return, it is all the more difficult to ask forgiveness from human beings whom *we* have wronged: In that context, no such openness is assured, and, on the contrary, the offender has every reason to fear that the victim will shun him or her.

OBSTACLES TO FORGIVING

Turning now to the sixth blessing, I asked the boys to tell me why the other side of the coin is also hard. Once again, I shall rephrase and add to the answers they gave me; but here too they were amazingly astute in identifying the factors that make forgiving someone hard:

1. You, as the victim, have to give up your claims to justice—that you have been wronged and that the offender owes you something. Some of the reluctance to do this stems from the human predilection to carry a grudge and to desire revenge—a characteristic that the Torah specifically requires us to suppress in commanding us "Do not take vengeance or carry a grudge, but rather love your neighbor as yourself; I am the Lord" (Lev. 19:18, Jewish Publications Society [JPL; cited hereafter]). Even if you can overcome your desire to get back at the offender in the "an eye for an eye" mode, you still may feel reluctant to forgive because you rightfully feel that he or she owes you something. That is, even if retribution may not be in order, compensation may be—and, indeed, the Rabbis of the Mishnah and Talmud specifically interpret "an eye for an eye" to mean *not* that the victim should exact retribution on the offender, but rather that the offender must compensate the victim monetarily (Mishnah [hereafter M.]. *Bava Kamma* 8:1; Babylonian Talmud [hereafter B.]. *Bava Kamma* 83b–84a).[1] To fulfill these legitimate expressions of the demand for justice, the victim may justifiably require the offender to pay monetary damages and perhaps also a fine (what we call today "punitive damages"). Even with such compensation, however, it is often hard to overcome the sense that no compensation can adequately make up for your loss—either because that actually is the case, as, for example, when something of emotional value has been damaged, or simply because you like the old and familiar thing rather than the new replacement.

2. You, the victim, have to overcome your feelings of vulnerability. After all, the offender has invaded your space, as it were, and has harmed you in a way that you were unable to avoid, thus compromising your own feelings of safety and integrity.

3. You have to trust that the offender will not harm you (or anyone else) again. Given the inherent fallibility and selfishness of people, there are no ironclad guarantees; this, combined with your own recent experience, makes it especially difficult to muster such trust with regard to the offender. Toward that end, you might require that, to the extent that it is possible, he or she take concrete steps to lessen the chances that the behavior will be repeated.

FACTORS PROMPTING FORGIVENESS

With all three of these factors mitigating the possibilities for forgiveness, why would anyone forgive anyone else? There too my twelve-year-olds had a keen sense of the matter — although I shall expand on their comments somewhat. You forgive someone else because:

1. You yourself do bad things and want to be forgiven when that happens. This was by far the most prevalent rationale for forgiving others offered by the members of the group, stemming from a painful recognition on their part that each of us is just as fallible as the next person.

2. You want to restore your relationship with the offender, albeit on a different footing. After all, if you never forgive people who wrong you, you will never have any friends.

3. You need to get past this incident to get on with your life. You therefore forgive the other person even if you would really prefer that the offender never darken your doorstep again. This is an admittedly selfish rationale for forgiveness, and it does not bode well for the future of your relationship with the offender; but you may decide that the relationship does not matter, especially if you were not that close to the person in the first place.

4. You want to do the right thing. Even if you still feel vulnerable and lack trust in the ability or even the intention of the offender to act differently in the future, you might forgive the person as an act of moral principle — or, as I suggested to the boys, as a way of imitating God.

PARDON/FORGIVENESS/RECONCILIATION

One other issue emerged from our discussion that day. The very words we were using needed to be more carefully defined so that we were sure to understand what we were thinking and saying.

The words "pardon" and "excuse" are often used interchangeably, as, for example, when you brush up against someone accidentally and say either "Pardon me" or "Excuse me." In legal contexts, the two terms are used in different settings, but nevertheless denote a similar phenomenon. Specifically, a person who violates the law may not be punished if he or she has a valid excuse—for example, running a red light to get a woman in labor to the hospital on time or killing someone in self-defense. The violation still stands, but no punishment is warranted. Similarly, when a governor pardons a prisoner, the record still shows that the prisoner violated the law—that does not go away; but the punishment is curtailed.

Forgiveness involves one more step: The original violation is itself removed, and thus certainly any punishment that might have resulted from that violation. The injured parties might still remember the transgression and even take steps to ensure that they will not suffer that way a second time; but if they forgive the perpetrator, they accept him or her into their good graces once again and treat him or her as they did before the violation—again, with the possible exception of taking precautions against a second violation of the same nature. That is, forgiveness prepares the parties for resuming their relationship as fully as they can.

Finally, in reconciliation the transgressor becomes part of the friendship, family, or community again, despite the bad feelings that have been generated by what he or she did. Neither pardon nor forgiveness alone produces reconciliation; they only help the parties set aside the bad feelings that have soured their relationship. Both pardon and forgiveness, in other words, bring the parties back to neutral ground. Once that is done, both parties must take positive steps to rebuild the relationship and restore genuinely good feelings. Note also that while forgiveness is totally within the power of the victim, reconciliation can happen only if both parties agree to resume their relationship.

Reconciliation can take place whether or not the sin remains—that is, whether the reconciliation has been preceded by pardon or forgiveness. The terms of the reconciliation, though, will usually be more generous and openhanded if the sin is wiped away—that is, if forgiveness, and not just pardon, has occurred.

If the sin remains and only pardon has been achieved, the conditions under which the transgressor may function in the relationship are often restricted. This, in effect, is what the United States does with felons who have served their time: They are returned to the community, but they may not become police officers or vote, and they must report their conviction each time they apply for employment. In contrast, Jewish law requires that once a transgressor has endured the punishment decreed by the court, members of the community may take precautions to ensure that they will not be subjected to the same transgression again by that person; but they may not mention the crime unless such mention is geared to the practical purpose of safeguarding the community from future violation. Speaking about the person's former crime to anyone for any other reason is, from the point of Jewish law, itself a violation of the commandment prohibiting us from oppressing our neighbors—this being a form of verbal oppression (M. *Bava Metzia* 4:10; B. *Bava Metzia* 58b).[2] In other words, Jewish law requires that transgressors be forgiven, not only pardoned.

This distinction between forgiveness and reconciliation based on pardon parallels exactly how the sin-offering worked in the sacrificial cult in the ancient Temple. As Professor Jacob Milgrom has noted, the offerings that the community, the chieftain, and the commoner bring, according to Leviticus 4, to induce God's forgiveness for an unintentional sin do not really bring forgiveness—i.e., the wiping away of sin—but rather bring reconciliation based on pardon:

> The rendering "forgive" for *salah* is, in reality, not accurate. When God grants *salah* to Moses' request for it (Num. 14:19–20), it cannot connote forgiveness, considering that God qualifies it by declaring that all of adult Israel, with the exception of Caleb, will perish in the wilderness (vv. 21–24). Furthermore, in the entire Bible only God dispenses *salah,* never humans. Thus, we confront a concept that must be set apart from anthropopathic notions: It does not convey the pardon or forgiveness that humans are capable of extending.

Finally, because Moses invokes God's dreaded attribute of vertical retribution (v. 18; cf. Exod. 34:7), he clearly does not have forgiveness in mind. All he asks is that God be reconciled with his people; punish Israel, yes, but do not abandon it. Indeed, in the episode of the golden calf, God answers Moses' request for *salah* by renewing the covenant (Exod. 34:9–10).

Similarly, the offender who brings the *hattat* [sin-offering] does so because he knows that his wrong, though committed inadvertently, has polluted the altar and hence, has alienated him from God. By his sacrifice he hopes to repair the broken relationship. He therefore seeks more than forgiveness. If God will accept his sacrifice, he will be once again restored to grace, at one with his deity (Milgrom, 1991, p. 245).[3]

I did not go over this biblical material with the boys, but we did distinguish between these various forms of rapprochement. At the end of this discussion, I scheduled another session with them and asked them to think, in the meantime, of the concrete things the two groups might do to overcome the obstacles to forgiveness — that is, those things that would open them up to forgiving others and those things that would prompt them to ask for forgiveness themselves. In that session, after hearing their suggestions, I explained that Judaism does not assume that we are perfect. On the other hand, it does not proclaim that we are innately sinful, either, very much contrary to the Christian doctrine of Original Sin. Instead, the Rabbis assert that we each have two inclinations, one to do good and one to do bad (M. *Berakhot* 9:5; M. *Avot* (*Ethics of the Fathers*) 4:1; B. *Berakhot* 61a-b; B. *Shabbat* 105b; B. *Sotah* 47a; B. *Avodah Zarah* 5b),[4] and that God gives us instruction in the Torah (the literal meaning of the word "Torah" is, in fact, "instruction") to help us control our penchant to harm others and to foster our desire to do good. That is, we cannot expect ourselves or others to be perfect; indeed, we ask God for forgiveness not only on the High Holy Days, when we concentrate on that part of our religious lives, but three times each day when we recite the three paragraphs of the Amidah that we had studied. We must, then, not be overly hard on ourselves or others — and, at the same time, we must demand of ourselves and others that we all do what we can to avoid or at least repair the wrong and to do the good. As Rabbi Tarfon said in one of my favorite rabbinic sayings, "Yours is not to finish the task, but neither are you free to desist from it."[5]

THE PROCESS OF RETURN (*Teshuvah*): BECOMING WORTHY OF FORGIVENESS

How does one make amends? The process is well described in the Jewish concept of *teshuvah*, meaning "return." *Teshuvah* is not just "repentance" (from the Latin root meaning "to pay back"). It is a full-blown return to the right path and to good standing with the community and, indeed, with God. Hence, the prayer that we had studied blesses God not only for accepting us back in His good graces when we endure a punishment, but says that God "desires return" — that is, a return to the relationship we had with God before sinning. Jewish sources then prescribe that the same process for returning to God be used when we need to repair our relationship with another human being.

To explain that concept, I handed out paragraphs from the famous formulation of it by Maimonides (1140–1204). This great rabbi, physician, and philosopher wrote a code of Jewish law, the *Mishneh Torah* (hereafter M.T.), in which he organized and summarized the Jewish legal tradition according to his time, combining elements from the Bible, Mishnah, Talmud, responsa (rabbinic rulings in specific cases), customs, and the ongoing tradition. In this section on the process of return, his philosophical and legal skills are in evidence in that he is careful to define the elements of return as clearly and carefully as possible. He does not, however, provide a simple list of the elements of return, as one might expect from a systematizer, undoubtedly because the appropriate process of return depends, in part, on the specific nature of the transgression. I nevertheless asked the boys to identify the elements of the process of return as they appear in these paragraphs and then to put them in the order in which they would most likely occur. I reproduce below an English translation of the sections I distributed to them from Maimonides' code in the section titled "Laws of Return." This section retains his masculine language to be true to the original, even though, as the first biblical passage Maimonides quotes makes clear, women are subject to the same laws in Judaism, whether as perpetrators or as victims.

Chapter One

1. [For] all of the commandments of the Torah, whether positive [that is, commanding someone to do something] or negative [commanding someone not to do something], if a person transgressed one of them, whether intentionally or unknowingly, when he goes through the process of return and returns from his transgression, he must confess before God, blessed be He, for the Torah says, "When a man or a woman commits any wrong toward a fellow person…he must confess the wrong that he has done" (Num. 5:6–7). This is a confession expressed in words [and not just thought]. Such a confession is a positive commandment. …And similarly anyone who injures his fellow or damages his property—even though he paid him what he owes him—does not atone until he confesses and returns [refrains] from ever doing anything similar again, for the Torah says, "*any* wrong [literally, "from *all* the wrongs of a person" or "from *all* the wrongs toward a fellow person"—and not just those against God]. . . .

3. In our time, when the Temple does not exist and we do not have its altar of atonement [through animal sacrifices], we have no alternative but the process of return. The process of return atones for all transgressions. Even if a person was wicked all his days and engaged in the process of return only in the end, we do not mention anything about his wickedness, as the Bible says, "the wickedness of the wicked shall not cause him to stumble when he turns back from his wickedness" (Ezek. 33:12). The essence of the Day of Atonement also atones for those who engage in the process of return, as the Torah says, "For on this day He will wipe your slate clean…" (Lev. 16:30).

Chapter Two

1. What is complete return? [It occurs when] a person encounters something in which he transgressed [previously] and it is possible

for him to do it [again] but he separates himself from it and does not do it, not because of fear and not because of failure of strength, but rather because he has undergone the process of return. For example, if a man had forbidden sexual relations with a woman, and after some time he was alone with her and still loved her and still had strength of body and was [even] in the same locale where he had transgressed previously with her, but he separated himself [from her] and did not transgress, that is a person who has effected complete return....And if he did not engage in the process of return until his old age, when it was impossible for him to do what he used to do, even though that is not the best kind of return, nevertheless it is effective for him and he attains the status of one who has returned. Even if he transgressed all his days and engaged in the process of return on the day of his death and then died in a state of return, all his sins are forgiven, as the Bible says, "Before the sun and light and moon and stars grow dark, and the clouds come back again after the rain" (Eccles. 12:2)—that is, the day of death. From this we learn that if he remembered his Creator and engaged in the process of return before he died, he is forgiven.

2. And what is return? It is that the sinner abandon his sin, remove it from his thoughts, and resolve in his heart that he will not do it anymore, as the Bible says, "Let the wicked give up his ways..." (Isa. 55:7). Moreover, he will have remorse over the fact that he transgressed, as the Bible says, "Now that I have turned back, I am filled with remorse" (Jer. 31:18 [31:19 in some English translations]). And he must swear to the One who knows all secrets that he will not return to this sin ever, as the Bible says ["Return, O Israel, to the Lord your God, for you have fallen because of your sin. Take words with you and return to the Lord. Say to Him, 'Forgive all guilt and accept what is good; instead of bulls we will pay the offering of our lips. Assyria will not save us...' "], nor ever again will we call our handiwork our god [since in You alone orphans find pity]" (Hos. 14:2–4). And he must make oral confession, articulating the resolutions that he made in his heart.

3. Anyone who confessed with words but did not resolve in his heart to forsake [his former ways] is like one who immerses himself [in a ritual pool of water to regain a state of ritual purity] but has a reptile in his hands [which makes him impure again immediately], for the immersion will not benefit him until he throws away the reptile. And so the Bible says: "[He who conceals his transgressions will not succeed, but] He who confesses and gives them up will find mercy" (Prov. 28:13). And he must spell out the sin in detail, as the Bible says, "Alas, this people is guilty of a great sin in making for themselves a god of gold" (Exod. 32:31) [thus specifying "the great sin"].

4. Some of the modes of manifesting repentance are: (a) the penitent cries continuously before God in tears and supplications; (b) performs acts of charity as much as he can; (c) distances himself greatly from the matter in which he sinned; (d) changes his name, as if to say: "I am a different person, not the same person who committed those deeds"; (e) changes all of his actions for the good and for the right path; and (f) exiles himself from his place [of residence], for exile wipes away sin, for it causes one to be submissive and to be humble and meek in spirit.[6]

5. It is highly praiseworthy in a penitent to make public confession, proclaiming his sins to them [the community], revealing his transgressions against other people [Rashi on B. *Yoma* 86b: so that they will intercede with the victim to ask him to forgive the perpetrator]. He [the one engaged in the process of return] says to them: "Truly, I have sinned against so-and-so, and did this and that to him, but today I repent [return] and feel remorse." He, however, who is proud and does not publish his trespasses but conceals them, has not achieved complete return, as the Bible says, "He who conceals his transgressions will not succeed" (Prov. 28:13). This only applies to transgressions of one person against another, but with regard to sins committed against God, the person need not publish them [to the community]. Indeed, it is a mark of effrontery on his part if he publicizes them [Rashi on B. *Yoma* 86b: for he diminishes the Name,

or reputation, of God through his public proclamation of his willful transgression of God's commands. Moreover, as B. *Berakhot* 34b maintains, publicly proclaiming sins against God makes it seem as if he is not embarrassed by them]. He should rather repent of them before the Almighty, blessed be He, declaring in detail his sins before Him, and make public confession in general terms; and it is well for him that his iniquity has not become known, as it is said, "Happy is he whose transgression is forgiven, whose sin is covered over" (Ps. 32:1). [Note: A contemporary of Maimonides, Rabbi Abraham ben David of Posquierres, maintains instead that if a person's sin against God is well-known, his process of return should be public as well. Maimonides, though, worries that even if many people know of the sin, others may not, and so it is better for God's reputation to keep both the sin and the process of return quiet.]

6. Even though return and supplication are always good, they are particularly so and are immediately accepted during the ten days between Rosh Hashanah (New Year) and Yom Kippur (the Day of Atonement), as the Bible says, "Seek the Lord when He may be found" (Isa. 55:6). This only applies, however, to an individual. But as for a community, whenever its members return and offer supplications with sincere hearts, they are answered, as the Torah says, "For what great nation is there that has a god so close at hand as is the Lord our God whenever we call upon Him?" (Deut. 4:7).

9. The process of return and the Day of Atonement only atone for transgressions against God, as, for example, when one has eaten a forbidden food or indulged in illicit sexual relations. But transgressions against another person—as, for example, if one wounds, curses, or robs someone—are never forgiven until the injured party has received the [monetary] compensation due him and has been appeased. Even if the perpetrator has compensated the victim, the wrongdoer must also appease the one he has injured and ask his forgiveness. Even if a person only annoyed another in words, he has to pacify the latter and entreat him until he has obtained his forgiveness. If, however, the injured party is unwilling to forgive, he [the

perpetrator] should bring three of his [the victim's] friends at one time, and they should entreat the person offended and solicit his pardon. If they fail, he [the offender] should take with him a second and even a third group. If the offended person continues obdurate, the wrongdoer leaves him alone and goes away; the one who refused to forgive is now the sinner. But if the victim was the offender's teacher, the pupil has to go to him again and again, even a thousand times, until pardon has been granted.

10. It is forbidden to be obdurate and not allow oneself to be appeased. On the contrary, one should be easily pacified and difficult to anger. Moreover, when asked by an offender for forgiveness, one should forgive with a sincere mind and a willing spirit. Even if one had been much vexed and grievously wronged, he is not to avenge nor bear a grudge (Lev. 19:18).

11. If a person sinned against another and the latter died before pardon was sought, the offender should bring ten men, station them at the grave of the deceased, and, in their presence, declare: "I sinned against the Lord, God of Israel, and against this individual, having committed such-and-such a wrong against him." If he owed the deceased money, he should pay it to the heirs. If he did not know any of the heirs, he should deposit the amount in court and confess.

What, then, are the elements of the process of forgiveness as described by Maimonides? While the order and even the elements on the list may differ according to the specific offense and the particular way in which one interprets Maimonides, one possible interpretation is this:

1. Acknowledgment that one has done something wrong.

2. Public confession of one's wrongdoing to both God and the community.

3. Public expression of remorse.

4. [Public announcement of] the offender's resolve not to sin in this way

again. (These first four may possibly take place amid crying and entreaties for forgiveness and, in the most serious of cases, may even include changing one's name.)

5. Compensation of the victim for the injury inflicted accompanied by acts of charity to others.

6. Sincere request of forgiveness by the victim—with the help of the victim's friends and up to three times, if necessary (and even more if the victim is one's teacher).

7. Avoidance of the conditions that caused the offense, perhaps even to the point of moving to a new locale.

8. Acting differently when confronted with the same situation in which the offender sinned the first time.

RETURN (*Teshuvah*): ITS PROBLEMS AND PROMISE

Avoidance versus Confrontation of Temptation

In the steps just delineated, numbers 7 and 8 are mutually contradictory, for offenders cannot possibly act differently in the same situation if they have intentionally removed themselves from tempting contexts. My own reading of this makes the proper course dependent on the circumstances. It is undoubtedly right and proper, for example, for pedophiles to remove themselves from children as much as possible. They will never be able to effect full return as a result, but they can surely accomplish a great measure of return, and it is more important to protect innocent children from abuse than to enable pedophiles to achieve full return. One would certainly not want to entrust such a person with a position of responsibility for children, such as teacher, coach, youth group leader, or camp counselor. Thus, the return of which Jewish sources speak is *not* necessarily to the same position that the person occupied before committing the offense; it is rather to good standing with God and within the community—albeit a standing that the community can and should limit for its own protection.

This strategy of avoidance is also commonly invoked in twelve-step programs for those addicted to alcohol, drugs, gambling, overeating, and the like. Similarly, placing a convicted gang member in a different city after his release from prison may remove the possibility of full return, in that we will never know whether he is now strong enough to resist all of the lures of the old neighborhood; but it may be completely acceptable if it also gives him a greater chance to begin a new life free from gang activities. On the other hand, where the risk cannot be avoided without curtailing human interaction altogether—for example, where the offense is gossip or petty theft or illicit sexual intercourse —then avoiding the risks of recurring sin is impossible (the "bad news"); however, full return becomes possible (the "good news").

The Duty versus the Grace to Forgive

Furthermore, forgiveness becomes the *duty* of the victim after the offender has done his or her best to make amends, act differently in the future, and has asked for forgiveness at most three times. In many cases, the victim may hesitate to forgive for all the reasons that we enumerated earlier; but where the offender has undergone the entire process of return, forgiveness is required, even when the wrong can never be righted fully.

It certainly makes sense that God should impose a duty on us to forgive each other. We thereby become closer replicas of Him, and we also overcome our alienation from each other. A good God would presumably want such things.

Forgiving, however, requires one to overcome feelings of hostility and vengefulness. Experientially, then, forgiveness seems more like an act that goes beyond moral duty, a supererogatory act rooted not in our sense of duty, but in our capability for charity and benevolence. How can these feelings be reconciled with Judaism's insistence that forgiveness is a moral duty?

The answer lies in the Jewish approach to moral education. Optimally, of course, you should do the right thing for the right reason. But when that is not possible, should you wait to act until you acquire the right motivation, or should you perform the right act now, even though it is for the wrong rationale? Immanuel Kant, who emphasizes intention as the key element in determining the moral character of an act, would say the former: Wait to act until you can do so out of a sense of moral principle. Judaism, however, stands at the opposite end of that spectrum: "A person should always do the right thing even for the wrong reason," the Rabbis say, "for in doing the right thing for an ulterior motive one will come to do it for the right motive (B. *Pesahim* 50b, *et. al.*)."[7] Thus, even though a victim may have no desire to forgive, he or she must do everything possible to forgive the transgressor once the transgressor has gone through the process of return. In such cases, it is duty that is at work rather than charity; at some point, the victim may be able to forgive out of a sense of charity, too.[8]

This means, of course, that for Judaism forgiveness is not exclusively, or even primarily, an internal, psychological process. Typical of Judaism's emphasis on action, the concept of forgiveness that emerges out of the Jewish tradition stresses the actions that the perpetrator must take to return to God and the community and, in turn, the actions that the community must take in welcoming him or her back. It is, in other words, an *inter*personal process, not an *intra*personal one. Judaism certainly harbors the hope that the feelings of both the perpetrator and the community will ultimately follow along, thereby creating the foundation for reconciliation and even renewed friendship; but the essence of forgiveness, for the Jewish tradition, is not acquiring a new feeling about each other, but rather acting on the demands that the duty of forgiveness imposes on us so that we can live together as a community worthy of God's presence.

The Scope of the Duty to Forgive

The Jewish tradition's description of the process of return also helps us define those cases in which forgiveness should not be granted. For example, if the offender never admits wrongdoing, the very first step in return has not been achieved, and no forgiveness can legitimately be demanded of the victims, even if the offender has served a prison term or some other form of punishment. I know of just such a case in which a Cub Scout leader of a synagogue was convicted of sexually abusing the boys in his den and served time in prison, but even after release he never admitted that he had done anything wrong. Under those circumstances, the community was under no obligation to restore his membership, and his accusers — now young men in their teens and twenties — were under no obligation to forgive him. On the contrary, to forgive him without demanding that he go through the process of return would both deny the claims of justice and undermine the legitimate social and religious pressure the offender should feel to take the steps of return. In such a case, forgiveness would be counterproductive — not only for society and the victims, but also for the offender.

Justice and Mercy

Even these cases, however, are not as easy to determine as they seem, for just as Judaism values justice, so too it values compassion and mercy. This flies in the face of many Christian stereotypes of Judaism that see Judaism as a religion of law and Christianity as a religion of love. Neither is exclusively true. Christianity speaks much of God's love, but it also values justice. Conversely, Judaism places great emphasis on justice and law, but only because it understands love to be most effectively expressed in families and societies that have and apply good laws.

Even so, sometimes the requirements of law must be set aside in an act of mercy. Thus, on the Day of Atonement, we Jews ask God Himself to move from his seat of justice to his seat of mercy in judging us; as God is our model, we too must manifest such compassion. The Rabbis say this explicitly:

> "To walk in all His ways" (Deut. 11:22). These are the ways of the Holy One: "gracious and compassionate, patient, abounding in kindness and faithfulness, assuring love for a thousand generations, forgiving iniquity, transgression, and sin, and granting pardon…" (Exod. 34:6-7). This means that just as God is gracious and compassionate, you too must be gracious and compassionate. "The Lord is righteous in all His ways and loving in all His deeds" (Ps. 145:17). As the Holy One is righteous, you too must be righteous. As the

Holy One is loving, you too must be loving (*Sifre Deuteronomy*, Ekev, on Deut. 11:22).

Note that the Rabbis, in this famous homily, cut off the biblical passage in the middle. According to the Bible, God is "gracious and compassionate…forgiving iniquity, transgression, and sin; yet He does *not* remit all punishment, but visits the iniquity of fathers upon children and children's children, upon the third and fourth generations" (Exod. 34:7). The Rabbis, in one of their most audacious moments, stop the sentence in the middle and thereby change the biblical view of God into a much more forgiving, rabbinic view—and it is this rabbinic editing of the biblical verse that is repeated many times in the High Holy Day liturgy. But even for the Rabbis, God is *both* righteous *and* compassionate, and His love is a product of His ability to balance both.

Similarly, while gross offenses should probably not be forgiven without sincere attempts to engage in the process of return, one might be prone to forgive more minor offenses without such a process both as a pragmatic way of getting on with one's life and possibly of restoring a friendship, and also as an expression of the religious demand that we imitate God. However, such free forgiveness becomes harder to justify as the offense grows larger, especially if it affects not only one's property, but one's person, or if its nasty effects persist. Then God's righteousness seems to be the divine attribute that we should emulate. But knowing just how to strike the requisite *balance* between justice and mercy in deciding when and whom to forgive is often easier said than done— and is itself an expression of the godly in us.

Limits to Forgiveness

Are there sins for which no forgiveness is justified, even after going through the process of return?

Communities. In defining who may, and who may not, join the Israelite community, the Torah itself forbids forgiveness to three specific communities, insisting that Israelites actively seek to destroy one of them:

No Ammonite or Moabite shall be admitted into the congregation of the Lord; none of their descendants, even in the tenth generation, shall ever be admitted into the congregation of the Lord, because they did not meet you with food and water on your journey after you left Egypt, and because they hired Balaam, son of Beor, from Pethor of Aram-naharaim to curse you. . . . You shall never concern yourself with their welfare or benefit as long as you live. . . .

Remember what Amalek did to you on your journey, after you left Egypt—how, undeterred by fear of God, he surprised you on the march, when you were famished and weary, and cut down all the stragglers in your rear. Therefore, when the Lord your God grants you safety from all your enemies around you in the land that the Lord your God is giving you as a hereditary portion, you shall blot out the memory of Amalek from under heaven. Do not forget! (Deut. 23:4–7; 25:17–19; see also Exod. 17:8–16).

On the other hand, that same passage in Deuteronomy prescribes that the Edomites be forgiven for not allowing the Israelites to pass through their territory on the trek from Egypt, "for he is your kinsman." Presumably, kinsmen are owed a greater measure of forgiveness than other people deserve. Deuteronomy even insists that the Israelites forgive the Egyptians—despite the fact that they enslaved the Israelites for hundreds of years—"for you were a stranger in [their] land." Thus, the fact that the Egyptians provided a place to live, albeit under terrible conditions, also requires the Israelites ultimately to forgive them. Nevertheless, in both cases, three generations must elapse before they can be fully admitted to the Israelite community, for by then the community that committed the trespasses and the community of Israelites that suffered them will have passed out of existence:

You shall not abhor an Edomite, for he is your kinsman. You shall not abhor an Egyptian, for you were a stranger in his land. Children born to them may be admitted into the congregation of the Lord in the third generation (Deut. 23:8–9).

Thus, apparently some communities do such egregious acts that they can never be forgiven, while other nations can and should be forgiven, at least after the passage of time. The Torah does not describe in any more detail the criteria by which to judge which communities of the future are to be forgiven their trespasses against the People Israel and which are not.

This, of course, raises major issues in our own time, when Jews need to decide how they are going to reconcile with present-day Germans, Poles, Austrians, and others. Many of the problems concern moral standing: The people asking for forgiveness — or at least for reconciliation — were, for the most part, not even born when the atrocities of the Holocaust were committed, let alone responsible for them; likewise, the people being asked for forgiveness were, for the most part, not even born during the Holocaust and therefore did not suffer directly from it — although members of their immediate or extended families may well have. Do we inherit our ancestors' guilt and thus their ability to ask for forgiveness? Conversely, do we inherit our ancestors' pain and injury and thus their standing to forgive? If not, is forgiveness possible a generation or two later? Even if forgiveness is impossible, is reconciliation attainable? I deal with these issues in another article (Dorff, 1992, pp. 193–218), but suffice it to say here that the Torah clearly draws distinctions between communities that can and should be forgiven and those that cannot and should not be; and the latter group constitutes a limit to the scope of forgiveness.

Individuals. As forgiveness is completely within the power of victims, they *can* forgive any offender, whether or not he or she deserves it — assuming, of course, that the victim survived the offense. Do any individuals *not* deserve forgiveness, even if they go through the process of return? That is, are any offenses so egregious that the process of return is not powerful enough to cleanse the offender and make him or her worthy of being restored to the community? Are there any offenses that even God does not and should not forgive?

Maimonides reflects the ambivalence of the tradition on this issue. On the one hand, relying on a number of talmudic passages, he compiles a list of offenses that are so heinous that even God does not forgive their perpetrators, and he states this in very strong language:

The following have no portion in the world to come, but are cut off and perish, and for their great wickedness and sinfulness are condemned for ever and ever: heretics and scoffing skeptics; those who deny the [authority of the] Torah, the resurrection of the dead, or the coming of the Redeemer; apostates; those who cause a multitude to sin; those who secede from the ways of the community; anyone who commits transgressions like [King] Jehoiakim, in high-handed fashion and openly; informers [against the Jewish community to the government]; those who terrorize a community for other than religious purposes; murderers and slanderers; and those who pull down their foreskin[s] [to obliterate the circumcision, the physical mark of Israel's Covenant with God] (M.T. Laws of Return 3:6).[9]

In the following paragraphs of his code, Maimonides defines each of these categories, specifying what each one means and the various classes of people who fall under them, for a total of twenty-four groups. At the end, he says this:

When it is said that one who commits any of these sins has no portion in the world to come, that statement is to be understood as applying only to the sinner who dies without going through the process of return. If he returned from his wickedness and died while in the process of return, though, he is of those who will have a portion in the world to come; for there is nothing that stands in the way of return....

When one thinks of contemporary history, Hitler and Stalin come to mind as people to whom forgiveness should be permanently denied. Similarly, those who have committed genocide in Cambodia, Bosnia, and Rwanda fall under this category. Their actions were depraved, repeated, and with malice aforethought, and we have no evidence of any remorse, let alone the other steps of return. But how far does this go? Would it *ever* be improper to forgive, for example, fathers who sexually abuse their daughters, or mothers who abandon their newborn infants in garbage dumps? What about mass murderers? More generally, is the number of people affected a factor? The seriousness of the offense? The lack of mitigating circumstances? The lack of remorse or any attempts at return? On the other hand, should there ever be those to whom we deny return altogether? Would that be in keeping with modeling ourselves after a just, but compassionate, God?

Jewish sources do not resolve these issues. What emerges is a strong belief that people can change for the better and that they must be given the opportunity to do so. This belief is grounded in Judaism's strong assertion of human free will. Maimonides, in fact, maintains that it is only "stupid gentiles and mentally incompetent Israelites" who deny that people have the ability to choose good or evil, for if that were not the case, he points out

> how could the Almighty have charged us, through the Prophets, "Do this and do not do that, improve your ways, do not follow your wicked impulses," when, from the beginning of his existence, his destiny had already been decreed, or his innate constitution irresistibly drew him to that from which he could not set himself free? What room would there be for the whole of the Torah? By what right or justice could God punish the wicked or reward the righteous? (M.T. Laws of Return 5:4).[10]

Along with free will comes responsibility, and so forgiveness is deserved only by those who accept responsibility for their wrongful actions, show remorse for them, and seek to make amends through the process of return. Even then, according to some sources, there are certain offenses for which no atonement is possible; people who commit them can never repair the wrong that they have done or warrant restoration to friendship and good standing in the community. These sources suggest that even God does not forgive such offenses. According to other Jewish sources, however, the possibility of return exists even for those who have committed the most egregious sins.

That tension in the sources, is, in my view, right on target; in truth, we do not know, in such cases, whether forgiveness is possible or warranted. Probably the most eloquent expression of that dilemma is Simon Wiesenthal's story, *The Sunflower*. In it, a Nazi, a member of the *Schutz-*

staffel (SS) who admitted, on his deathbed, to having killed Jews asks Wiesenthal to be his confessor and grant him forgiveness. The story is followed by a symposium of thirty-two people, including such important religious thinkers as Edward Flannery, Abraham Heschel, Primo Levi, Martin Marty (see Chapter 1), John Oesterreicher, and Cynthia Ozick. While some of the respondents are sure that Wiesenthal had the right to forgive and then take differing stances as to whether or not he should have, others are not sure that he even has that standing in the first place. What emerges from the symposium is, thus, not clear guidance at all, but rather deep ambivalence—an ambivalence that is, in my judgment, exactly appropriate. Sometimes we simply do not know who, if anyone, has the authority to forgive; at other times we know who can forgive, but do not know whether forgiveness is warranted.

EPILOG

Fortunately, in most of our lives, the violations for which we are called upon to grant or request forgiveness are not nearly as serious as the mass murders committed by the SS man asking for forgiveness on his deathbed. Moreover, usually it is the victim who is asked for forgiveness, not a surrogate, thus eliminating the difficult issue of whether anyone can forgive an offense against someone else, even a relative. Forgiving is often hard, as is asking for forgiveness; but, fortunately, in most of our lives, the degree of difficulty does not approach that of Wiesenthal's story. For that alone, we should be thankful.

To return to the boys whose conflict started this story, I surely cannot report utopian results. Following our sessions, however, the boys did find ways to become civil to one another and even to do some things *together* with a sense of cooperation, respect, and, yes, by the end of the summer, even friendship. Through it all, it was truly amazing for this rabbi to see how the liturgy and the recipe for return in classical Jewish sources could take on deep emotional, intellectual, and practical meanings in their lives.

NOTES

1. For a translation and discussion of those passages, see Dorff and Rosett, 1988, pp. 152–179.

2. Here the Rabbis deduce this prohibition from Leviticus 25:17 (as the prohibition against oppressing another in monetary matters has already been stated in Leviticus 25:14, and the rabbis presume that nothing in the Torah is superfluous).

3. Professor Milgrom continues to translate the Hebrew *salah* as "forgive" on the grounds that he cannot think of a better substitute, but I think that our discussion would suggest "pardon."

4. The "evil" impulse, however, is not evil in the normal sense, as this rabbinic statement attests: "'And God saw everything that He had made and, behold, it was very good' (Gen. 1:31). 'Very good' indicates both the good impulse and the evil impulse. But is the evil impulse very good? Were it not for that impulse, a man would not build a house, marry a wife, beget children, or conduct business affairs" (*Genesis Rabbah* 9:7). Thus, the "evil impulse" does not denote our penchant to do immoral things; it is rather, the self-directed inclination in us, in contrast to the other-directed impulse in us, which is termed the "good impulse." It may indeed be the case that self-directed actions are more likely to result in immorality than other-directed actions are, but they surely do not always do so, as the examples in this last rabbinic source make clear. The "evil impulse," therefore, makes human free will possible (and thus "there is no evil impulse in animals," according to *Avot d'Rabbi Nathan* 16) and indeed, as it includes our sexual urges, life itself depends on it (cf. B. *Avodah Zarah* 5a). Because the evil impulse, so defined, was created by God for the preservation of the human species, in the life to come, when there is no further need for it, God will slay it (B. *Sukkah* 52a). In the meantime, however, "You should love the Lord your God with all your heart" (Deut. 6:5), where "heart" is spelled unusually with two, rather than one, of the Hebrew letter *bet* and interpreted on that basis by the Rabbis to mean "with two impulses" — the good and the evil" (*Sifre Deuteronomy* on Deut. 6:5). For further discussion, see Cohen, 1949, pp. 88–93; cf. pp. 54–55.

5. M. *Avot* (*Ethics of the Fathers*) 2:21.

6. The four modes of return delineated as (a), (b), (d), and (e) are based on the remark of Rabbi Yitzhak in Babylonian Talmud *Rosh Hashanah* 16b. That exile wipes away sin (f) is found in B. *Sanhedrin* 37b.

7. I would like to thank Professor Lewis Smedes (see Chapter 10) for calling my attention to the tension that I am discussing in this section.

8. There is an interesting discussion in Jewish sources—and, interestingly, in Kant—as to whether an act is more or less morally worthy when done out of a sense of duty or out of one's own desire. Both the Talmud and Kant maintain that the act is more morally worthy—and for Kant *only* morally worthy —if done out of a sense of duty. The Rabbis do not go that far: An act can have moral worth if it conforms to duty, even if one acts out of one's desire to do the right or good thing. It is just that acting out of a sense of duty recognizes the authority of God more fully. Pragmatically, the chances that good will be done are greater if people recognize a duty to do so, whether or not they want to act that way. See B. *Kiddushin* 31a.

9. Most of the talmudic passages on which Maimonides relies come from the eleventh chapter of the tractate *Sanhedrin*.

10. Maimonides calls those who deny free will "stupid" and "mentally incompetent" (actually, he uses the word *golem*; that is, a human mass totally directed by the will of its master) in 5:2.

REFERENCES

Babylonian Talmud (edited c. 500 C.E.).

Cohen, A. (1949). *Everyman's Talmud*. New York: Dutton.

Dorff, E.N. (1992). Individual and communal forgiveness. In D.H. Frank (Ed.), *Autonomy and Judaism: The individual and the community in Jewish philosophical thought*. Albany: State University of New York Press.

Dorff, E.N., & Rosett, A. (1988). *A living tree: The roots and growth of Jewish law*. Albany, NY: State University of New York Press.

Maimonides. *Mishneh Torah* (completed 1177 C.E.).

Marty, M.E. (1998). The ethos of Christian forgiveness. In E.L. Worthington, Jr. (Ed.), *Dimensions of forgiveness: Psychological research aand theological perspectives* (pp. 9–28). Philadelphia, PA: Templeton Foundation Press.

Milgrom, J. (1991). *Leviticus 1–16: A new translation with introduction and commentary*. New York: Doubleday [The Anchor Bible, Vol. 3].

Mishnah (edited c. 200 C.E.).

Smedes, L.B. (1998). Stations on the journey from forgiveness to hope. In E.L. Worthington, Jr. (Ed.), *Dimensions of forgiveness: Psychological research and theological perspectives* (pp. 341–354). Philadelphia, PA: Templeton Foundation Press.

PART II

✦

Forgiveness in Basic
Social Processes

CHAPTER 3

Forgiveness as a Method of Religious Coping

Kenneth I. Pargament and Mark S. Rye

According to the "Law of the Instrument," if you have a hammer in your hand, you are likely to see nails all around you (Kaplan, 1964). This law applies to social scientists as well as those they study.

For example, one of our colleagues was conducting an evaluation of a spiritual intervention group for women with breast cancer to compare the spirituality group with a cognitive-behavioral comparison group. In her effort to obtain a sample of patients, she approached a major university-based hospital for support. However, the review committee refused, stating that the design failed to control for expectancy effects. They maintained that those in the spiritual group could improve, not because of the treatment itself, but because of the *expectancy* that the spirituality intervention would be helpful. The research committee went on to recommend the addition of a "sham-spirituality" group to control for this effect.

We believe that the research committee erred. They applied an experimental methodology—a "hammer"—derived from the natural sciences to something other than a "nail," a topic that requires a different instrument of study.

Science is not a value-free business, but the illusion that it is can damage our deepest values. Complex human phenomena must be approached with sensitivity and appropriate paradigms of concepts and methods. We suggest that forgiveness is a method of religious coping for many people. Although this is not the only way to conceptualize forgiving, our task as scholars and professionals interested in advancing this topic of study is not to zero in on the single best perspective, definition, or measure of forgiveness, but to identify valuable theories and methodologies that can shed some light on this multifaceted construct. We believe that conceptualizing forgiveness as a way of religious coping does justice to the richness of this construct, links it to an established body of research, raises interesting insights, and points to potential pitfalls and important questions to guide further study.

Two key points are implicit in our thesis: (1) Forgiving is a method of coping. (2) Forgiveness is, in some sense, a religious pursuit.

FORGIVING AS A METHOD OF COPING

A Definition of Coping

We begin with the definition of coping as *a search for significance in stressful times.*[1] This definition makes the assumption that everyone is engaged in a search for significance.

Significance is both subjective and objective. Subjectively, it involves the experience of caring or attraction. Objectively, significance can be attached to a variety of things—physical (houses, cars, money, our bodies, physical health); psychological (a sense of meaning,[2] personal identity, comfort, growth); social (children, closeness with others, social justice, a commitment to making the world a better place); or spiritual (closeness to God, sacred matters). But significant objects are not necessarily good; we can care about things that aren't very good for us—such as drugs, alcohol, or social status at the expense of others.

By referring to coping as a "search," we mean that people try to find and hold onto (conserve) or, when necessary, transform the things they value. Coping involves the steps people take to conserve or transform significance in the face of situations that pose a challenge, threat, or potential harm to the things they most care about.

Conservational and Transformational Methods of Coping

In difficult situations, our first reaction is *conservational*. This is not a new idea. Many years ago, Jean Piaget observed this tendency in his studies of children. But children aren't the only ones who try to hold onto their ways of viewing and dealing with the world. Adults also try to find ways to conserve the things they want.

Take the example of one young couple that badly wants to have their own children. Faced with the trauma of infertility, the couple may take a number of coping steps to protect their cherished goal: gathering information about infertility, committing to expensive infertility treatments, going to an infertility support group. Fortunately, in many instances, conservational methods of coping work; the couple of this example may succeed in their efforts to have children. But in other cases, old dreams are no longer viable; then, goals have to be changed.

Such situations call for transformation. The couple above may fail in all of their efforts. Their task for coping is to come to terms with their inability to have their own biological children. What will they do? Perhaps they will be able to transform their desire for children from a biological to a general, more psychological goal and seek to adopt a child or become foster parents. Or, perhaps they will shift to entirely new objects of significance in life. Examples of coping methods that may facilitate this process include psychotherapy, prayer for new religious direction, or involvement in a ritual of loss (i.e., a grieving process).

It is important to stress that transformation—change in the things we strive for in life—is exceptionally difficult. Think about how you would respond if asked to give up one of the objects of greatest significance in your life. Often transformation is a last resort, a method of coping used only when all attempts to conserve what matters most fail.

Researchers and theorists of coping have generally focused more on methods of conservation than on methods of transformation (see Aldwin, 1994; Lazarus & Folkman, 1984). The emphasis has been on how people resolve problems or how they maintain themselves emotionally in response to major life crises, rather than on how they let go of previously cherished objects and find new things to care about. Methods of transformation, however, deserve further study. Forgiving is one method of transformation.

Forgiving as Transformational

In the case of forgiving, we are talking about coping with the stressor of abuse, betrayal, or victimization. As with other stressors, the initial reaction of most people is not transformational, but conservational, as shown in Table 1.

Table 1. Forgiving as a Method of Transformational Coping		
	MEANS OF COPING	ENDS OF COPING
PHASE ONE: CONSERVATION	Anger Fear Hurt Resentment	Self-Protection Justice
PHASE TWO: TRANSFORMATION	Reframing Humanizing Empathizing Reappraisal Social Facilitation	Peace

Although we may not think of emotions in a functional sense, feelings do serve important purposes. Anger, fear, hurt, and resentment are, at least in part, conservational strategies (Simon & Simon, 1990). Anger can be a source of energy and power that counteracts feelings of paralysis and loss of control that often accompany mistreatment. Fear and suspiciousness serve to "protect" the individual from the repeated pains of the past. Feelings of hurt can be a source of comfort, a reminder that the individual is a decent person who deserves better out of life. Resentment can bring with it a clear explanation for the person's present predicament. And expressions of all of these feelings remind others of the individual's plight.

Unfortunately, these strategies are only partially successful. With anger comes the realization that the person was powerless in the past. With fear comes the reality that terrible things could happen again. With hurt comes the question of one's own true value. And with resentment comes an underlying sense of shame. In each of these expressions of distress, the pain from the past continues to intrude on the present. Empirical studies also suggest that quite a price is paid for the protection offered by the negative emotions of anger, fear, hurt, and resentment (e.g., Diamond, 1982).

From a coping perspective, forgiving is transformational in both the ends that are sought and in the means that are used to reach these ends. Forgiveness involves a transformation in motivation (see also McCullough, Worthington, & Rachal, 1997). Implicit in the act is the effort to change direction from self-protection as the object of greatest significance to what Kolnai (1968) called a "boldly, venturesomely, aspiring, and active pursuit of Value" (cited in Rowe et al., 1989, p. 236). Put another way, forgiving is an attempt to shift from a life devoted to avoiding further pain and the memory of injustice to one dedicated to pursuing peace. Forgiveness offers the possibility of two types of peace: peace of mind—the potential healing of old emotional wounds, and peace with others—the possibility of new, more gratifying relationships in the future.

Forgiveness involves more than a transformation of ends or motivations. The means or methods of forgiving are also transformational in nature. This is not as simple as saying, "I forgive you." Augsberger (1981) described forgiveness as one of the hardest things in the world to do. To let go of justified anger and hurt, to think about the betrayal and the betrayer in a new light, to give up the well-deserved right to hurt back— all of these call for change at many levels: cognitive, affective, relational, behavioral, volitional, and spiritual.

Forgiving actually encompasses many subtypes of coping. Enright and colleagues have identified several psychological variables involved in this process (Enright & the Human Development Study Group, 1991). They include emotional ventilation, a reframing of the offender and victim, empathy with and humanization of the offender, and reappraisal of the costs of not forgiving and the benefits of forgiving.

Another implicit, but often overlooked, ingredient of forgiving is social facilitation. Much of what we know about the process of forgiving comes from studies in which we have tried to facilitate forgiveness through education, encouragement, and therapy. It is reasonable to ask whether forgiveness, in the transformational sense used here, can take place outside of a facilitative context. Radical change isn't easy.

It may not be surprising then that forgiveness is a complex method of coping, one that subsumes many subtypes of coping. Radical change requires many methods.

We should add a qualification here. Once an individual has made this type of radical change, forgiveness may become something less radical, more a way of life, a method that is regularly practiced without as much tumult and turmoil. In fact, forgiving may become relatively automatic, a response that quickly mitigates the offensiveness of egregious acts. In this sense, a forgiving attitude, once deeply established, may become a form of anticipatory coping that preempts mistreatment.

What enables this sort of change? Let us suggest here that forgiving is often empowered by religion.

FORGIVING AS A RELIGIOUS PURSUIT

A Definition of Religion

It is important to preface this discussion with a definition of religion. Few terms elicit stronger and more diverse reactions among people in society than this one (see Pargament, Sullivan, Balzer, Van Haitsma, & Raymark, 1995). For some, religion refers to a set of beliefs; for others, it is a set of practices; and for still others, it is a way of life. Some view religion as a force for good, and others see it as a source of repression and pain. Historically, psychologists have defined religion as a broadband construct, a multifaceted phenomenon made up of institutional, behavioral, affective, cognitive, experiential, and motivational dimensions. More-over, psychologists have remarked on religion's capacity for both good and bad. More recently, however, "religion" has taken on a narrower meaning. It is increasingly used to refer to institutionalized beliefs and practices that restrict and inhibit human potential (see Zinnbauer et al., 1997). Now, the term "spirituality" is becoming differentiated from "religion" as an expression of the greatest of human capacities.

We believe that these recent developments are overly simplistic and polarize processes that are fundamentally interrelated (see Pargament, in press, for discussion). Religion has both individual and institutional expressions and offers the potential for both good and bad. Thus, we return to the classic broadband tradition and define religion as *a search for significance in ways related to the sacred* (Pargament, 1997).

There is a close connection between religion and times of stress, as we hear in old sayings and aphorisms, such as "Man's extremity is God's opportunity" and "There are no atheists in foxholes." Our favorite is: "Dear God, help me get up; I can fall down by myself." Social scientists have also noted the connection between religion and stressful times, but they have tended to view religion stereotypically as a source of conservation rather than transformation.

Religion, according to Freud (1927/1961), is merely a defense against anxiety and uncertainty, a refuge people seek in response to powerful, uncontrollable forces in the universe. And there is some truth to this notion. The religions of the world provide their adherents with a number of methods of coming to grips with the most basic—and terrifying—of life's problems. Theologies offer ways to sustain a sense of meaning even in the face of the most seemingly incomprehensible events. Rituals of purification help people who may have strayed from their paths return to lives of integrity. The services of most religious congregations are filled with hymns, prayers, and stories of solace and consolation that offer support for the suffering. And, we should add, a number of empirical studies have shown that these methods of religious coping are uniquely helpful to people in their efforts to keep themselves together through life's most difficult trials (see Pargament, 1997, for a review).

But the power of religion goes beyond conservation. Earlier in this century, psychologist George Coe (1916) wrote: "Possibly the chief thing

in religion…is the progressive discovery and reorganization of values"
(p. 65). Religion is often intimately involved in the search for new
sources of significance when old ones are lost or no longer tenable.
Through religious rites of passage, people are encouraged to give up old
social roles (e.g., through Bar/Bat Mitzvah) or loved ones (e.g., through
mourning rituals). Through mystical or conversion experiences, individuals may find new visions and purpose to replace shattered dreams
and lives. Forgiving can be another method of religious transformation.

Religious Characteristics of Forgiveness

What makes forgiving religious? Virtually every religious tradition
places extraordinary value on love, kindness, and compassion and warns
against the unbridled emotions of hatred and bitterness. Forgiveness is
explicitly addressed within Christianity (see Marty, Chapter 1) and Judaism
(see Dorff, Chapter 2). Both traditions encourage their adherents to
return good for evil and practice acts of forgiveness. The great Jewish sage
Maimonides said that the failure to forgive someone who sincerely requests
it is as offensive as the original transgression (Minkin, 1987). Within the
New Testament, the reader is frequently encouraged to forgive others:
"Forbearing one another, and forgiving one another, if any man may
have a quarrel against any; even as Christ forgave you, so also do ye" (Col.
3:13, King James Version [KJV; cited herafter]). Empirical studies indicate
that people who are more religiously involved continue to place more value on forgiveness than their less religious counterparts (Gorsuch & Hao,
1993; Rokeach, 1973).

Sanctification of Forgiveness. Forgiveness can be profoundly religious in
two ways. First, it represents an act that can take on sacred qualities; put
another way, forgiveness can be sanctified. The power of religion goes
beyond belief in God or worship of the divine. Other seemingly secular objects can become imbued with divine-like qualities by virtue of
their association with God (see also Emmons, in press; Pargament, 1997).
And once sanctified, these objects may be sources of extraordinary
power. For instance, our research group recently examined whether
sanctified marriages are, in any sense, different from marriages that are

less sanctified (Mahoney et al., 1997). They were. Couples who viewed their marriages as sacred vows experienced higher levels of marital satisfaction and greater marital commitment, and they made use of more effective problem-solving strategies for dealing with marital conflict than did couples who saw their marriages as less sacred.

Similarly, forgiving can be sanctified. According to many religious traditions, human relationships are working models of an ideal relationship—that between the individual and God. From this perspective, a breach between two people that goes unhealed represents an offense against the sacred. Repairing the damage, in turn, signifies a spiritual as well as an interpersonal healing process. Forgiving then can become invested with sacred meaning, a practice that is integral to a vision of spiritual community in which we all require forgiveness and need to be forgiving (e.g., Patton, 1985).

Another kind of sanctification is directly relevant to forgiving—the sanctification of what it means to be human. Enright (1994) argues convincingly that forgiveness rests on a moral view that we all are fundamentally human in spite of differences in the ways we behave. And, as human beings, we are worthy of respect, dignity, and love. But many might ask, Why? What makes humanity inherently worthy of anything? The notion of inherent human worth is a fundamentally religious concept based on the belief that each of us contains a divine spark. Each of us is, in some sense, a manifestation of a power that goes beyond ourselves. As bearers of that divine spark, we are equally and inherently worthy of compassion, love, and respect. It is this sanctification of what it means to be human that helps make forgiveness possible.

Religious Models of Forgiveness. Religion contributes to forgiving in a second way: It provides models, methods, and resources for forgiving. From Joseph, to Hosea, to Jesus Christ, religious literature is filled with examples of remarkable individuals who transcended their own pain and reached out to others with compassion rather than perpetuate their suffering.

Religious traditions also contain worldviews that set the stage for forgiveness. Embedded in these worldviews are new ways to think about or "reframe" offenders and their relationships to victims. On the one hand, misdeeds of the perpetrator can be reattributed to ignorance rather than malice, as illustrated by Jesus' last words: "Father, forgive them; for they know not what they do" (Luke 23:34). On the other hand, we are reminded that none of us is without our own foibles ("He that is without sin among you, let him first cast a stone at her" (John 8:7) and that each of us requires purification and forgiveness. Thus, religious worldviews can provide radically different ways of thinking that encourage the spiritualization rather than the demonization of the offender and the healing rather than the fragmentation of community (see also Batson et al., 1989).

The decision to forgive itself can be conceptualized within a religious frame of reference as a "leap of faith," an opportunity to let go of negativity. There can be no guarantee of the outcomes, just as there can be no guarantee of God's existence. But viewed as a matter of faith, the act of forgiving is placed in a larger spiritual context of hope, surrender, trust, and goodwill.

Finally, people can draw on several religious resources to facilitate the process of forgiving, such as prayer, ritual, services, and the religious congregation (see Kinens, 1989). It is important to add that, for some, forgiving is less a conscious act of self-direction than it is a revelation.

Take the case of Corrie Ten Boom (1971), who, years after her imprisonment in a concentration camp, encountered one of her former Nazi *Schutzstaffel* (SS) guards at a church service. When he came up to shake her hand after the service, she was unable to respond initially. But after she prayed for the strength to forgive, she recounted this experience: "From my shoulder along my arm and through my hand a current seemed to pass from me to him, while into my heart sprang a love for this stranger that almost overwhelmed me" (p. 238). Ten Boom experienced her forgiveness as a gift from God.

It could be argued that forgiveness is religious only for those who come from or identify with a religious tradition. But keep in mind that most people in the United States do, in fact, come from a religious tradition, and most maintain some involvement in religious beliefs and practices (Gallup & Castelli, 1989). Even those who do not, however, may continue to sanctify forgiveness and draw on religious resources to facilitate it. Although the individual may have removed himself or herself from organized religion, forgiveness may have developed a "religious functional autonomy" of its own; it retains sacred value even though the individual has separated from the institutions and beliefs that gave birth to the value.

This point was illustrated in Rye's doctoral dissertation (Rye & Pargament, 1997). Rye wanted to know whether a religiously integrated forgiveness intervention would be helpful to women in college who felt they had been wronged in a romantic relationship. He compared the efficacy of this intervention to a secular forgiveness intervention that was virtually identical with the exception of the religious elements, as well as to a no-intervention comparison group. Both the religiously integrated and the secular forgiveness groups resulted in significant positive change in several dimensions, including measures of hopefulness, religious well-being, existential well-being, and three measures of forgiveness. The two treatment groups did not differ from each other in their degree of efficacy.

At first glance, this result might suggest that forgiving does not have to occur in a religious context to be successful. But Rye also asked the women in each of the groups how they went about the business of forgiving. Interestingly, the women identified religious resources as the first and third most frequent sources of assistance in the forgiveness process. The most commonly reported forgiveness strategy was to ask God for help and/or support in efforts to forgive. The second most common strategy was relying on support from friends. The third most common strategy was to pray for the person who had wronged the woman.

These female college students, from a state university in the Midwest, were not highly religious as a group. Also, participants in the secular and comparison conditions used religious forgiveness strategies more often than other strategies. Thus, the findings suggest that it may be very difficult to remove forgiveness from its spiritual context; in fact, the notion of a secular forgiveness group may be, for many people, an oxymoron.

Implications of Forgiving as a Method of Religious Coping

Thinking about forgiving as a method of religious coping has several interesting implications. We would like to focus on two of them here.

No Single Key to Good Coping. From the perspective of coping theory, there is no single key to good coping, no single panacea for everyone or for the full range of life's problems. Coping is a transactional process, involving a complex interplay of personal, situational, and larger social forces.

There can be no single key to good coping for a number of reasons: First, the value of any coping method cannot be disentangled from the demands raised by the situation. For instance, in the early stages of a heart attack, denial (a method of conservation if there ever was one) has devastating consequences. However, after the coronary, denial has been tied to lower anxiety, shorter hospitalization, and even lower risk for morbidity and mortality (Fowers, 1992). Similarly, active problem-focused efforts at coping have been found more helpful in controllable than uncontrollable situations; conversely, less active emotion-focused efforts at coping have been found more helpful in uncontrollable than controllable situations (Vitaliano, DeWolfe, Maiuro, Russo, & Katon, 1990).

We might expect forgiveness to vary in its value across situations as well. In this vein, McCullough and Worthington (1994) suggest that forgiveness may be inappropriate when the wounds from a personal assault are too fresh, when the violation is too severe, or when the mistreatment is ongoing. From the perspective of coping theory, we need to learn not only when to forgive, but when *not* to forgive.

Second, there is no single key to good coping because the value of any coping method is intimately tied to the values of the individual. As noted earlier, coping theory rests on the assumption that we do not seek the same ends out of life. People vary in choosing their objects of significance. The same methods of coping, then, are not necessarily appropriate to different people. Forgiveness may be a powerful method of coping for those interested in finding peace in their lives. Not everyone, however, is interested in this goal.

For instance, Baures (1996) interviewed twenty well-known survivors who had faced exceptionally difficult situations. All of these survivors had coped successfully with their ordeals. Yet not all took the same path. Through forgiveness, some were able to let go of their pain. Others, however, did not cope through forgiveness. Rather than letting go of their pain, they used it, revisited it, reworked it, and shared it with others in an attempt to create a more compassionate, more just world. Was their method of coping any less effective than those who forgave? We think not. They found a way of coping that was more helpful to them in their own search for significance.

There is one final reason why it is difficult to identify "panaceas" when it comes to coping. Many of the choices that we must make when confronted with major life stressors are far from simple. Any way of coping may be associated with both advantages and disadvantages. Thus, evaluations of the efficacy of any coping method should be alert to the potential for tradeoffs, both positive and negative outcomes that mirror, in essence, the difficult choices people face in times of trouble. For example, earlier we noted studies that indicate that denial can be helpful to heart attack sufferers later in their recovery. There is, however, an important downside. Empirical studies indicate that, while the patient in denial may be less depressed and more engaged in life, the spouse of the patient in denial is at greater risk of emotional trouble. In essence, the spouse takes on the burden of an illness the patient refuses to acknowledge (Stern & Pascale, 1979).

Forgiveness may also be associated with positive and negative outcomes simultaneously. To this point, research has focused on the impact of forgiveness on the forgiver. Important as he or she is, the forgiver represents only one relevant source of information. Forgiveness has profound interpersonal as well as personal implications (see Baumeister, Exline, & Sommer, Chapter 4). It is critically important to determine the impact of forgiving on others. Perhaps being forgiven facilitates a transformation as powerful in the perpetrator as it does in the forgiver. On the other hand, being forgiven may simply reinforce the perpetrator's negative behavior. Thus, at this time, we cannot dismiss this possible troubling scenario: a forgiveness that facilitates the well-being of the forgiver, but at the same time supports the perpetrator's misbehavior. We know of no studies that examine the effects of forgiving on the behavior of others. We need to extend the focus of our research beyond the forgiver to the world of the perpetrator.

Forgiving Is a Religious Value. A second implication of thinking about forgiving as a method of religious coping has more to do with religion than with coping. This point was illustrated in a story Baumeister told at the American Psychological Association in 1997. He was talking with a colleague about his plans to serve as a discussant on a panel focused on forgiveness. Her response was, "Oh, I don't believe in forgiveness." The belief was not stated in tentative scientific form of the kind we might expect from a social scientist. She didn't ask: What is your operational definition of forgiveness? She didn't say: I wonder what people mean by forgiveness, and I wonder about its effects. Instead, she made a statement that revealed her most fundamental beliefs and values.

This statement serves as a reminder that forgiveness is more than a method. It is a value, and, for many, a religious value. Her statement was, in certain respects, profoundly religious. This woman's view was not testable; it was not falsifiable. She simply did not believe in forgiveness, just as some do not believe in God, astrology, or the stock market.

Forgiveness should be understood within its religious context. Unfortunately, as Meek and McMinn (1997) note, many psychologists have detached forgiveness from its religious foundation, "so that it might be more acceptable to nonreligious clients and therapists" (p. 60). However, forgiving is more than a therapeutic technique, and it should not be treated as simply another method of change akin to systematic desensitization, hypnosis, or autogenic training (Jones, 1995).

Clinicians who work with clients struggling with mistreatment need to be especially sensitive to the value-laden questions that accompany this topic. It is important to remember that clinical interventions that promote forgiving are also encouraging fundamental changes in significance. We are not saying that we shouldn't be doing just that at times; helping is not value-free. But helping professionals must be very explicit with clients about their professional values and respectful of their clients' right to accept or reject these values.

In a related sense, it is important to be aware of the differences in the values and meanings of forgiveness to different religious groups. Members of different religious traditions may have generally favorable views toward forgiving. But they may think about and approach forgiving in different ways. For instance, for many Christians, forgiveness may be an unconditional value, an act of love and compassion offered to others regardless of the context or situation (Phillips, 1986). Many Jews, however, may see forgiveness more conditionally, depending on whether the perpetrator has shown remorse; the severity of the violation; or the length of time since the assault (Friedlander, 1986).

We need to learn more about how different religious and nonreligious groups view and approach forgiveness. In the process, we may find that religiously integrated forgiveness interventions are especially helpful to highly religious individuals. We may also find that forgiveness interventions should be tailored to fit within the worldviews of particular religious groups. And we may find that forgiveness interventions are simply inappropriate for some groups that place other values higher within their hierarchy of significance.

It is also important to remember that forgiveness is a value for researchers and practitioners as well as those they study and help. Our own models of forgiveness are embedded within our particular worldviews and values. We should be especially sensitive to the dangers of espousing as universal any models of forgiveness that grow out of specific faith traditions.

Two other potential value-related dangers exist. First, some, like Baumeister's colleague above, may be likely to reject the study of forgiveness out-of-hand. Indiscriminate *anti*-forgiveness values represent one potential roadblock to progress in this area of study. But indiscriminate *pro*-forgiveness values represent another potential pitfall. Researchers and practitioners who view forgiving as an "unqualified good" may be less than open to the hard questions and critical scrutiny that are so necessary to advance the field. Similarly, they also run the risk of overlooking other important values. What, for instance, happens to values of justice, fairness, and equity if we focus on forgiveness to the exclusion of these concerns? Enright's (1994) efforts to address the interface between the values of justice and forgiveness are particularly important here. To say that for too long we have focused on justice concerns to the exclusion of forgiveness is certainly true; but to substitute one set of imbalanced values for another seems a poor solution.

Obviously, our own values are showing here. We believe that the single-minded devotion to any end can become a problem when that end is defined narrowly or excludes other values (see James, 1902). A need for intimacy unbalanced by a need for autonomy can turn into a desperate dependency. The search for control can turn into fanaticism when it is unbalanced by a concern for others. The pursuit of meaning can become cold and obsessive when it is removed from other interests. And, we believe, the search for peace through forgiveness can become destructive when it is unbalanced by the values of responsibility and justice. Ultimately, forgiveness cannot be studied effectively if it is isolated from other values and methods of coping.

Thinking about forgiving as a way of religious coping, then, alerts us to a host of terribly important value-related questions—not only for those we study and serve, but for ourselves as well.

CONCLUSIONS

Forgiveness is unlike other methods of coping in one important respect: the way it has been studied. Within the coping literature, literally hundreds of studies have addressed basic questions: How do people cope? What situations elicit coping? How does coping change over time? What forms of coping are associated with beneficial and detrimental outcomes? Only recently, however, have researchers begun to develop coping interventions. The situation is just the reverse for forgiveness. A limited number of forgiveness interventions have been conducted (see Part III of this volume), but very little in the way of basic research has been done. Of course, we don't need to know why a solution works to go ahead with it. (John Snow was able to prevent cholera without an understanding of the etiology of the disease.) But if this area of study is to advance, we will need to lay a deeper foundation of basic knowledge.

Exciting basic questions about forgiving persist: What do various groups of people mean by forgiveness? Just how common is forgiving in the profound sense that we are using here? When does forgiveness occur, and under what conditions? Who is likely to forgive? Who is not? What are the implications of forgiving for ourselves, for those we forgive, for marriages, families, communities, and society more generally?

We would like to conclude with a more general comment about our own discipline—psychology. At the risk of stereotyping, American psychology is largely a psychology of personal control (Pargament, 1997). As a profession, we have developed a number of ways to enhance our control over what is not controlled. Psychodynamic practitioners try to make the unconscious conscious. Behaviorists try to help people master the contingencies of their lives. Cognitive therapists teach people how to gain control over their thoughts and feelings. Wonderful advances have been achieved in many areas. But our field is less knowledgeable and helpful when it comes to the uncontrollable — when we face situations that are less amenable to further action, when we have to come to terms with fundamental human limitations.

Religion is more helpful here. Religion speaks a language unfamiliar to psychology — forbearance, surrender, letting go, conversion, faith, finitude, suffering, meaning, hope — and, of course, forgiveness. These terms grow out of confrontation with the deepest crises of existence. They are terms that reflect our response to human frailty and mortality.

In spite of, or perhaps because of, these different worldviews, psychology (with its focus on the controllable) and religion (with its focus on the uncontrollable) have much to offer each other. Our capacities and our limitations are both part of the human condition; and, as we cope with life's most troubling problems, we have to struggle with both the possible and the futile.

Perhaps one of the reasons why psychology has largely overlooked the potential for significant transformation in coping is because many of the most powerful transformational mechanisms — from rites of passage to conversion — are rooted in religion. But psychology has much to gain by broadening its boundaries to include religious values and methods of coping. In opening itself up to these methods, new to psychology, but very old to the world, the field of psychology may be in for some surprises; paradoxically, it is through some of these methods of religious coping that people may be able to achieve their most profound changes.

Psychology has something to offer the religious world, in turn, when it shifts its sights to religious methods of coping, such as forgiving. By applying its critical thinking skills, research methods, and background in psychological intervention to the topic of forgiving, psychology may be able to work in concert with the members of many religious communities searching for significance in stressful times. In this sense, the study of forgiving may help to build a bridge between psychological and religious worlds, two worlds that have been separated for too long.

NOTES

1. Much of the discussion is a shorthand description of material presented in Pargament's book on the psychology of religion and coping (1997).

2. Note that the concept of "significance" is broader than the concept of "meaning," a construct that has a cognitive and favorable connotation; in our framework, meaning is only one possible object of significance.

REFERENCES

Aldwin, C.M. (1994). *Stress, coping and development: An integrative perspective.* New York: Guilford Publications.

Augsberger, D. (1981). *Caring enough to forgive: Caring enough not to forgive.* Scottsdale, PA: Herald Press.

Batson, C.D., Oleson, K.C., Weeks, J.L., Healy, S., Reeves, P.J., Jennings, P., & Brown, T. (1989). Religious prosocial motivation: Is it altruistic or egoistic? *Journal of Personality and Social Psychology, 57,* 873–884.

Baumeister, R.F., Exline, J.E., & Sommer, K.L., (1998). The victim role, grudge theory, and two dimensions of forgiveness. In E.L. Worthington, Jr. (Ed.), *Dimensions of forgiveness: Psychological research & theological perspectives* (pp. 79–104). Philadelphia, PA: Templeton Foundation Press.

Baures, M.M. (1996). Letting go of bitterness and hate. *Journal of Humanistic Psychology, 36,* 75–90.

Coe, G.A. (1916). *The psychology of religion.* Chicago: University of Chicago Press.

Diamond, E.L. (1982). The role of anger in essential hypertension and coronary heart disease. *Psychological Bulletin, 92,* 410–433.

Dorff, E. The elements of forgiveness: A Jewish approach. In E.L. Worthington, Jr. (Ed.), *Dimensions of forgiveness: Psychological research & theological perspectives* (pp. 29–55). Philadelphia, PA: Templeton Foundation Press.

Emmons, R.A. (in press). Assessing spirituality through personal goals: Implications for research on religion and subjective well-being. *Social Indicators Research.*

Enright, R.D. (1994). Piaget on the moral development of forgiveness: Identity or reciprocity. *Human Development, 37,* 63–80.

Enright, R.D., & the Human Development Study Group (1991). The moral development of forgiveness. In W. Kurtines & J. Gewirtz (Eds.), *Handbook of moral behavior and development* (Vol. 1, pp. 123–152). Hillsdale, NJ: Erlbaum.

Fowers, B.J. (1992). The Cardiac Denial of Impact Scale: A brief self-report research measure. *Journal of Psychosomatic Research, 36,* 469–475.

Freud, S. (1927/1961). *The future of an illusion.* New York: Norton.

Friedlander, A.H. (1986). Judaism and the concept of forgiving. *Christian Jewish Relations, 19,* 6–13.

Gallup, G., Jr., & Castelli, J. (1989). *The people's religion: American faith in the 90's.* New York: Macmillan.

Gorsuch, R.L., & Hao, J.Y. (1993). Forgiveness: An exploratory factor analysis and its relationship to religious variables. *Review of Religious Research, 34,* 333–347.

James, W. (1902). *The varieties of religious experience: A study in human nature.* New York: Modern Library.

Jones, L.G. (1995). *Embodying forgiveness: A theological analysis.* Grand Rapids, MI: William B. Eerdmans.

Kaplan, A. (1964). *The conduct of inquiry.* San Francisco: Chandler.

Kinens, J.J. (1989). What is lost shall be found. In J.T. Clemons (Ed.), *Sermons on suicide* (pp. 71–78). Louisville, KY: Westminster/John Knox Press.

Lazarus, R.S., & Folkman, S. (1984). *Stress, appraisal, and coping.* New York: Springer.

Mahoney, A.M., Pargament, K.I., Scott, E., Swank, A., Emery, E., Hipp, K., Rye, M., & Butter, E. (1997). S*acred vows: The sanctification of marriage and its psychosocial implications.* Paper presented at the American Psychological Association, Chicago, IL.

Marty, M.E. The ethos of Christian forgiveness. In E.L. Worthington, Jr. (Ed.), *Dimensions of forgiveness: Psychological research & theological perspectives* (pp. 9–28). Philadelphia, PA: Templeton Foundation Press.

McCullough, M.E., & Worthington, E.L., Jr. (1994). Encouraging clients to forgive people who have hurt them: Review, critique, and research prospectus. *Journal of Psychology and Theology, 22,* 3–20.

McCullough, M.E., Worthington, E.L., Jr., & Rachal, K.C. (1997). Interpersonal forgiving in close relationships. *Journal of Personality and Social Psychology, 73,* 321–336.

Meek, K.R., & McMinn, M.R. (1997). Forgiveness: More than a therapeutic technique. *Journal of Psychology and Christianity, 16,* 51-61.

Minkin, J.S. (1987). *The teachings of Maimonides.* Northvale, NJ: Aronson.

Pargament, K.I. (1997). *The psychology of religion and coping: Theory, research, practice.* New York: Guilford Publications.

Pargament, K.I. (in press). The psychology of religion and spirituality? Yes and no. *International Journal for the Psychology of Religion.*

Pargament, K.I., Sullivan, M.S., Balzer, W.E., Van Haitsma, K.S., & Raymark, P. H. (1995). The many meanings of religiousness: A policy-capturing approach. *Journal of Personality, 63,* 953–983.

Patton, J. (1985). *Is human forgiveness possible? A pastoral care perspective.* Nashville: Abingdon Press.

Phillips, A. (1986). Forgiveness reconsidered. *Christian Jewish Relations, 19,* 14–21.

Rokeach, M. (1973). *The nature of human values.* New York: Free Press.

Rowe, J.O., Halling, S., Davies, E., Leifer, M., Powers, D., & Van Bronkhorst, J. (1989). The psychology of forgiving another: A dialogical research approach. In R.S. Valle & S. Halling (Eds.), *Existential-phenomenological perspectives in psychology: Exploring the breadth of human experience* (pp. 233–234). New York: Plenum Press.

Rye, M. S., & Pargament, K. I. (1997). *Forgiveness and romantic relationships in college.* Paper presented at the American Psychological Association, Chicago, IL.

Simon, S. B., & Simon, S. (1990). *Forgiveness: How to make peace with your past and get on with your life.* New York: Basic Books.

Stern, M. J., & Pascale, L. (1979). Psychosocial adaptation post-myocardial infarction: The spouse's dilemma. *Journal of Psychosomatic Research, 23,* 83–87.

Ten Boom, C. (1971). *The hiding place.* Toronto: Bantam Books.

Vitaliano, P.P., DeWolfe, D.J., Maiuro, R.D., Russo, J., & Katon, W. (1990). Appraised changeability of a stressor as a modifier of the relationship between coping and depression: A test of the hypothesis of fit. *Journal of Personality and Social Psychology, 59,* 582–592.

Zinnbauer, B.J., Pargament, K.I., Cole, B., Rye, M.S., Butter, E.M., Belavich, T.G., Hipp, K.M., Scott, A.B., & Kadar, J.L. (1997). Religion and spirituality: Unfuzzying the fuzzy. *Journal for the Scientific Study of Religion, 36,* 549-564.

CHAPTER 4

The Victim Role, Grudge Theory, and Two Dimensions of Forgiveness

Roy F. Baumeister, Julie Juola Exline, and Kristin L. Sommer

W HEN ONE PERSON DOES SOMETHING to hurt another, the relationship between the two of them can be permanently damaged. Because people are imperfect, such transgressions are probably inevitable, and so the prospects for human relationships to survive and flourish over a long period of time may seem dim. Forgiveness offers an alternative, however: If the victim can forgive the transgressor, the relationship may be repaired and possibly even saved from ending. At the interpersonal level, the essence of forgiveness is that it creates the possibility for a relationship to recover from the damage it suffers from one person's transgressions against the other. Forgiveness is thus a potentially powerful prosocial phenomenon. It benefits human social life by helping relationships to heal.

Another way of looking at forgiveness is as an individual, or intrapsychic, phenomenon. Forgiveness in this view is something that occurs inside the mind and heart of the victim. The victim has suffered at the hands of the perpetrator and must choose between two paths. One involves sustaining anger and resentment (i.e., holding a grudge) toward the perpetrator. The other involves forgiving, which entails an effort to bring such feelings to an end and replace them with positive thoughts, feelings, and actions. Because sustaining anger and resentment over time can be unpleasant, stressful, and unhealthy, forgiveness may be beneficial to the victim even apart from whatever effect it has on the relationship between the two people. Indeed, forgiveness of this sort may be important and beneficial in cases where the perpetrator has vanished or even died, and so no relationship exists to be salvaged. The victim's peace of mind is benefit enough.

Thus, forgiveness can be conceptualized at two different levels. This chapter will treat them as two dimensions of forgiveness: (1) the inner, intrapsychic dimension involving the victim's emotional state (and the cognitive and behavioral accompaniments), and (2) the interpersonal dimension involving the ongoing relationship within which forgiveness takes place or fails to do so. Although the majority of past work has focused on the inner dimension of forgiveness, we think the interpersonal dimension is too fundamental and important to neglect, and so we shall seek to give the interpersonal dimension its due.

Because forgiveness (in both dimensions) depends on how the victim responds to a transgression, it is important that forgiveness theory pay careful attention to the role of the victim and to the costs and benefits it contains. Early research showed that victims suffer from their traumas and seek to make sense of them. More recent work has begun to shed light on how victims think and on some of the appeal of remaining in the victim role, as well as on the price people may have to pay for remaining in that role. This chapter will summarize what research on victimization and the victim role has to offer forgiveness theory.

In particular, it is important to understand the barriers to forgiveness that go beyond mere stubbornness. If holding a grudge is the opposite of forgiveness, then it is essential to analyze the appeal and the potential (or perceived) benefits of holding a grudge. Grudge theory and forgiveness theory thus constitute mirror images of each other. Our analysis of the victim role offers one useful basis for constructing grudge theory, which in turn offers a useful perspective for understanding forgiveness.

The precise nature of forgiveness remains elusive, and indeed the definitional difficulties suggest that the very concept of forgiveness has some contradictions or problems at its core. Does forgiveness mean agreeing to act as if the transgression never happened? Does it mean that the perpetrator need not feel guilty anymore? Does it mean that no restitution is needed? That no revenge will be sought? That the victim will not feel upset or angry about the transgression anymore? That the perpetrator is free to do it again? Careful philosophical distinctions may be made, but do people actually respect and abide by them? And if the answer to many of those questions is "no," then in what sense is the transgression forgiven? That is, if the person will continue to condemn the action and the further interactions between the two people are changed because of it, then has the transgression been forgiven at all? We think that analyzing the victim role and paying due attention to the two different dimensions of forgiveness enable us to make sense of some of these questions and to understand why forgiveness may mean one thing to victims and something different to perpetrators—with the potential for serious misunderstandings as a result.

TRANSGRESSION

If there were no transgressions, there would be no need for forgiveness. Forgiveness theory is an extension of the theory of evil in an important sense. The theory of evil explains why transgressions occur and how they are perceived, as well as their consequences (e.g., Baumeister, 1997). In the aftermath of a transgression, however, forgiveness involves bringing to an end the detrimental effects of the transgression. Ideally, the relationship can return to something akin to the normal, positive state that it enjoyed before the transgression took place.

Transgression involves a perpetrator and a victim. The problem of forgiveness can therefore be understood as a question of whether the victim forgives the perpetrator. As a choice by the victim, forgiveness is a rejection of the victim role and a gesture of return to normalcy. The alternative is to hold a grudge against the perpetrator, thereby altering the relationship and continuing to identify oneself in terms of victimization.

Victims are not the only ones who face a choice point in the aftermath of a transgression. Perpetrators also can respond in widely different ways. Some perpetrators want forgiveness, feel genuinely sorry for what they have done, can promise sincerely never to repeat the transgression, and are willing to do whatever they can to make up for it. Others are thoroughly unrepentant and do not even acknowledge their wrongdoing. Many others fall between these extremes, and yet others are long out of touch or even dead. The perpetrator's position on this must inevitably make a huge difference to the victim and hence to forgiveness theory as well.

The perpetrator's options can be understood in terms of guilt over the transgression. Guilt involves negative affect associated with possible condemnations of one's actions (Baumeister, Stillwell, & Heatherton, 1994; Tangney, 1991, 1992). The perpetrator may or may not acknowledge guilt; that is, the perpetrator may recognize the act as wrong and may apologize or make amends—or, at the other extreme, may refuse to acknowledge any wrongdoing.

The German word for guilt is *Schuld*, and the same word is used to refer to debt. Indeed, the Lord's Prayer (Matt. 6:9-13) in some English versions (e.g., New Revised Standard Version [NRSV], 1989) use the word "debt" in just this seemingly odd way to refer to guilt over transgressions; but the German basis makes this more intelligible. The resemblance between guilt and debt is more than superficial, and an interpersonal analysis can make the two concepts almost interchangeable.

In that analysis, forgiveness means canceling, as of a debt. Indeed, it is noteworthy that the word "forgive" is used for both canceling someone's guilt and for canceling someone's debt. At the interpersonal level, a transgression within an ongoing relationship creates a debt: If I have wronged you, I owe you something that will make up for it.

Clearly, there is some cost to forgiving a debt, because the victim in effect agrees to be "poorer" in some sense. If you don't have to pay me back, I will have less money than I would have if you did. If one starts forgiving a lot of such debts, or even a few large ones, one could end up in financial difficulties. The same applies to transgressions. If you forgive all the wrongs that have been done to you, you relinquish the social equivalent of the debts the transgressors owed you. Your right or power to extract concessions, compromises, or compliance from them on future occasions is reduced.

This leads us to the final theoretical relative of forgiveness theory—

what we call "grudge theory." Some recent works on guilt (e.g., Freedman & Enright, 1996; McCullough, Sandage, & Worthington, 1997; McCullough, Worthington, & Rachal, 1997) have emphasized the positive, desirable features of forgiveness, and to be sure these need to be studied and explicated. Yet it is essential to realize that people often have important, compelling reasons for withholding forgiveness. Refusing to forgive entails holding a grudge, and there are presumably some advantages to holding the grudge as opposed to forgiving. A balanced theory must recognize the reasons that hold people back from forgiving.

VICTIM AND PERPETRATOR

It is crucial to appreciate that victims and perpetrators have different perspectives and are prone to interpret the same events differently. Recent work has documented systematic ways in which perpetrators and victims perceive things from different points of view (Baumeister, Stillwell, & Wotman, 1990; Mikula, 1994; Stillwell & Baumeister, 1997). Moreover, both roles seem to contain motivated biases that can twist the facts to fit a preferred view.

Not surprisingly, the main thrust of differences between victims and perpetrators is that victims exaggerate the severity of the transgression, while perpetrators tend to minimize and downplay it. Victims tend to see the act as possessing severe consequences, as part of an ongoing pattern of misbehavior, as inexcusable and immoral, and as gratuitous (i.e., as having no valid reason other than sheer meanness or arbitrary cruelty). In contrast, perpetrators perceive their transgressions as involving extenuating and mitigating circumstances, tend to downplay the consequences, divide blame among many parties (including themselves), and describe their actions as arising from motives that were understandable and sometimes legitimate. These differences have been established by content coding of personal narratives and confirmed by statistical tests (Baumeister et al., 1990; Exline, Yali, & Lobel, 1997; Mikula, 1994).

These differences are likely to complicate the issue of forgiveness. The average perpetrator is much more eager than the victim to consider the matter settled and to forget the incident. For example, the ongoing consequences of the transgression may be quite salient to the victim—certainly more so than to the perpetrator—and so forgiving requires the victim to discount those consequences in some way. Meanwhile, the perpetrator may not even be aware of some of these consequences and hence not recognize the difficulty of forgiving; that is, the perpetrator may fail to give the victim credit for discounting these consequences.

Another difference between victim and perpetrator was observed by Baumeister (1997) in his survey of evil. What he termed "the magnitude gap" signifies a general pattern in which the victim loses more than the perpetrator gains. This, too, exacerbates the difficulty of forgiveness because the debt cannot be precisely repaid in a way that will satisfy both parties. (Hence the tendency for vendettas and other conflicts to become unresolvable over time: As soon as one payback makes one party think that the two sides are now even, the other party is likely to think that the ledger is egregiously out of balance and that some retaliation is warranted.) It is as if a debt were created by one person lending $100, but somehow the borrower received only $50; what amount should be repaid? Neither sum would satisfy both parties.

Traditional wisdom holds that perpetrators lie and dissemble to escape punishment, while victims tell the truth. The assumption is that victims are free from the biases that distort the perpetrators' accounts, so victims can be trusted. Recent work challenges this view, however. Stillwell and Baumeister (1997) gave participants identical information about an incident involving a transgression and instructed them to retell the story in the first person as if they were either the victim or the perpetrator (after being assigned at random to one or the other role). Control participants were told simply to tell the story in the third person without identifying with either role or taking sides. By comparing the participants' stories with the original, objective information, it was possible to see who distorted the incident.

The results revealed that both victims and perpetrators distorted the narrative; that is, both made an average of twenty-five errors in their stories compared with only seventeen errors in the control condition. Victims and perpetrators distorted the story in different ways, of course: For example, perpetrators tended to leave out some of the bad consequences that the victim suffered, whereas victims tended to omit some of the mitigating circumstances that reduced the perpetrator's blame. Still, the net distortion was almost exactly the same. Hence, both victim and perpetrator roles contain biases in how people perceive and interpret events.

Forgiveness, therefore, must face a formidable set of obstacles. The victim, in effect, has to cancel a debt that is larger than the one the perpetrator acknowledges. To the extent that forgiveness is an interpersonal act, it must be negotiated between two people who interpret and evaluate things in systematically different ways.

TWO DIMENSIONS OF FORGIVENESS

Our explication of the different perspectives of victim and perpetrator indicates that forgiveness must be understood both as something that occurs inside people (victims) and between people (victim and perpetrator). To give both of these their due entails recognizing that forgiveness has at least two major dimensions. These may be assumed to have distinct causes, properties, and consequences, and so it is confusing (if not misleading) to lump all of forgiveness together and treat the topic as if it were a unitary phenomenon.

On the one hand, forgiveness refers to an emotional attitude based on cognitive appraisals and interpretations. To forgive someone means to cease feeling angry or resentful over the transgression. This form of forgiveness is thus essentially intrapsychic: It involves states and processes inside the mind of the victim. In this sense, it is even meaningful to speak of forgiving someone who is dead or absent or who, for other reasons, would have no way of knowing whether he or she has been forgiven. The emotional dimension of forgiveness is probably mediated in most cases by cognitive processes, such as framing the transgression so as not to seem so bad, or making oneself understand the perpetrator's point of view.

On the other hand, forgiveness is a social action that happens between people. It is a step toward returning the relationship between them to the condition it had before the transgression. Forgiveness signifies that the victim will not seek further revenge or demand further reparations, and it may mean that the perpetrator does not have to feel continually guilty or to change his or her behavior to make it up to the victim. Like many social acts, forgiveness can occur on a specific occasion and can even be publicly witnessed by others.

In a nutshell, then, forgiveness may best be understood as having two distinct dimensions: It is both an internal mental/emotional state and an interpersonal act. It can be a process that goes on entirely inside the mind of the victim, or it can be a transaction that occurs between two people, even without much in the way of inner processing.

These two dimensions of forgiveness can be considered orthogonal; that is, they are in principle independent of each other, and so the actual social situation may contain either, or both, or neither. (Undoubtedly, they do correlate and overlap to some extent in reality.) In effect, this creates a "matrix" of possibilities, as shown in Table 1. These are worth considering separately.

Table 1. Two Dimensions of Forgiveness: Possible Combinations

Interpersonal Act	+	No Intrapsychic State	=	Hollow Forgiveness
Intrapsychic State	+	No Interpersonal Act	=	Silent Forgiveness
Intrapsychic State	+	Interpersonal Act	=	Total Forgiveness
No Intrapsychic State	+	No Interpersonal Act	=	No Forgiveness

Hollow Forgiveness

One possible combination would involve the interpersonal act without the intrapsychic state; that is, the victim may express forgiveness to the perpetrator, but not actually feel this forgiveness privately. The victim may continue to harbor some resentments or hurts even after having said, "I forgive you" to the perpetrator. Enright and his colleagues speak of "making the commitment to forgive," which signifies the beginning of the intrapsychic process of forgiving—but perhaps only the beginning (Enright & the Human Development Study Group, 1991; see also Al-Mabuk, Enright, & Cardis, 1995). When one makes the commitment to forgive, one may well express this to the perpetrator, particularly if the perpetrator is a partner in a close relationship, is someone whom one sees frequently, and who may also be anxious to secure forgiveness. Indeed, expressing forgiveness is probably an integral part of making the commitment to forgive.

What we know about the gaps between victims and perpetrators makes this discrepancy especially likely. The transgression looms larger to the victim than to the perpetrator, and so the victim may find it hard to get rid of all hard feelings. In contrast, the perpetrator is often all too ready to put the transgression behind and cease thinking about it. Therefore, the words "I forgive you" may mark only the beginning of the process to the victim, whereas to the perpetrator they signify that the matter is ended. The perpetrator may then comfortably go on acting as if the transgression never happened, perceiving that the relationship is back on its pretransgression footing, whereas the victim continues to harbor hurts and resentments.

Moreover, these hurts and resentments may be all the more troublesome because the victim now feels prohibited from expressing them. Once the victim has expressed forgiveness, he or she will not, supposedly, bring the transgression up again as if it were an unpaid debt. Yet, to the victim, the matter may not be so easily settled. The victim may have resolved only to begin to *try* to put the matter behind and not continue feeling upset. This resolve is likely to be imperfectly maintained. Victims may think they have forgiven, only to have resentful or hurt feelings crop up again; and perpetrators may remain unaware of the victim's inner conflicts.

Ironically, it is now especially costly to bring up the transgression again. A major advantage of the victim role (see below) is that it confers a position of moral superiority. Transgressors have done something bad and so must carry the load of guilt or shame that attends what they did, whereas the victims are presumably innocent and are entitled to positive treatment for what they have suffered. Yet, if the victim expresses forgiveness but still continues to bring up the transgression in a re-proachful fashion, then the victim in effect sacrifices some moral high ground—the perpetrator can reproach the victim for going back on his or her word. To pursue the debt analogy, the victim who brings up continuing hurt after expressing forgiveness is like someone who has agreed to cancel the other's debt but then later requires repayment.

If forgiveness is understood essentially or exclusively in intrapsychic terms, then this combination of public expression despite private reluctance would be regarded as pseudoforgiveness, or in some other way as not real forgiveness. Again, however, that is a one-sided and problematic way of looking at the issue. A public statement of forgiveness is likely to be very real and meaningful to the perpetrator, especially if he or she is kept in the dark about any continuing hard feelings the victim may have. Hence, we favor a term such as "hollow forgiveness" or "outer forgiveness" that acknowledges the interpersonal action despite the lack of inner emotional concurrence.

The concept of hollow forgiveness draws attention to a theoretically and practically important discrepancy between the two dimensions. Intrapsychic forgiveness has two steps: one in which the victim begins to forgive, and a second in which the forgiveness is more or less fully achieved and the victim no longer feels anger or resentment. Interpersonal forgiveness does not, however, normally recognize two steps, but instead focuses on the single act of expressing forgiveness. This mismatch is a potential source of conflict and misunderstanding; when the victim says "I forgive you" to the perpetrator, the victim's inner processes may be only starting the process of forgiving. It might facilitate mutual understanding, and indeed the healing process between victim and perpetrator, if victims learned to express forgiveness in two steps so that they could say, "I will start trying to forgive you" without letting the perpetrator entirely off the hook.

Silent Forgiveness

A second possible combination is the reverse of the first: intrapsychic forgiveness without interpersonal expression. In this case, the victim may have ceased to feel angry or hostile toward the perpetrator, but neglects to express this. The victim thus allows the perpetrator to continue feeling guilty and may in fact continue to act as if the perpetrator is in the wrong (i.e., owes an apology or restitution).

Silent forgiveness seems manipulative and even hypocritical, although it has certain pragmatic considerations to recommend it. Indeed, as we shall see from grudge theory, it may be a very useful course from the victim's point of view—it enjoys the advantages of forgiveness (cessation of negative affect), but avoids the disadvantages (loss of the other's concessions and restitution). In some situations, such as that of an abusive spouse, the victim may wish to be very cautious about expressing forgiveness out of a genuine fear that it could lead to further harm.

Clark and her colleagues have made a distinction between two kinds of human relationships (Clark, 1984; Clark & Mills, 1979; Clark, Mills, & Powell, 1986). Communal relationships are defined by a norm of mutual concern for each other's needs and wants. Exchange relationships are governed by norms of equity and payback, so that each favor should be returned or compensated. Exchange relationships may be especially fertile grounds for this sort of unstated forgiveness because to release the other from a debt or obligation (unilaterally and without getting anything) goes against the relationship norms. Even in communal relationships, however, people may occasionally want to influence the other's behavior by using a sense of debt or obligation that may accompany past transgressions ("After all I've sacrificed for you..."), even if those people do not privately harbor lingering resentment or hurt.

Total Forgiveness and No Forgiveness

Two other combinations of the two dimensions are possible, of course. One involves both intrapsychic and interpersonal forgiveness: total forgiveness. The victim ceases to feel upset or resentful about the transgression, and the perpetrator is released from further obligation and guilt. In this case, the relationship may indeed return fully to its pretransgression state.

The final combination would involve neither intrapsychic nor interpersonal forgiveness. This is the "total grudge" combination. The complete lack of forgiveness requires some consideration and analysis.

Many writers have touted the benefits of forgiveness, including benefits to the forgiver (e.g., McCullough, et al., 1997a). In view of those benefits, why would someone fail to forgive? For this, we need to understand the contingencies that govern relationships in the wake of transgressions that make grudges appealing.

GRUDGE THEORY: WHY FORGIVE?

Suppose someone has wronged you. You face a choice: Either you forgive the transgression or you hold a grudge. Why would you choose the latter course?

Claims on Rewards and Benefits

An obvious reason for sustaining a grudge is that the victim seeks practical or material benefits from the perpetrator. If the other person has wronged you, he or she owes you something. To forgive is, in essence, to relinquish such claims. A transgression that has been forgiven is, by definition, not one for which further claims are pending.

The analogy to debt is instructive here. Forgiving a debt entails that the debtor no longer has to pay it back. The forgiver thus agrees to make do with less money than he or she would otherwise be entitled to have. Whether the debt is $0.50 or $50,000, to extend forgiveness means that you will not get it back. In a similar fashion, expressing forgiveness for a crime or trespass implies that you will not press charges or sue for damages.

A story told by Tavris (1989) exemplifies how interpersonal transgressions can lead to material benefits. A husband was sexually unfaithful to his wife on one occasion, and the wife refused to forgive him afterward, even though he confessed, apologized, and sought to make amends. Nothing he did seemed able to reduce her anger and resentment. Eventually, they sought marital therapy. The therapist helped them work out an explicit contract by which the husband agreed to perform a definite set of extra chores and favors for the wife (e.g., cleaning the bathroom on a specified set of occasions), in return for which she agreed to forgive him and consider the matter settled. Although this case is extreme in the way an explicit contract was made, many other cases may involve implicit versions of the same thing: A transgression is forgiven when the perpetrator performs a recognizable set of acts to benefit the victim.

Still, Tavris' story shows that the victim can derive tangible benefits by holding onto the grudge. If the woman had immediately expressed forgiveness toward her husband, he would never have had to make that contract and perform those extra chores and favors for her. The more general point remains that to forgive can be costly, in both interpersonal and intrapsychic terms. It is no wonder that people are sometimes reluctant to do it.

The rewards do not have to be material. In some cases, the perpetrator owes the victim other forms of restitution and seeks to make amends in a variety of ways. Guilt does motivate people to express forgiveness. By doing so, one releases the person from guilt and relinquishes all the things the person might have done in order to make amends.

Another nonmaterial reward of refusing to forgive is a possible sense of moral superiority. The victim can claim a valuable moral high ground by maintaining a sense of righteous indignation, but to forgive is willingly to abandon that advantageous position. Moreover, the moral superiority issue may depend on whether one is concerned with inner forgiveness or intrapsychic forgiveness. With inner or intrapsychic forgiveness, the victim willingly relinquishes the moral high ground. Expressing forgiveness interpersonally, however, may even enhance the victim's claim to moral superiority, because the act of forgiveness is itself seen as morally commendable.

To Prevent Recurrence

The victim role is primarily one of looking backward, defined as it is by an event that occurred in the past. Yet some victims look to the future, and how the future appears to them is of considerable importance. Indeed, Holman and Silver (1998) have emphasized the forward versus backward orientation of victims as one of the defining criteria of whether they are coping and adjusting well. Hence, when a victim begins to recover and is ready to resume life in a positive spirit, he or she may begin to look to the future.

Inevitably, perhaps, an important consideration for a victim who begins to look forward is whether the victimization will happen again. If one recovers from one trauma only to face another—and especially if one can anticipate a long series of such abuses stretching out for years ahead—the prospect is dim. Regardless of how one feels about a past trauma, future traumas have to be considered. Moreover, whatever has happened before is generally more likely to happen again (and harder to dismiss from the realm of the possible) than is something that has never happened. Therefore, a victim may well wonder: Will this person do this to me again?

Forgiving may well increase the probability that something will happen again. To be sure, forgiving does not necessarily entail totally forgetting about the transgression or returning the relationship to precisely where it stood before the transgression. Still, the idealized forms of forgiveness and reconciliation do suggest those criteria: The relationship returns to exactly the same condition and situation it had before the transgression. Obviously, that original situation made the transgression possible, because that situation is precisely the one in which the transgression occurred. Hence, if you could return to precisely that state, the transgression would be just as likely to occur as it was previously.

In contrast, by refusing to express forgiveness, the victim may hope to exert some influence on the perpetrator not to repeat that transgression. If I tell you that I forgive you for forgetting my birthday, I essentially release you from all guilt; there may thus be little to prevent you from forgetting my next birthday. In contrast, if I refuse to express forgiveness, such as if I continue to tell you how hurt or disappointed I was that you forgot it, you may be much less likely to forget my next birthday.

In particular, as long as the victim refuses to express forgiveness, the victim can continue reminding the perpetrator of the transgression. If you have forgiven the person, you are not supposed to bring the matter up any more or to induce guilt through such reminders. Expressing forgiveness thus restricts the options available to the forgiver, especially for controlling the further behavior of the perpetrator. By refusing to behave in a forgiving manner, the victim retains greater ability to exert such influence.

An important implication of this is that the perpetrator's attitude makes a big difference. Some perpetrators may apologize, accept responsibility for what they did, acknowledge that it was wrong, and implicitly or explicitly promise not to repeat the transgression. Such cases are probably rather easy to forgive, in both interpersonal and intrapsychic terms, because one of the major barriers to forgiveness is removed.

Other perpetrators may deny their wrongdoing or insist that they had a right to do what they did. To express forgiveness toward such persons is much riskier and costlier to the victim. If the perpetrator does not see anything wrong in his or her actions, then there is no reason that those actions will not be repeated—other than the punishing actions by the victim. If the victim expresses forgiveness, then the last obstacle to repeating the transgression is removed.

In an important sense, then, blaming the other person can be viewed as a substitute for the other's deficiency in self-blame. If the perpetrator does not accept blame, and the victim forgives the perpetrator, then there is no blame at all and no reason to think that the transgression will not be repeated. It is rational and self-protective for the victim to behave in a grudging manner until the perpetrator acknowledges his or her guilt, such as by apologizing, because such actions carry the implicit promise that the transgression will not be repeated.

In support of this analysis, Exline and her colleagues (1997) found that the perpetrator's response was the single largest predictor of forgiveness, and a perpetrator's apology correlated with high forgiveness. Other studies have also demonstrated the value of apologies in eliciting forgiveness (Darby & Schlenker, 1982). Confessions likewise promote forgiveness (Weiner, Graham, Peter, & Zmuidinas, 1991). Although these studies examined intrapsychic forgiveness rather than interpersonal expressions of it, the findings confirm the view that there are reasons to hold a grudge when the perpetrator refuses to acknowledge wrongdoing.

Continued Suffering

Undoubtedly, one barrier to forgiveness is the continuation of suffering or other consequences of the transgression. If someone murdered your spouse or child, how could you truly forgive that person, whether in interpersonal or intrapsychic terms? The murder has irrevocably deprived you of the relationship with the deceased person, and you continue to suffer that deprivation for the rest of your life.

In principle, the continuation of consequences is not a determining factor of forgiveness. People may forgive or not, regardless of whether they suffer continuing consequences of the transgression.

Yet the time frame of forgiveness is quite relevant. One way to understand the goal of forgiveness is to consign the transgression to the past in a way that does not have an adverse effect on the relationship's future. But if the consequences of the transgression continue into the present and future, it is clearly much more difficult to bury the transgression in the past. The transgression, if its consequences persist, affects the relationship's future, and so forgiveness is at best a valiant effort to pretend—to the self or the other person—that this is not so.

In other words, when one continues to suffer adverse consequences, the transgression continues to be quite relevant, and indeed it takes its place as one determining factor for the state of one's present and future life. To forgive and forget would be to pretend that the transgression had not occurred. Such a pretense is clearly easier to maintain if the transgression is not such a determining factor.

Thus, the magnitude and duration of the consequences of the transgression should help determine forgiveness. To forgive when one will continue to suffer adverse consequences is probably quite difficult, and indeed it may even be illusory. How can one continue to suffer without blaming the person who caused the suffering? How can one expect to forgive if suffering occurs over that deed every day?

A variation on this possibility is that the transgression changes the victim's perception of the perpetrator in some fundamental, far-reaching way. It becomes therefore impossible to revert to the prior relationship. Transgressions that violate trust may provide a good example of this. The transgression itself may be of little consequence, but trust is gone; therefore, it is impossible to resume the relationship in its previous form. Even if intrapsychic forgiveness occurs, reconciliation may not be possible.

Pride and Revenge

Many transgressions involve blows to the victim's self-esteem or pride. Victims of such transgressions may feel that to forgive—whether in intrapsychic or interpersonal terms—would be to accept a loss of face or even lower self-esteem. If you intrapsychically forgive someone who has wounded your pride, you may regret the fact that you did not stand up for your own rights. And if you are too quick to behave in a forgiving way toward someone who mistreated you, others may perceive you as a fool.

The concern over how one is evaluated by others can make the interpersonal dimension of forgiveness important. What we have called "silent forgiveness" may reflect the concern over public appearances: The victim may have recovered from the transgression and have mostly ceased to feel hostility or resentment toward the perpetrator, but may still be reluctant to make a public expression of forgiveness because it will be interpreted as a loss of face. Such public expression might become a particularly potent regret if the transgressor refuses to apologize or acknowledge wrongdoing. Wounded pride or loss of face may make the victim unwilling to take any first step toward reconciliation, and, in particular, may make the victim unwilling to express forgiveness.

Another way of putting this is that forgiveness may make the person appear weak. People who want or need to maintain an image of strength may be reluctant to express forgiveness—at least with some kinds of transgressions, such as ones that include blows to one's self-esteem. A grudge would therefore be maintained out of pride.

A variation on this theme is the desire for revenge (see Stuckless & Goranson, 1992, 1994). Forgiveness entails the relinquishing of any claim on or quest for revenge, whereas a grudge may be explicitly aimed at getting even. Revenge offers the satisfaction of feeling vindicated and of having restored equity or justice. The desire for those positive outcomes may be a reason to hold a grudge.

Although revenge and pride may seem like separate concepts, in the actual occurrence of transgressions they are often linked. Brown (1968) showed that a loss of face or a blow to pride is a powerful stimulus to revenge-seeking, and Baumeister (1997) concluded from a review of

evidence that the attempt to avenge a blow to one's self-esteem constitutes one of the major causes of interpersonal violence and evil. Forgiveness theory (like grudge theory) can probably not afford to ignore
the overlap between pride and revenge, and should therefore consider
the role that wounded pride plays in creating formidable obstacles to
forgiveness.

Clearly, the quest for revenge after a loss of face is an interpersonal
act, and as such it is most relevant to the interpersonal dimension of forgiveness. Yet it could also apply to the intrapsychic dimension. People
may privately nurse a grudge for years over a blow to their pride. The
intrapsychic processes of forgiveness may demonstrate that concern over
self-esteem is a major obstacle to releasing anger and other hard feelings.

Principled Refusal

The final set of reasons for holding a grudge involves adherence to firm
principles or standards of justice. Moral standards condemn certain
actions as unacceptable, and some people may well believe that intrapsychic or interpersonal forgiveness of such actions betrays those standards.

In particular, people may believe that a general pattern of forgiving
certain acts will amount to condoning them. If a certain category of
transgression is invariably, routinely forgiven, it may cease to seem
wrong. Hence, people may feel that isolated instances can be forgiven,
but it remains essential to withhold forgiveness in the majority of cases.

To be sure, some theorists of forgiveness (Freedman & Enright, 1996;
McCullough, Sandage, & Worthington, 1997) assert that forgiving is not
the same as condoning. Yet the distinction may be a subtle and imperfect one; it is likely that the two overlap substantially and correlate highly.
Even though forgiving and condoning are quite different in principle,
especially as intrapsychic processes, in interpersonal practice the perpetrator may blur the distinction. If the victim does not acknowledge the
unacceptability of the transgression or the damage it wrought, the perpetrator may interpret forgiven behavior as having been condoned, and
as a result the perpetrator may feel free to commit the same transgression again.

Even more important for the present argument, people may believe that regular expressions of forgiveness will lead to condoning—or will amount to about the same thing. If transgressors learn to expect that their transgressions will be forgiven—and frequent forgiveness would almost certainly generate such expectations, just as any regular pattern comes to be expected—then any principle that condemns such transgressions will lose most of its moral force. In such cases, it would be risky to express forgiveness.

In short, strong adherence to high standards of justice may well imply that some acts should not be forgiven. To some people, the category of such actions may be limited to extremes such as genocide, torture, and child abuse, while for others it may extend to more ordinary transgressions such as extramarital sex or cheating at poker. In either case, people may hold a grudge indefinitely.

A prediction of this view is that forgiveness will depend on the moral magnitude of the transgression and on the victim's perception of the importance of the principle involved. Personal experiences and emotional attitudes may exert a considerable influence over which moral principles are perceived as most important, so there could be considerable idiosyncratic variation as to what sins are seen as unforgivable.

When firm moral principles are at stake, the perpetrator's attitude may make a substantial difference. The victim is reluctant to forgive because he or she wants to maintain and honor the principle that condemns such actions. If the perpetrator affirms that same principle by acknowledging the wrongness of the transgression, the moral burden on the victim is reduced, and the victim may find it easier to begin forgiving. In contrast, if the perpetrator refuses to acknowledge wrongdoing, the victim may feel that he or she (the victim) is the only one standing up for the principle. For the victim to forgive without the perpetrator's acknowledging the wrong might be tantamount to abandoning the principle.

Costs of Holding a Grudge

We turn now to consider the other side of the coin. The previous sections detailed some of the attractions and benefits to sustaining a grudge.

This section will examine the costs that attend doing so. In effect, the intrapsychic act of holding a grudge preserves the victim role; this section explores the price paid for remaining a victim.

A first, substantial cost is the continuation of negative affect. We noted in the preceding section that continued suffering is one reason that may cause people to hold a grudge. The relationship is probably reciprocal, however: Holding a grudge, at least in intrapsychic terms, may also perpetuate suffering and distress.

This cost pertains to the victim role generally. To privately identify oneself as a victim is to embrace suffering, weakness, and distress as part of one's identity. Indeed, the phrase "happy victim" is probably an oxymoron. To cling to the victim role, therefore, is to relinquish important possibilities for happiness.

The intrapsychic act of holding a grudge exemplifies this affective choice. When one holds a grudge, each contact with the person is likely to activate the hard feelings toward that person, and so the grudge holder (i.e., the victim) is obliged to feel them again. Most likely, various other cues or situational events will remind the person of the grudge, reactivating the set of negative feelings. If nothing else, holding a grudge is a commitment to remain angry (or to resume anger periodically), so one has at least to endure the corrosive, unpleasant, and unhealthy effects of anger (Williams & Williams, 1993).

The emotional cost of refusing to forgive is undoubtedly a central reason that therapists and others extol forgiveness. In particular, continuing to feel angry toward distant or unresponsive (e.g., dead) perpetrators over transgressions that can no longer be rectified may create a cycle of negative emotion that persists in a futile and pointless manner. Such a grudge does nothing but make the holder (the victim) miserable. Under such circumstances, intrapsychic forgiveness would release the victim from further unpleasantness and would hence be felt as a welcome relief.

It must be acknowledged that the corrosive effects of negative affect and the victim role may have costs beyond the emotional distress itself. The victim role is associated with misfortune and passivity, and identifying oneself with it can conceivably undermine people's functioning in a variety of spheres. In other words, holding a grudge might reduce one's chances for success and happiness even in domains that have no direct relation to the transgression.

As evidence for that view, recent work suggests that the victim role tends to breed passivity and failure. In a series of experiments, Tice and colleagues (1997) planted the idea of victimization in people's minds through unconscious priming. These people then performed worse on a problem-solving (anagram) task compared with control subjects. Although there was no apparent meaningful connection between the victim-role manipulation and the anagram task, the thought of victimization appears simply to have made people more passive, slower, and more willing to give up as soon as they encountered difficulties.

In other circumstances, there may be interpersonal costs to holding a grudge. These would primarily take the form of relationship damage. A grudge is an antagonistic relationship, and as such it is incompatible with optimal intimacy and positive social bonds. It is unlikely that two spouses, colleagues, neighbors, or the like could continue to have an extremely positive relationship if one of them holds a serious grudge against the other for a long period of time.

It is, of course, a matter of partly arbitrary definition whether one says that it is the transgression or the grudge that creates the damage to the relationship. It seems likely that perpetrators and victims would disagree about this (insofar as each would tend to shift blame onto the other). Either way, however, our thesis has been that forgiveness is an effort to heal a relationship that has been damaged by transgression. In that analysis, forgiveness is good for the relationship, whereas refusing to forgive (i.e., holding a grudge) is fundamentally antisocial.

In some cases, holding a grudge can probably lead to the termination of the relationship. To some extent, this was institutionalized in restrictive divorce laws that permitted divorce only if one person (or both) had done something unforgivably bad. More generally, it appears that grudges can lead to relationship dissolution by its effects on either person. The victim who holds a grudge may eventually lose all pleasure in and desire for the perpetrator's companionship because of the negative affect associated with the grudge. The perpetrator may resent the interpersonal expression of the grudge as unfair. He or she might also cease to tolerate the aversive interaction patterns that are linked to reminders of the grudge.

Grudge Theory and Two Dimensions of Forgiveness

The costs and benefits of grudge holding, and conversely of forgiveness, are not evenly distributed between the two kinds of forgiveness that we noted. This asymmetry has implications for what is adaptive and how people are likely to respond.

We noted one intrapsychic and one interpersonal cost of holding a grudge. The interpersonal cost is, however, derivative of the intrapsychic cost, insofar as the relationship damage follows because the victim continues to feel upset at the perpetrator. Thus it is the continuation of negative emotional states on the part of the victim (who holds the grudge) that constitutes the fundamental, primary cost of refusing to forgive. Put another way, the main cost of the grudge is intrapsychic.

In contrast, the benefits of holding the grudge are primarily interpersonal. The potential claim on rewards or benefits, such as restitution and the exertion of pressure to prevent the transgression from recurring, refer to the interpersonal relationship between the victim and the perpetrator. Any revenge seeking is likewise interpersonal. The other reasons we listed for holding a grudge—the fact that the victim continues to suffer adverse consequences from the transgression and the sense that forgiveness would compromise one's moral principles—may have both intrapsychic and interpersonal aspects; but they do not actually constitute benefits of refusing to forgive and so are less relevant.

Thus, in this analysis, the benefits of holding a grudge are primarily interpersonal, while the costs are mainly intrapsychic.

One self-protective pattern in many cases would therefore be to strive for intrapsychic forgiveness while maintaining the grudge at the interpersonal level. This was the pattern we termed "silent forgiveness." By striving privately to stop feeling angry, hurt, or resentful, the victim may enjoy substantial affective improvements and genuinely feel better. Meanwhile, by refusing to express forgiveness to the partner, the victim may be better positioned to exact concessions or restitution and to influence the perpetrator not to repeat the transgression.

The perpetrator's attitude alters these contingencies and may, therefore, again make a major difference as to what degree (and what kind) of forgiveness is adaptive. In many cases, presumably, the victim would benefit by resuming a good relationship with the perpetrator, and so forgiveness would be desirable. If this can be achieved without incurring the interpersonal costs of forgiveness, the result would be to the victim's maximum advantage. Hence, if the perpetrator acknowledges the misdeed, makes amends, and implicitly or explicitly promises not to repeat the transgression, then there is little to be gained by holding a grudge. Interpersonal forgiveness would be beneficial to all parties under those circumstances.

To be sure, forgiveness may still not be forthcoming, such as if the victim takes a principled stance that the transgression is unforgivable. Still, the effects of shifting costs and benefits are likely to be noticeable, and so it seems fair to predict that interpersonal forgiveness will be much greater when the perpetrator acknowledges and tries to make up for the transgression.

In contrast, if the perpetrator refuses to acknowledge the misdeed, there may be more usefulness in holding onto the grudge. And if the perpetrator acknowledges the misdeed but is unable to make full restitution, the victim may even benefit, because the grudge may operate as a nonspecific debt that can be invoked to influence the other's behavior whenever needed.

Thus, the future course of the relationship may depend on whether a particular transgression is forgiven, and that in turn may depend heavily on the perpetrator's attitude. Whether the perpetrator acknowledges the transgression and apologizes will therefore have a substantial impact on the interpersonal dimension of forgiveness. As for the intrapsychic dimension of forgiveness, the perpetrator's attitude is not necessarily decisive; but in practice it can make a major difference. Undoubtedly, victims find comfort in knowing that the perpetrator regrets the transgression. By revealing how the perpetrator feels about the relationship and what his or her intentions are, such regrets may have an impact (if an indirect one) on the victim's inner processes, including forgiveness.

CONCLUSION

This work has sought to approach the topic of forgiveness by analyzing the victim role and the discrepant perspectives of victim and perpetrator.

It has also sought to establish the psychological problem of forgiveness in a network of related topics: evil, the victim role, and grudge theory.

The important work by McCullough and his colleagues (McCullough, Sandage, & Worthington, 1997) has established many positive benefits of forgiveness. Reading that evidence, one cannot help but wonder: If forgiveness is so good, why do many people find it so difficult?

We have sought to answer this question by examining the costs of forgiveness and the attractive appeal of holding a grudge. If holding a grudge is the opposite of forgiveness, then phrasing the problem of forgiveness in terms of the appeal of holding the grudge makes it easier to understand some of the important obstacles that can prevent people from forgiving. In particular, people may hold grudges because they want to exact rewards, benefits, or concessions from the perpetrator; because they believe that holding the grudge will help prevent the transgression from being repeated; because they continue to suffer the consequences of the transgression, and therefore cannot easily put the transgression behind them; because their wounded pride would make forgiving seem an admission of weakness or a loss of face; or because they hold to high moral principles that would be compromised by forgiving an act that remains unacceptable to them.

Despite the appeal of holding a grudge, it also carries costs, such as the continuation of hard, unpleasant feelings; the damage to one's health and well-being that such feelings confer; and the damage to close relationships that a long-standing grudge can cause. To forgive is to step out of the victim role; but relinquishing the victim status has both costs and benefits. To understand why a given person forgives or refuses to forgive, it becomes vital to understand how the costs and benefits of the victim role pertain to the individual case.

To provide an adequate theoretical account of the victim role, it was necessary to distinguish between two major dimensions of forgiveness: (1) the inner, or intrapsychic, dimension that refers to the victim's feelings about the transgression, as well as the cognitive processes that mediate those feelings; and (2) the outer, or interpersonal, dimension of forgiveness that involves the social transactions between the victim and perpetrator and its effects on the relationship between them. Forgiveness has benefits at both levels: It may help the victim to escape from the burden of hard, aversive feelings, and it may ultimately heal the relationship and allow it to survive. Yet forgiveness also has costs, particularly on the interpersonal dimension. An adequate appreciation of these costs will help explain why many victims are slow to forgive.

REFERENCES

Al-Mabuk, R.H., Enright, R.D., & Cardis, P.A. (1995). Forgiveness education with parentally love-deprived late adolescents. *Journal of Moral Education, 24,* 427–444.

Baumeister, R.F. (1997). *Evil: Inside human violence and cruelty.* New York: W.H. Freeman.

Baumeister, R.F., Stillwell, A.M., & Heatherton, T.F. (1994). Guilt: An interpersonal approach. *Psychological Bulletin, 115,* 243–267.

Baumeister, R.F., Stillwell, A., & Wotman, S.R. (1990). Victim and perpetrator accounts of interpersonal conflict: Autobiographical narratives about anger. *Journal of Personality and Social Psychology, 59,* 994–1005.

Brown, B.R. (1968). The effects of need to maintain face on interpersonal bargaining. *Journal of Experimental Social Psychology, 4,* 107–122.

Clark, M.S. (1984). Record keeping in two types of relationships. *Journal of Personality and Social Psychology, 47,* 549–557.

Clark, M.S., & Mills, J. (1979). Interpersonal attraction in exchange and communal relationships. *Journal of Personality and Social Psychology, 37,* 12–24.

Clark, M.S., Mills, J., & Powell, M.C. (1986). Keeping track of needs in communal and exchange relationships. *Journal of Personality and Social Psychology, 51,* 333–338.

Darby, B.W., & Schlenker, B.R. (1982). Children's reactions to apologies. *Journal of Personality and Social Psychology, 43,* 724–753.

Enright, R.D., & the Human Development Study Group (1991). The moral development of forgiveness. In W. Kurtines & J. Gerwitz (Eds.), *Moral behavior and development* (Vol. 1, pp. 123–152). Hillsdale, NJ: Erlbaum.

Exline, J.J., Yali, A., & Lobel, M. (1997). *Correlates of forgiveness.* Unpublished data, State University of New York at Stony Brook.

Freedman, S.R., & Enright, R.D. (1996). Forgiveness as an intervention goal with incest survivors. *Journal of Consulting and Clinical Psychology, 64,* 983–992.

Holman, E.A., & Silver, R.C. (1998). Getting "stuck" in the past: Temporal orientation and coping with trauma. *Journal of Personality and Social Psychology, 74,* 1146–1163.

McCullough, M.E., Sandage, S.J., & Worthington, E.L. (1997). *To forgive is human: How to put your past in the past.* Downers Grove, IL: InterVarsity Press.

McCullough, M.E., Worthington, E.L., & Rachal, K.C. (1997). Interpersonal forgiving in close relationships. *Journal of Personality and Social Psychology, 73,* 321–336.

Mikula, G. (1994). Perspective-related differences in interpretations of injustice by victims and victimizers: A test with close relationships. In M.J. Lerner & G. Mikula (Eds.), *Entitlement and the affectional bond: Justice in close relationships* (pp. 175–203). New York: Plenum.

Stillwell, A.M., & Baumeister, R.F. (1997). The construction of victim and perpetrator memories: Accuracy and distortion in role-based accounts. *Personality and Social Psychology Bulletin, 23,* 1157–1172.

Stuckless, N., & Goranson, R. (1992). The Vengeance Scale: Development of a measure of attitudes toward revenge. *Journal of Social Behavior and Personality, 7,* 25–42.

Stuckless, N., & Goranson, R. (1994). A selected bibliography of literature on revenge. *Psychological Reports, 75,* 803–811.

Tangney, J.P. (1991). Moral affect: The good, the bad, and the ugly. *Journal of Personality and Social Psychology, 61,* 598–607.

Tangney, J.P. (1992). Situational determinants of shame and guilt in young adulthood. *Personality and Social Psychology Bulletin, 18,* 199–206.

Tavris, C. (1989). *Anger: The misunderstood emotion.* New York: Simon & Schuster (Touchstone).

Tice, D.M., Hastings, S., & Sommer, K.L. (1997). *Effects of priming the victim role on task performance.* Unpublished findings, Case Western Reserve University.

Weiner, B., Graham, S., Peter, O., & Zmuidinas, M. (1991). Public confession and forgiveness. *Journal of Personality, 59,* 281–312.

Williams, R., & Williams, V. (1993). *Anger kills.* New York: Random House.

PART III

✦

Forgiveness in Interventions

CHAPTER 5

The Pyramid Model of Forgiveness: Some Interdisciplinary Speculations about Unforgiveness and the Promotion of Forgiveness*

Everett L. Worthington, Jr.

R ESEARCH ON INTERVENTIONS to promote forgiveness is in its infancy, with only six extant studies (Al-Mabuk, Enright, & Cardis, 1995; Coyle & Enright, 1997; Freedman & Enright, 1996; Hebl & Enright, 1993; McCullough & Worthington, 1995; McCullough, Worthington, & Rachal, 1997). However, two major programs of intervention have been investigated. Enright (see Chapter 6) and his colleagues have developed a multistep process model of promoting forgiveness. McCullough and his colleagues, of which I am one, have developed an intervention focusing on empathy as a necessary condition for promoting forgiveness.

I will summarize my version of the empathy model, which I call the Pyramid Model of Forgiveness (previously the Empathy-Humility-Commitment Model; Worthington, 1998), which is an intervention pro-

---

*In this chapter, I present the five-step Pyramid Model of Forgiveness and summarize some of the research on its effectiveness. With each step, I speculate about possible neurobiological reasons why unforgiveness occurs and persists and why the Pyramid Model might be effective in fostering forgiveness. However, these speculations are intended to be a stimulus for researchers and theoreticians to articulate an integrated, multidisciplinary model, not a definitive account of the neurobiology of unforgiveness and forgiveness.

gram that has promoted forgiveness in people who have experienced hurts. The Pyramid Model of Forgiveness differs from empathy-based forgiveness, which was developed by McCullough and Worthington (1995) and McCullough, Worthington, and Rachal (1997), in that it is more comprehensive and has a different structure.

We have some experimental evidence that the model works and that empathy is centrally involved in why it works, and I will briefly summarize that evidence. However, before I discuss our model, I would like to speculate about a neurobiological foundation for why the model might work, which articulates the initial description of a theory about unforgiveness and the promotion of forgiveness.

NEUROBIOLOGICAL FOUNDATION FOR UNFORGIVENESS AND FORGIVENESS

Forgiveness is a motivation to reduce avoidance of and withdrawal from a person who has hurt us, as well as the anger, desire for revenge, and urge to retaliate against that person. Forgiveness also increases the pursuit of conciliation toward that person if moral norms can be reestablished that are as good as, or even better than, they were before the hurt (McCullough, Rachal, Sandage, Worthington, Brown, & Hight, 1998; McCullough, Sandage, & Worthington, 1997; McCullough, Worthington, & Rachal, 1997).

In describing the Pyramid Model of Forgiveness, I will speculate about some of the mechanisms that might be occurring during unforgiveness and the promotion of forgiveness. I describe the treatment in five steps that are represented by the acrostic **REACH:** **R**ecall the hurt, **E**mpathize with the one who hurt you, [offer the] **A**ltruistic gift of forgiveness, [make a] **C**ommitment to forgive, and **H**old onto the forgiveness. Although I present the model in a series of steps, I do not believe that the steps need to be followed in invariant order; for example, steps **E** and **A** are particularly subject to being joined.

Because I am interested in *interventions to promote forgiveness*, certain aspects of my explanation, of course, may not reflect naturally occurring instances of forgiveness. For example, in naturally occurring forgiveness,

I would expect that whether someone forgives depends to some degree on (a) the person's personality, (b) the characteristics of the relationship before the hurtful act, (c) the events that occurred during the hurtful episode and afterward (e.g., presence of confession, apology, and the like), and (d) psychological processes that might be associated with the development of a sense of empathy and humility and the intention to forgive. I have summarized many of these factors in Table 1.

Table 1. Conditions Associated with Forgiveness in Natural Situations

INHIBITORY CHARACTERISTICS

PERSONALITY FACTORS

+ Sensitivity to sensory stimulation
+ Rumination
+ Narcissism
+ Self-monitoring
+ Susceptibility to fear
+ Trait anxiety
+ Trait anger
+ Type A chronic hostility
+ Neuroticism
+ Introversion (versus extraversion, which is expected to promote forgiveness)
+ Reactivity to stress
+ Shame-proneness (Tangney, 1995)

FOSTERING CHARACTERISTICS

+ Trait humility
+ Trait gratitude
+ Trait empathic concern (Davis, 1996)

+ Interpersonal trust
+ Openness
+ Agreeableness
+ Guilt-proneness (Tangney, 1995)

PRE-EXISTING RELATIONSHIP VARIABLES

RELATIONAL
FACTORS

+ Closeness (which might involve other variables such as obligation, duty, norm compliance, liking, loyalty, guilt, reciprocity in present and future, desire for relationship maintenance [Batson et al., 1997])
+ Commitment to the relationship (Rusbult, Bissonnette, Arriaga, & Cox, 1998; Rusbult & Buunk, 1993)
+ Beliefs about the relationship, such as covenantal or contractual stance (Bromley & Busching, 1988; Bromley & Cress, 1998; Browning, Miller-McLemore, Couture, Lyon, & Franklin, 1997; Ripley, 1998; Witte, 1997); sacredness with which the relationship is viewed (Mahoney et al., 1996); willingness to sacrifice in a close relationship (Van Lange et al., 1997); satisfaction with the relationship; satisfaction with alternatives to the relationship; investments in the relationship; and salience of the relationship (Rusbult, Johnson, & Morrow, 1986)
+ Length of time the relationship existed before the hurt occurred
+ Degree of love (passion, closeness, commitment) (Sternberg, 1986)
+ History of hurts and how they were handled previously
+ Experiential skill repertoire for handling hurts (learned from parents, siblings, significant adults in the past, friends, previous romantic partners)
+ Declarative knowledge about how to handle hurts (learned from books, teachers, television, educational sources, therapists or psychoeducators)

HURTFUL EVENT CHARACTERISTICS

EVENT
FACTORS

+ Degree of perceived hurt, pain, and trauma
+ Perceived intentionality of the hurt (accident, negligence, intention)
+ Objective or subjective nature of the hurt
+ Number of hurts
+ Perceived level of hurtfulness

POST-HURT EVENTS

+ Time since the hurt
+ Stance of the person who inflicted the hurt (justification, excuse, confession and repentance, contrition)
+ Verbal expression of apology
+ Verbal expression of intent not to reharm
+ Recognized expression of implicit overtures toward reconciliation (de Waal, 1989a, 1989b, 1996)
+ Degree and type of tender touch (i.e., "grooming," de Waal, 1989a)
+ Buildup of additional hurts
+ Reciprocal hurts inflicted by the person who had been harmed
+ Level of relationship deterioration (criticism, contempt, defensiveness, stonewalling) (Gottman, 1994)
+ Attempts to forgive
+ Success or failure of the attempts to forgive
+ Attempts at reconciliation
+ Success or failure of the attempts to reconcile
+ Accumulation of mutual post-event trustworthy behaviors

PSYCHOLOGICAL PROCESSES ASSOCIATED WITH EMPATHY

EMPATHY & HUMILITY	✦ Inclusion of other in one's sense of self (Aron & Aron, 1986; Cialdini, Brown, Lewis, Luce, & Neuberg, 1997; Hamilton, 1964; Neuberg, Cialdini, Brown, Luce, & Sagarin, 1997; cf. Batson, 1997; Batson et al., 1997)
	✦ Similarity
	✦ Sense of "we"-ness
	✦ Sense of "one"-ness
	✦ Sense of shared experience
	✦ Degree of kinship
	✦ Humility

In intervention research, however, the objective is to create a superpotent sequence of stimulus events—a treatment so powerful that *all* people respond positively to it. Thus, to the extent that intervention researchers are successful, they should not be investigating personality traits, relational factors, or events, as much as inducing psychological states. In the case of the Pyramid Model of Forgiveness, we seek to induce states of empathy and humility (including guilt, gratitude for having been forgiven in the past, and the decision to give a gift of forgiveness). In actual practice, however, no intervention is so powerful that everyone reacts positively to it, so wise intervention researchers are always looking for treatment interactions that suggest which personality attributes predict who will respond most strongly (and positively) to the intervention and which attributes predict nonresponse or antipathy.

Now, let's examine the five steps of the Pyramid Model of Forgiveness.

THE PYRAMID MODEL OF FORGIVENESS

Step 1: Recall the Hurt

The Mechanics of Fear Conditioning. When people are hurt, they are classically fear conditioned in a classical conditioning sense, somewhat like a rat in a cage. The rat hears a tone (conditioned stimulus) and, at the end of the tone, receives a painful shock to the feet (unconditioned stimulus). With one trial, if the painful stimulus is strong, or with several trials, if the painful stimulus is mild, the rat associates the tone alone with fear (conditioned response).

Examine the rat's fear-response system once it has been fear conditioned. First, when the rat hears the tone, it immediately orients and freezes. Second, corticosteroid releasing factor is excreted and signals the hypothalamus to stimulate the pituitary to turn on the stress-response system; this system releases stress hormones, such as glucocorticoids, cortisol, and others, and sprays the brain with various neurotransmitters in various locations. Third, the rat tries to escape or withdraw, if possible. If prevented from avoiding the threat, the rat will engage in defensive fighting (see Berkowitz, 1983). If the rat cannot win the fight, perhaps because the dominance hierarchy is too well established, it might make a submissive gesture (see Seligman's [1975] seminal helplessness paradigm). This same pattern is, of course, observed in primates in both captivity and in the wild: freeze, ignite the stress system, withdraw, fight, and perhaps submit (LeDoux, 1996; de Waal, 1989b).

Consider an unforgiving person. The person receives a hurt, offense, injustice, or rejection (unconditioned stimulus) from an offender (conditioned stimulus). Afterward, the unforgiving person sees the offender again. First, he or she becomes tense, a vestige of orienting and freezing. Second, the stress-response system is activated. Third, the person tries to avoid or withdraw from the offender—to have little or no contact. Fourth, if withdrawal is not possible—because of inclusion in the same family or work unit—then anger, retaliation, and defensive fighting occur. Fifth, if such fighting is unwise, self-destructive, or futile, the person might exhibit the human equivalent of a submissive gesture— depression, which declares that the person is weak and needs succor.

Neural Pathways Activated by Fear Conditioning. One brain pathway that is emotionally conditioned probably runs through the amygdala, if my reasoning—that fear conditioning is the *beginning* of unforgiveness— is true. A direct pathway exists from sense organs to thalamus to amygdala (LeDoux, 1996). The thalamus relays the incoming signals to sensory cortices, which send additional signals to the hippocampus, which then integrates the signals into a more refined picture. The pathways also project to the prefrontal cortex, where information is processed, feelings pass through working memory, and decisions are made. LeDoux has described the neural pathways activated by fear conditioning, concentrating particularly on the amygdala. Damasio (1994) has also focused on the whole-body emotional response. He has shown that decisions are not merely cognitive activities. Instead, decisions involve the emotions and gut feelings. Information from the body is relayed to the ventromedial portion of the prefrontal cortex, which seems to be one crucial area that facilitates (or even makes possible) decision making.

Imagine that you are walking in the woods. You hear a rustle in the leaves. You immediately leap back and freeze, adrenaline and other stress hormones course through your body, and neurotransmitters flood various areas within your brain. This happens without conscious thought and is a product of fear conditioning of the amygdala. As you scan the surroundings alertly, you integrate sights and sounds (in the hippocampus) into a more coherent picture of what is occurring. The image and projections of the stimuli come into focus more sharply as your brain routes neural impulses (originating from your perceptions of the context and from your body) to the prefrontal cortex. You decide whether there is danger and, if so, whether you must withdraw, fight, or act submissively.

Some Indirect Preliminary Evidence of Fear Conditioning. In some psychometric studies, we have developed a measure of forgiveness that has two subscales: avoidance and revenge (McCullough et al., 1998). Using structural equation modeling, we showed that the scales are moderately intercorrelated, but not explainable by a single forgiveness factor. While such factors could arise from sampling, measurement error, or a host of other reasons, the scales may be measuring the interrelated parts of the fear-conditioned biological system. Causes of the activation of different aspects of the biological motivational system depend on many factors, not merely biology (see Table 1).

Note the subscales—avoidance and revenge. These are similar to the fear-response system. Theoretically, when someone is hurt, the person freezes or tenses in the presence of the offender. If the person can *avoid* or escape contact with the offender (i.e. avoidance), the person does so. If the person is forced to remain in contact with the offender, the person might retaliate or exact revenge.

Resistance of Fear Conditioning to Extinction. When someone is hurt or unjustly wronged, let's assume that the person is fear conditioned. One way to reduce fear conditioning is through extinction; however, extinction does not eliminate fear conditioning. Extinction probably occurs in the prefrontal cortex, where the brain *controls* the fear-response system rather than *eliminates* the fear-conditioned pathway through the amygdala (see LeDoux, 1996); that is, extinction may change one's response to the unconditioned stimulus, but does not eliminate the emotional conditioning.

To understand that, recall how difficult it is to extinguish fear conditioning in a rat. The rat is placed on an extinction schedule; that is, it is placed back in the cage and subjected to the tone repeatedly until it no longer responds. The conditioned fear response is gone, but is the fear-conditioned pathway in the amygdala eliminated? No. To show that fear conditioning still exists, put the rat in the cage and sound the tone. It freezes. Spontaneous recovery has occurred. Fear conditioning is still present.

Next, the rat is placed in its cage repeatedly and the tone sounded (with no shock) so often that spontaneous recovery no longer happens. Is the fear conditioning gone? No. But place the rat in a different cage and shock it without ever playing the tone again. Now, if the rat is put back in the original cage and the tone sounded, spontaneous recovery occurs.

Or, take a rat, with an extinguished fear response and subject it to extreme stress. The extreme stress can potentiate the fear response. Further, we also know that fear conditioning is permanent because it can be quickly reinstated through pairing of a tone and even the mildest, almost harmless shock. Fear conditioning, once it occurs, is stubbornly maintained.

Note again the similarity to the person who has been hurt or offended: The person forgives an offender (i.e., unforgiveness is extinguished). Then, the person sees the offender again; spontaneous recovery occurs.

Even after spontaneous recovery no longer occurs, if the person is rejected by someone else the old hurts flood back. If the person is under stress, the old wounds are reopened. It takes very little additional hurt by the original offender to reinstate the fear conditioning.

The fear conditioning would be even greater in an unforgiving person because fear would be potentiated by the unforgiveness. Lang (Drobes & Lang, 1995) and others have shown that when a person is fearful, he or she will respond more strongly to a fear-inducing stimulus than when not fearful. I am not equating fear conditioning and unforgiveness, but I am hypothesizing that fear conditioning is at the root of much unforgiveness, even though unforgiveness requires additional emotional and cognitive manipulation.

An Objection. Some might object that anger more than fear characterizes an unforgiving person (Davenport, 1991; Fitzgibbons, 1986); that is, a counterhypothesis to the fear-conditioning model of unforgiveness would be that unforgiveness is anger-based rather than fear-based.

First, it is not clear that the unforgiving person experiences anger more than fear or hurt as a response to perceived offense or interpersonal injury. No published data have addressed this in an epidemiological study. Most evidence that anger is the primary emotion associated with unforgiveness comes form the clinic. Recall that intervention studies create events that direct the participants' attention in theory-relevant directions. In addition, people who volunteer for *treatment* might be a selected subpopulation of unforgiving people, such as those in whom anger is prevalent. Thus, observations by therapists (e.g., Davenport, 1991; Fitzgibbons, 1986), while accurate according to their experiences within the therapeutic setting, are not a reliable indication of what takes place in naturally occurring unforgiveness.

Second, examine the following prediction of a fear-based conception of unforgiveness. The unforgiveness response should be expected to parallel the fear response. In the presence of the conditioned stimulus in actual form (i.e., seeing or hearing the offender) or in symbolic form (i.e., thinking about, imagining, or remembering the offender, the offensive act, or associations with either), an unforgiving person should tense and orient to the stimulus. Then, unforgiveness should be correlated with activity in the stress–response system (e.g., elevations in epinephrine, corticosteroids, and other stress hormones), regardless of whether unforgiveness is consciously admitted. Then, parallel to avoidance as a first physical defense in fear, the psychological defense of choice is hypothesized to be *cognitive avoidance* of the stimulus (person). That is, denial, repression, and suppression are expected as early defensive reactions.

However, it is not as easy for most people to avoid symbolic representation of a conditioned stimulus (i.e., thoughts, images, and memories of the offender) as it is to avoid the actual person. So, cognitive avoidance is likely to be ineffective in many people. In fear, when physical avoidance fails, defensive fighting occurs. Similarly, when cognitive avoidance fails, they will engage in *cognitive defensive fighting* and anger. Finally, some people who are unable to avoid thoughts about the offender and unable to control anger and thoughts of defensive fighting (i.e., bitterness, thoughts of revenge, or obsessive desire for justice) will experience depression.

From this analysis, we can see that unforgiving people who *can* cognitively and psychodynamically defend against unforgiving, bitter thoughts are likely to experience little anger, hatred, or desire for revenge. Those less successful will experience more anger, hatred, and desire for revenge and are more likely to be troubled by unforgiveness. Thus, they will consequently seek interventions to promote forgiveness. Alternatively, they will be more likely to pursue justice or revenge.

Using the Fear-Conditioning Model of Unforgiveness to Promote Forgiveness. Using the first step in the Pyramid Model (**R**ecall the hurt), we help people recall the hurts and elaborate on them *within a supportive, nonhurtful atmosphere* (McCullough & Worthington, 1995; McCullough, Worthington, & Rachal, 1997) without reexperiencing the associated pain (i.e., extinction). We help people talk about the hurt and try to keep the emotional level relatively low and the support high. The hurt might be discussed supportively and empathically in a group (McCullough, Worthington, & Rachal), with a couple (McCullough, 1997), or in individual counseling. Importantly, repetition of the conditioned stimulus—cognition about the person who inflicted the hurt—without reexperiencing the full depth of pain is crucial. This *extinction* actually occurs throughout the intervention protocol, but is concentrated in the early stage of intervention. Recalling the hurt involves extinction, which does not eliminate the fear conditioning, but does change the response to the unconditioned stimulus; this is the *beginning* of forgiveness. As one might expect, the duration of treatment might play an important part in how effectively extinction occurs. I will present data on that later.

Step 2: Empathize with the One Who Hurt You

Empathy constitutes the key step in our model. Because fear conditioning is an emotional response, we combat it to some degree by creating cognitive and emotional conditions that activate other emotional systems. State-empathy is such an emotion. I am not referring to a trait of empathy, although I would expect such a trait to have a modest effect on who can benefit by our method; in addition, the study of this trait may indicate who would develop a sense of unforgiveness strong enough to seek help for it. Certainly, people who are incapable of empathy—perhaps those with narcissistic, borderline, or antisocial personality disorders—would be expected to have particular difficulty forgiving.

Rather, our method rests on creating a *state of empathy* for the person who harmed the client. We create a state of empathy through helping people think what the other person might have been thinking, and feel what the other person might have been feeling, during the hurtful event. For example, we might have the person

✦ speculate about what the offender might have been thinking or feeling during the hurtful event;

✦ write a letter of explanation, assuming reasonable motives on the offender's part;

✦ recall good experiences with the offender;

✦ actively imagine interacting with the offender during more pleasant times; and

✦ breathe deeply and slowly (activating parasympathetic nervous system responses) during the memory or imagery.

We also use a variety of stories and analogies, which might affect the prefrontal cortex through other pathways, notably through the right side of the cortex more heavily than the left.

The idea of creating a state of empathy, of course, is not as straightforward as it initially appears. Science uses and investigates empathy (Levenson & Ruef, 1992) in at least three ways. *Empathic accuracy* is being able to discern the thoughts and feelings of another person. *Empathic identification* goes a step further and feels with the person, sharing a similar emotional and mental state. *Empathic compassion* combines the first two with feeling compassion and caring for the other person. Empathic compassion is the type of empathy we aim to produce.

The prefrontal cortex is one key to forgiveness. While unforgiveness *begins* with fear conditioning, it is not *merely* fear conditioning. Unforgiveness is a complex emotion—what Damasio (1994) calls a secondary emotion—that is nuanced by thinking about the original event; manipulating it cognitively; and reexperiencing the fear through the body and through the "as-if" system of symbolic representation, which bypasses the body but allows us to "remember" what the body felt like. If one thinks or imagines long enough, one can often experience actual bodily responses through activation of the "as-if" system.

The prefrontal cortex holds working memory, where we receive a representation of all our emotional feedback. (Technically, the different sources of information do not "come together" in the prefrontal cortex as a center of simultaneous experience. Experiences occur at different points in the brain and seem to be integrated in the prefrontal cortex and unified; Damasio, 1994.)

At least eight sources of feedback from the body maintain an emotional experience. Thus, unforgiveness involves feedback from eight sources:

- facial muscles (indicating fear, anger, depression, and empathy-induced compassion, care, etc.) (Izard, 1992a, 1992b);

- skeletal muscles (responses to our actions);

- viscera (pounding heart, twisted gut; or calming heart rate, relaxing gut);

- the hormone signature of emotional experience (fear, anger, depression, stress; or empathy-induced calm, compassion, care) (Sapolsky, 1994);

- aspects of neurochemical stimulation of the brain (neurochemicals are strongly active in various brain sites as indicated by studies on rhesus monkeys by Kalin and his colleagues) (Kalin & Shelton, 1989) (Kalin, Shelton, & Takahashi, 1991);

- the ever-changing environment (other people's actions, changing conditions, the context of the hurtful behavior);

- the content of thinking about the issue and the associations made in the associative portions of the brain with other memories, situations, responses, and outcomes; and

- the flow of consciousness, including the flow of feelings, through the working memory.

We try, through empathy inducement, to affect as much positive emotional associative feedback as possible. We expect that a strong sense of compassionate empathy, which affects the above sources of feedback, will necessarily change the emotion and experience of unforgiveness. The transformation is not necessarily full-blown forgiveness (at this point), but the experience of unforgiveness will have been modified. As one might expect, inducement of compassionate empathy takes *time*—as did the extinction (Step 1, **R**ecall the hurt). Creating an emotional state of empathic compassion changes all of the above parts of the person's experience. New facial expressions, skeletal muscle tension, visceral activity, hormonal patterns, neurochemical patterns, environmental stimuli, thoughts and associations, and flows of consciousness are all created.

Producing such experiences cannot help but change the person's experience of unforgiveness. Indirect support for this approach comes from over thirty years of research on systematic desensitization of phobic fears. Lang (see Drobes & Lang, 1995, for a review) has investigated the physiological aspects of such "emotional reconditioning" treatments of fear-based disorders for at least twenty years. While we have not shown empirically that unforgiveness is a fear-based state and that our treatment will reduce the fear at the root of unforgiveness, studies are under way to investigate that hypothesis.

In our research, we have found that an empathy-based treatment can produce more forgiveness than does a strong forgiveness treatment based on a rationale to forgive, because forgiveness is good for the individual. (For example, we suggest that forgiveness *might* reduce stress, lower chronic anger and fear, lower the risk of cardiovascular problems, and improve immune system functioning relative to chronic and severe unforgiveness, citing Kaplan, Munroe-Blum, & Blazer, 1993. Also see McCullough & Worthington, 1995; McCullough, Worthington, & Rachal, 1997).

For now, I will present the results of three studies that have compared these two treatments (see Table 2). The conclusions are extremely tentative and await additional investigations before I would be confident that this hypothesized dose-effect relationship is stable.

The self-focused treatment has powerful effects in a brief treatment of 1 hour (McCullough & Worthington, 1995), but it has essentially the same effect in 6 (Sandage, 1997) or 8 hours (McCullough, Worthington, & Rachal, 1997). Whatever occurs in those forgiveness-as-self-enhancement groups apparently occurs quickly. With the empathy-inducing group, we find a different pattern. Its effects increase with time as people elaborate on their emotional experience of empathy and allow its effects to counter the emotion of unforgiveness. This is supported, too, as we look at the follow-up data. Again, the effects of empathy groups, even the brief ones, do not decay as fast as the self-focused group.

Table 2. Estimated Effect Sizes for Three Completed Intervention Studies on Forgiveness

	EMPATHY GROUP		SELF-ENHANCEMENT GROUP	
	PRE-POST	PRE-FOLLOW	PRE-POST	PRE-FOLLOW
STUDY 1	WADE (MCCULLOUGH & WORTHINGTON, 1995) Treatment = 1 hour; Follow-up after 1 month			
Avoidance	.03	.17	.09	.29
Revenge	.12	.33	.43	.67
Conciliation	.01	.24	.91	.78
Mean	.05	.25	.44	.58
STUDY 2	ENRIGHT FORGIVENESS INVENTORY (EFI, FULL-SCALE; SANDAGE, 1997) Treatment = 6 hours; Follow-up after 6 weeks			
Total	.52	.49	.49	.38
STUDY 3	EFI (FIVE ITEMS; MCCULLOUGH, WORTHINGTON, & RACHAL, 1997) Treatment = 8 hours; Follow-up after 6 weeks			
FIVE items	1.12	.83	.28	-.04

For those who have seen the recent debate in the *Journal of Personality and Social Psychology* between Batson's and Cialdini's groups over whether Batson's empathy-altruism hypothesis or Cialdini's absorption-of-the-other-into-self model of altruism, our research might have some relevance (Batson, 1997; Batson et al., 1997; Cialdini etal., 1997; Neuberg, Cialdini, Brown, Luce, & Sagarin, 1997). Batson's and Cialdini's different results arise from experiencing empathy and altruism within a limited time frame. While Cialdini's procedure does not induce a strong state of empathy, Batson's produces empathic compassion rather than empathic identification. Predictably, from my point of view, Batson's protocol demonstrates a stronger connection between empathy and altruistic helping. We have drawn on Batson's research as one basis for our treatment: We attempt to induce a state of empathic compassion, which should be expected to lead to altruistic forgiving.

Step 3: Altruistic Gift

In our research (McCullough, Worthington, & Rachal, 1997), we have found that empathy mediates forgiveness, the granting of which we see as an act of altruism. This is true not only in the empathy-induction group, but also of people who forgive successfully, even in the self-enhancement group. They forgive to the extent that they empathize with the offender, even though the group does not explicitly lead them to empathize with him or her.

A person might empathize with the offender, understand his or her actions from the offender's point of view, imagine the feelings of the offender and feel with him or her in imagination, and even feel empathic compassion for the offender. Yet, the person might still not forgive. To move the person further along the road to forgiveness, we attempt to induce a state of humility (Means, Wilson, Sturm, Biron, & Bach, 1990). That state will lead through three experiences, which I label *guilt*, *gratitude*, and *gift*.

Guilt. Importantly, I am using guilt as a healthy sense of one's own wrongdoing, rather than as a more self-involved sense of shame (see Tangney, 1995; cf. O'Connor, Berry, Weiss, Bush, & Sampson, 1997). Guilt is the experience, in humility, that one is capable of inflicting pain, harm, or suffering on another. In an ideal sense, the person might realize that he or she has actually harmed the offender in the same way as the offender harmed him or her. Usually, though, even with couples, we encounter less defensiveness and resistance to our intervention if we induce the participant to consider another person whom he or she has harmed, but who has forgiven him or her. We move to the consideration of reciprocal hurtfulness only (a) after substantial reflection about another

person, and (b) if the consultant (i.e., group leader, counselor, or therapist) evaluates the likelihood of resistance as small. Realization that one
has participated in reciprocal hurtfulness can enhance the humility and
empathic identification (to the extent that one does not justify one's
own hurtfulness on the basis of what the offender did to one).

However, such a specific epiphany is not necessary to experiencing
humble guilt. The person could come to experience that he or she is
capable of inflicting such harm, or even is *capable of desiring to inflict* such
harm. The person might even realize that he or she *has harmed others* in
very different ways—perhaps more severely or perhaps not as severely.
The emotion we hope to engender is guilt, not shame. Tangney and others have strongly differentiated guilt and shame (Tangney, 1995; Tangney,
Wagner, Barlow, & Marschall, 1996). Guilt is more event-focused, while
shame is personalized blame for wrongdoing. In many ways, guilt is
associated with better mental health and behavioral outcomes than is
shame.

Gratitude. In our intervention, after we ask the participant to reflect on
his or her guilt for a period, we invite the person to recall what it would
be like to be granted forgiveness for that transgression. The person recalls
and describes aloud, in writing, or both, a specific time that a parent,
employer, teacher, friend, or acquaintance offered forgiveness for a clear
transgression. Then the person dwells on the sense of release, freedom,
and relief that was experienced upon receiving that forgiveness, as well
as on the gratitude that he or she has for having been forgiven.

When that sense of gratitude is recalled and vividly elaborated, at
least three things will probably occur. First, the person's emotional state
changes to one consonant with joy, love, and positive emotions. Positive feelings are experienced in working memory and positive emotions
throughout the body, brain, and mind. Those positive emotions and
feelings are associated with the offender merely because this experience is occurring within the context of a treatment that purports to promote forgiveness for that offender.

Second, the feeling and emotion of gratitude is juxtaposed against the
offender, and what I might term an *empathic projection* occurs. In empathy,
the person tries to understand (empathic accuracy), experience and

identify with (empathic identification), and feel compassion and caring toward (empathetic compassion) the other person, who in our case is the offender. In the empathic projection, the person has good feelings (about being grateful for having been forgiven) and seeks intentionally to project those onto the other person. In recent studies on the self, people in close relationships have been found to incorporate the other within the sense of self (Aron & Aron, 1986; Aron, Aron, Tudor, & Nelson, 1991). My focus remains more on the emotional projection rather than on the cognitive schema of the self, but I hypothesize that a sense of "one-ness" between people (or "we-ness") increases (Davis, Conklin, Smith, & Luce, 1996), which is the third part in the induction of a sense of gratitude.

Gift. Empathy plus the guilt and gratitude of humility create an aroused motivational state. The person identifies with the experience of the offender (through empathy) and sees the other as needy (through humility). The facilitator in our forgiveness intervention makes explicit what is implicit in the situation by inviting the person to forgive the offender by saying something like, "You can see that the person needs your forgiveness. You can see what a gift it is to have received forgiveness yourself. Would you like to give him (or her) a gift of forgiveness?" If the person is ready to offer such a gift of forgiveness to the offender, then the person is invited to proceed to the fourth step.

Step 4: Commitment to Forgive

While, at this point, the person might have forgiven the offender in his or her *heart*—and I use the term deliberately to emphasize that the forgiveness is an emotional event—the forgiveness is covert; that is, forgiveness is observed by an $n = 1$ audience. Being covert, forgiveness is subject to later doubts. This becomes especially important when we consider that the fear conditioning that associates the offender with the fear response is still present, and fear of hurt *will* be reexperienced at some future time. The person might have substantially rearranged his or her cognition and experience in the prefrontal cortex through this experience. Because he or she is continually getting feedback from the face, skeletal muscles, viscera, hormones, situation, thoughts, and feelings, and because all of those might be different at this point (than when feeling more painful unforgiveness), the person might be experiencing forgiveness.

However, the fear-conditioned pathway through the amygdala still exists. Recall that the unconscious fear conditioning will lead to a sudden sense of fear being reinstated or spontaneously recovering under the conditions if (a) the offender is seen, (b) the person is hurt by someone else in the same way, (c) the person is under high stress, or (d) the offender offends the person again. When the person experiences that fear, the person will—as humans do—think about it. The natural thoughts that might occur are that the forgiveness that the person thought himself or herself to have experienced must have been mistaken. In other words, the fear conditioning leads the person to draw an incorrect conclusion about his or her experience of forgiveness.

To make the later denial of the experience of forgiveness more difficult, the person should make a public commitment that states his or her experience of forgiveness to an audience that is broader than the $n = 1$ of the private mind. We attempt to induce this public commitment through a graduated series of steps:

1. We ask the person to talk about his or her experience of forgiveness.

2. Then, we invite the person to write a certificate stating the date of granting forgiveness. That certificate is retained for later reference.

3. The person is invited to write a letter of forgiveness explicitly forgiving the person for the harm *as if* the person were going to send the letter.

4. The person is invited to read the letter aloud to the psychoeducational group (which is a group of virtual strangers), the therapist, a family member, or a partner.

5. The person is asked to consider whether it is possible and wise to send the letter or some edited version of it to the offender. This fifth step, though, begins reconciliation, because it involves a step

that might lead to the rebuilding of trust; therefore, it can be a continuation of forgiving within the reconciliation process—but it is not necessary to forgiveness.

Numerous social psychological theories explain why making a public commitment to forgive using the steps outlined might produce a stronger (more lasting) sense of forgiveness (see Worthington, 1998). These include general cognitive dissonance theory (Festinger, 1957), self-perception theory (Bem, 1968), commitment theory (Kiesler, 1971), cognitive dissonance through counter-attitudinal behavior (e.g., Lord, Ross, & Lepper, 1979), or cognitive dissonance through arousal of hypocrisy (Aronson, 1992).

If we speculate about what might be happening in the brain and body during these commitment exercises, we can see that new bodily experiences are caused (affecting facial, skeletal, and visceral feedback to working memory), new stress responses are generated (affecting hormonal and neurochemical feedback to working memory), new thoughts and attributions are experienced in working memory, and new associations are forged in the association areas of the cortex. The body and brain work together to modify the person's experience of unforgiveness into forgiveness.

Step 5: Holding Onto Forgiveness

As I have suggested, maintaining forgiveness is no easy task. In fact, an onslaught against one's belief that he or she has *really* forgiven the offender is inevitable because of the lingering presence of fear-conditioned, amygdala-mediated responses to both the offender and the situation in which the offense occurred. Thus, explicit attention needs to be applied to maintaining the forgiveness.

The avenues of holding onto forgiveness run through six experiences:

1. The point must be made that recalling the hurt—and even being afraid that one will experience a similar hurt again—are not the same thing as unforgiveness. Recalling the hurt will inevitably provoke emotions and feelings of pain, fear, anger, and sadness.

Those feelings will be transient unless the person dwells on the negative emotional state.

2. The facilitator explains that one cannot stop feelings through conscious effort. Wegner's (1994) white-bear studies are discussed, showing that focal attempts to stop thoughts generally have the exact opposite effect of increasing those thoughts.

3. Emotion-management techniques are taught. Specifically, the person imagines pleasant scenes with the offender to combat fear (Drobes & Lang, 1995) and to engage in cognitive-behavioral anger-management strategies to ameliorate anger (Novaco, 1975).

4. The facilitator explains that concentrating on the accomplished task of forgiveness, through reexamining the certificate of forgiveness and perhaps the written letter, might be enough to refocus thoughts.

5. If that is not enough, then the person is coached to work through the forgiveness pyramid again rather than dwell on the unforgiving emotions and thoughts.

6. Finally, the facilitator shares that additional forgiveness sometimes is indeed necessary. The person might recall another hurt and might want to reexperience the forgiveness pyramid to deal with that hurt.

If it has not come up earlier in the treatment, the facilitator makes the distinction between forgiving a hurt and forgiving in a relationship that is hurtful—that is, full of hurts. The person is told that it is impossible to recall and work through all of the hurts within a hurtful relationship—and, in fact, that it is unnecessary to do so. The person can use symbolic hurts as proxies for the myriad hurts in a hurtful relationship. However, sometimes in a hurtful relationship, previously undealt with hurts might become salient and need direct attention.

FORGIVENESS AND ITS CONNECTION
TO RECONCILIATION

Forgiveness is not the same thing as reconciliation (Enright & the Human Development Study Group, 1994; McCullough & Worthington, 1994a). Forgiveness is a motivation (McCullough, Worthington, & Rachal, 1997) empowered by basic emotion (Worthington, 1998); reconciliation is relational. Forgiveness happens inside an individual; reconciliation happens within a relationship. Forgiveness exists as a gift that is granted to someone who has harmed one (although that does not mean that the gift will be received); reconciliation, which is a restoration of violated trust, is earned through mutually trustworthy behavior. Forgiveness and reconciliation are obviously related, but separate, processes.

One could conceptualize them in a "2 x 2 matrix," with the presence or absence of forgiveness along one side and the presence or absence of reconciliation along the other (see Table 3). Given that forgiveness and reconciliation are distinct from each other, there are four logical possibilities: no forgiveness and no reconciliation, forgiveness without reconciliation, reconciliation without forgiveness, and forgiveness with reconciliation. When no forgiveness and no reconciliation occur, usually

Table 3. Forgiveness and Reconciliation:
Possible Combinations

FORGIVENESS		RECONCILIATION	
		No	Yes
	No	Neither forgiveness nor reconciliation	Reconciliation without forgiveness
	Yes	Forgiveness without reconciliation	Reconciliation and forgiveness

people are either (a) seeking revenge or retaliation, which is pursuing vigilante justice; (b) seeking social justice; (c) seeking mediation; (d) simply accepting the hurt and trying to move on with their lives; (e) insincerely saying they forgive while not forgiving privately; or (f) remaining mired in bitterness and unforgiveness. When forgiveness without reconciliation occurs, it is usually because people cannot reconcile (because an offender might be dead or might have moved) or because it is not safe to reconcile (because an offender is a rapist or physical abuser). When reconciliation without forgiveness occurs, it might be because people are forced to forgive, simply decide to get on with their relationship without giving much thought to forgiveness, or feel the hurtful act was too insignificant to worry about or might be too difficult to forgive.

Forgiveness can help promote reconciliation. In a paper currently in press (McCullough et al., 1998), we measured relationships in which people had experienced someoffense or harm in the past. People rated length of offense and pre-offense closeness; impact of the offense and depth of the hurt; time since the offense occurred and whether an apology had occurred, and forgiveness (two subscales: avoidance and revenge). In a hierarchical regression analysis (see Table 4), variables were entered in those four steps. After the third step (just before the measures of forgiveness were entered), the relationship variables, offense variables, and post-hurt variables accounted for 22% of the variance in rating of current closeness (our measure of reconciliation). When the forgiveness measures were entered at a final step, they accounted for 39% of the additional variance in reconciliation. Forgiveness is not necessary for reconciliation, but it appears to facilitate it greatly. (Note: In the article, we reported and tested a more thorough structural equation model.)

Table 4. Hierarchical Multiple-Regression Equation Predicting Reconciliation (Current Relationship Closeness)

Using Measures of the Early Relationship, Characteristics of the Hurtful Event, Occurrences Since the Hurtful Event, and Forgiveness

		R^2tot	R^2chg	Fchg	Beta
STEP 1	(Early Relationship)	.13	.13	13.02*	
	Length of relationship				.36*
	Pre-offense closeness				.09
STEP 2	(Characteristics of Hurt)	.15	.02	2.03	
	Impact of offense				−.09
	Depth of hurt				−.08
STEP 3	(Events Since Hurt)	.22	.07	6.85*	
	Apology				.26*
	Time since offense				−.08
STEP 4	(Forgiveness)	.61	.39	33.21*	
	Revenge				.02
	Avoidance				−.72*

*$p < .001$

FINAL THOUGHTS

As I have described, the Pyramid Model of Forgiveness is based on an understanding of unforgiveness as a fear-based secondary emotion that motivates avoidance and revenge. Unforgiveness is thought to arise from fear conditioning that serves as the basis for a secondary emotion of unforgiveness involving the body, brain, and mind. The treatment that we have developed is based on creating a choreographed set of emotional, cognitive, and behavioral experiences that change the person's emotional experience, producing in turn states of calm openness (Step 1, *R*ecall the hurt); empathy (Step 2, *E*mpathize with the one who hurt you); humility—guilt, gratitude, and altruistic gift-giving (Step 3, *A*ltruistic gift of forgiveness); public commitment to forgiveness (Step 4, *C*ommitment to forgive); and perseverance (Step 5, *H*old onto the forgiveness). The Pyramid Model of Forgiveness is not the only avenue to the prefrontal cortex and, eventually, to the amygdala. Forgiveness can occur through many routes, including those that are spontaneous or unconscious over time.

The scientific study of forgiveness can be advanced most effectively through scientific studies of forgiveness at both the intervention level, which we have done with the Pyramid Model of Forgiveness, and at the basic-science level, including social psychological, brain-, and mind-science approaches. I have sketched a hypothetical neurobiology of unforgiveness with some hints about a possible neurobiology of forgiveness. I believe there is a psychoneuroimmunology of forgiveness, too. Forgiveness—as opposed to unforgiveness—results in different patterns of stress hormones in the bloodstream and different brain chemistry, which certainly affect many biological processes, including immune system functioning. Forgiveness reduces chronic and acute anger, which has been linked to cardiovascular trouble (Kaplan et al., 1993; Williams, 1989).

There might even be animal models of forgiveness. We certainly have good animal models for the neurobiology of fear and of reconciliation among chimpanzees, rhesus monkeys, and bonobos (de Waal, 1989a, 1989b, 1996). The central challenge in that area seems to be to examine implicit and explicit reconciliation and operationally define the difference in nonhuman primates between reconciliation (as getting along, grooming, and social alliances) versus what forgiveness might look like in animals.

I began this chapter with the caveat that much of what I had to say involved frank speculation. Nonetheless, I hope that the present inter-disciplinary approach to unforgiveness and the induction of forgiveness will be heuristic and will stimulate thought, discussion, and empirical research.

REFERENCES

Al-Mabuk, R.H., Enright, R.D., & Cardis, P.A. (1995). Forgiveness education with parentally deprived late adolescents. *Journal of Moral Education, 24,* 427–444.

Aron, A., & Aron, E.N. (1986). *Love and the expansion of self: Understanding attraction and satisfaction.* Washington, D.C.: Hemisphere.

Aron, A., Aron, E.N., Tudor, M., & Nelson, G. (1991). Close relationships as including other in self. *Journal of Personality and Social Psychology, 60,* 241–253.

Aronson, E. (1992). The return of the repressed: Dissonance theory makes a comeback. *Psychological Inquiry, 3,* 303–311.

Batson, C.D. (1997). Self-other merging and the empathy-altruism hypothesis: Reply to Neuberg et al. (1997). *Journal of Personality and Social Psychology, 73,* 517–522.

Batson, C.D., Sager, K., Garst, E., Kang, M., Rubchinsky, K., & Dawson, K. (1997). Is empathy-induced helping due to self-other merging? *Journal of Personality and Social Psychology, 73,* 495–509.

Bem, D.J. (1968). Self-perception theory. In L. Berkowitz (Ed.), *Advances in Experimental Social Psychology* (Vol. 6). New York: Academic Press.

Berkowitz, L. (1983). Aversively stimulated aggression: Some parallels and differences in research with animals and humans. *American Psychologist, 38,* 1135–1144.

Bromley, D.G., & Busching, B. (1988). Understanding the structure of contractual and covenantal social relations: Implications for the sociology of religion. *Sociological Analysis, 49,* 15–32.

Bromley, D.G., & Cress, C.H. (1998). Locating the corporal punishment debate in the context of conflicting forms of social relations. *Marriage and Family: A Christian Journal, 1*, 152–164.

Browning, D.S., Miller-McLemore, B.J., Couture, P.D., Lyon, B., & Franklin, R.M. (1997). *From culture wars to common ground: Religion and the American family debate.* Louisville, KY: Westminster John Knox Press.

Cialdini, R.B., Brown, S.L., Lewis, B.P., Luce, C., & Neuberg, S.L. (1997). Reinterpreting the empathy-altruism relationship: When one into one equals oneness. *Journal of Personality and Social Psychology, 73*, 481–494.

Coyle, C.T., & Enright, R.D. (1997). Forgiveness intervention with post-abortion men. *Journal of Consulting and Clinical Psychology, 65*, 1042–1046.

Damasio, A. (1994). *Descartes' error: Emotion, reason and the human brain.* New York: Grosset/Putnam.

Davenport, D.S. (1991). The functions of anger and forgiveness: Guidelines for psychotherapy with victims. *Psychotherapy, 28*, 140–144.

Davis, M.H. (1996). *Empathy: A social psychological approach.* Boulder, CO: Westview Press.

Davis, M.H., Conklin, L., Smith, A., & Luce, C. (1996). The effect of perspective taking on the cognitive representation of persons: A merging of self and other. *Journal of Personality and Social Psychology, 70*, 713–726.

Drobes, D.J., & Lang, P.J. (1995). Bioinformational theory and behavior therapy. In W. O'Donahue & L. Krasner (Eds.), *Theories of behavior therapy: Exploring behavior change* (pp. 229–257). Washington, D.C.: American Psychological Association.

Enright, R.D., & Coyle, C.T., (1998). Researching the process model of forgiveness with psychological interventions. In E.L. Worthington, Jr. (Ed.), *Dimensions of forgiveness: Psychological research & theological perspectives (pp. 139–161).* Philadelphia, PA: Templeton Foundation Press.

Enright, R.D., & the Human Development Study Group (1994). Piaget on the moral development of forgiveness: Identity or reciprocity? *Human Development, 37*, 63–80.

Enright, R. D., Santos, M. J., & Al-Mabuk, R. (1989). The adolescent as forgiver. *Journal of Adolescence, 12*, 95–110.

Festinger, L. (1957). *A theory of cognitive dissonance.* Stanford, CA: Stanford University Press.

Fitzgibbons, R.P. (1986). The cognitive and emotive uses of forgiveness in the treatment of anger. *Psychotherapy, 23*, 629–633.

Freedman, S.R., & Enright, R.D. (1996). Forgiveness as an intervention goal with incest survivors. *Journal of Consulting and Clinical Psychology, 64*, 983–992.

Gottman, J.M. (1994). *What predicts divorce? The relationship between marital processes and marital outcomes.* Hillsdale, NJ: Lawrence Erlbaum Associates.

Hamilton, W.D. (1964). The genetic evolution of social behavior. *Journal of Theoretical Biology, 7,* 1–52.

Hebl, J.H., & Enright, R.D. (1993). Forgiveness as a psychotherapeutic goal with elderly females. *Psychotherapy, 30,* 658–667.

Izard, C.E. (1992a). Basic emotions, relations among emotions, and emotion-cognition relations. *Psychological Review, 99,* 561–565.

Izard, C.E. (1992b). Four systems for emotion activation: Cognitive and noncognitive. *Psychological Review, 100,* 68–90.

Kalin, N.H., & Shelton, S.E. (1989). Depressive behaviors in infant rhesus monkeys: Environmental cues and neurochemical regulation. *Science, 243,* 1718–1721.

Kalin, N.H., Shelton, S.E., & Takahashi, L.K. (1991). Depressive behaviors in infant rhesus monkeys: Ontogeny and context-dependent selective expressions. *Child Development, 62,* 1175–1183.

Kaplan, B.H., Munroe-Blum, H., & Blazer, D.G. (1993). Religion, health, and forgiveness: Traditions and challenges. In Jeffrey S. Levin (Ed.), *Religion in aging and health* (pp. 52–77). Thousand Oaks, CA: Sage Publications.

Kiesler, C.A. (1971). *The psychology of commitment.* New York: Academic Press.

LeDoux, J. (1996). *The emotional brain: The mysterious underpinnings of emotional life.* New York: Simon & Schuster.

Levenson, R.W., & Ruef, A.M. (1992). Empathy: A physiological substrate. *Journal of Personality and Social Psychology, 3,* 234–246.

Lord, C.G., Ross, L., & Lepper, M.R. (1979). Biased assimilation and attitude polarization: The effects of prior theories on subsequently considered evidence. *Journal of Personality and Social Psychology, 37,* 2098–2109.

Mahoney, A., Pargament, K.I., Scott, E., Jewell, T., Swank, A., Emery, E., Hipp, K., Rye, M.S., & Butter, E. (1996, August). *Sacred vows: The sanctification of marriage and its psychosocial implications.* Paper presented at the meeting of the American Psychological Association, Chicago.

McCullough, M.E. (1997). Marriage and forgiveness. *Marriage and Family: A Christian Journal, 1,* 81–96.

McCullough, M.E., Rachal, K.C., Sandage, S.J., Worthington, E.L., Jr., Brown, S.W., & Hight, T.A. (1998). Interpersonal forgiving in close relationships II: Theoretical elaboration and measurement. *Journal of Personality and Social Psychology,* in press.

McCullough, M.E., Sandage, S.J., & Worthington, E.L., Jr. (1997). *To forgive is human: How to put your past in the past.* Downers Grove, IL: InterVarsity Press.

McCullough, M.E., & Worthington, E.L., Jr. (1994a). Encouraging clients to forgive people who have hurt them: Review, critique, and research prospectus. *Journal of Psychology and Theology, 22,* 3–20.

McCullough, M.E., & Worthington, E.L., Jr. (1994b). Models of interpersonal forgiveness and their applications to counseling: Review and critique. *Counseling and Values, 39,* 2–14.

McCullough, M.E., & Worthington, E.L., Jr. (1995). Promoting forgiveness: A comparison of two brief psychoeducational group interventions with a waiting-list control. *Counseling and Values, 40,* 55–68.

McCullough, M.E., Worthington, E.L., Jr., & Rachal, K.C. (1997). Interpersonal forgiving in close relationships. *Journal of Personality and Social Psychology, 73,* 321–336.

Means, J.R., Wilson, G.L., Sturm, C., Biron, J.E., & Bach, P.J. (1990). Humility as psychotherapeutic formulation. *Counseling Psychology Quarterly, 3,* 211–215.

Neuberg, S.L., Cialdini, R.B., Brown, S.L., Luce, C., & Sagarin, B.J. (1997). Does empathy lead to anything more than superficial helping? Comment on Batson et al. (1997). *Journal of Personality and Social Psychology, 73,* 510–516.

Novaco, R.W. (1975). *Anger control: The development and evaluation of an experimental treatment.* Lexington, MA: Lexington Books.

O'Connor, L.E., Berry, J.W., Weiss, J., Bush, M., & Sampson, H. (1997). Interpersonal guilt: The development of a new measure. *Journal of Clinical Psychology, 53,* 73–89.

Ripley, J.S. (1998). *Marriage contracts and covenants: The effects of marital values on outcomes of marital-enrichment workshops.* Doctoral dissertation, Virginia Commonwealth University, Richmond.

Rusbult, C.E., Bissonnette, V.L., Arriaga, X.B., & Cox, C.L. (1998). Accommodation processes during the early years of marriage. In T.N. Bradbury (Ed.), *The developmental course of marital dysfunction* (pp. 74-113). New York: Cambridge University Press.

Rusbult, C.E., & Buunk, B.P. (1993). Commitment processes in close relationships: An interdependence analysis. *Journal of Social and Personal Relationships, 10,* 175–204.

Rusbult, C.E., Johnson, D.J., & Morrow, G.D. (1986). Predicting satisfaction and commitment in adult romantic involvements: An assessment of the generality of the investment model. *Social Psychology Quarterly, 49,* 81–89.

Rusbult, C.E., Verette, J., Whitney, G.A., Slovik, L.F., & Lipkus, I. (1991). Accommodation processes in close relationships: Theory and preliminary evidence. *Journal of Personality and Social Psychology, 60,* 53–78.

Sandage, S.J. (1997). *An ego-humility model of forgiveness*. Unpublished doctoral dissertation, Virginia Commonwealth University, Richmond.

Sapolsky, R. (1994). *Why zebras don't get ulcers: A guide to stress, stress-related diseases, and coping*. New York: W.H. Freeman.

Seligman, M.E.P. (1975). *Helplessness: On depression, development, and death*. San Francisco: W.H. Freeman and Co.

Sternberg, R. (1986). A triangular theory of love. *Psychological Review, 93,* 119–135.

Tangney, J.P. (1995). Shame and guilt in interpersonal relationships. In J.P. Tangney & K.W. Fisher (Eds.), *Self-conscious emotions: Shame, guilt, embarrassment, and pride* (pp. 114–139). New York: Guilford Press.

Tangney, P.P., Wagner, P., Barlow, D.H., & Marschall, D.E. (1996). Relation of shame and guilt to constructive vs. destructive responses to anger across the life span. *Journal of Personality and Social Psychology, 70,* 797–809.

Van Lange, P.A.M., Rusbult, C.E., Drigotas, S.M., Arriaga, X.B., Witcher, B.S., & Cox, C.L. (1997). Willingness to sacrifice in close relationships. *Journal of Personality and Social Psychology, 72,* 1373–1395.

de Waal, F. (1989a). *Chimpanzee politics: Power and sex among apes*. Baltimore: The Johns Hopkins University Press.

de Waal, F. (1989b). *Peacemaking among primates*. London: Penguin Books.

de Waal, F. (1996). *Good natured: The origins of right and wrong in humans and other animals*. Cambridge, MA: Harvard University Press.

Wegner, D.M. (1994). *White bears and other unwanted thoughts: Suppression, obsession, and the psychology of mental control*. New York: Guilford Press.

Williams, R.B. (1989). *The trusting heart*. New York: Random House.

Witte, J. (1997). *From sacrament to contract: Marriage, religion and law in the Western tradition*. Louisville, KY: Westminster John Knox Press.

Worthington, E.L., Jr. (1998). An empathy-humility commitment model of forgiveness applied to family dyads. *Journal of Family Therapy, 20,* 59–76.

Worthington, E.L., Jr., & DiBlasio, F.A. (1990). Promoting mutual forgiveness within the fractured relationship. *Psychotherapy, 27,* 219–223.

CHAPTER 6

Researching the Process Model of Forgiveness Within Psychological Interventions

Robert D. Enright and Catherine T. Coyle

THE QUESTION OF HOW PEOPLE LEARN to forgive is among the most important in the social sciences. When we speak to audiences on the issue of forgiveness, we equate the search for ways to forgive with the search for a way to cure cancer. While this may seem to be hyperbole for some, it is not for us. Those who seek a cure for cancer are working to end human suffering on a global scale. Those who pursue ways to forgive are striving to end deep human misery.

We are perplexed that, until quite recently, the scientific community has not noticed the link between forgiving and the alleviation of such distresses as depression, anxiety, hopelessness, and low self-esteem. People who do not forgive may be at risk not only for continual emotional disruption, but also for damaged relationships and perhaps even physical complications (Fitzgibbons, 1986; Hope, 1987). The question about psychological interventions on forgiveness, then, should be taken seriously by a wide variety of helping professionals.

We are happy to report that, over the past decade, social scientists and those in the helping professions are beginning to take seriously the ideas about interpersonal forgiveness. Evidence of this interest is found (1) in the development of psychological theory (Enright, Eastin, Golden,

Sarinopoulos, & Freedman, 1992; Enright & the Human Development Study Group, 1991a; Linn & Linn, 1978; Smedes, 1984); (2) in clinical practice (Brandsma, 1982; Enright & the Human Development Study Group, 1991b; Fitzgibbons, 1986; Hope, 1987; Worthington & DiBlasio, 1990); and (3) in research (Al-Mabuk, Enright, & Cardis, 1995; Coyle & Enright, 1997; Enright, Santos, & Al-Mabuk, 1989; Freedman & Enright, 1995; Hebl & Enright, 1993; Hepp-Dax, 1996; McCullough, Worthington, & Rachal, 1997; Trainer, 1981/1984).

Our intent in this chapter is to review two prototype psychological interventions on forgiveness that we and our colleagues have developed at the University of Wisconsin–Madison. We first define forgiveness, then turn to a description of our intervention model. Following this, we describe each research-based intervention and conclude with our recommendations for those entering this challenging line of investigation.

FORGIVENESS DEFINED

As interest in forgiveness continues to grow, it becomes increasingly imperative to adequately define the construct. Forgiveness may be defined as an interpersonal process—a process occurring between people rather than between people and an object or event (such as a natural disaster). It also is critical to differentiate genuine forgiveness from pseudo forms and concepts similar to but distinct from it. In genuine forgiveness, one who has suffered an unjust injury chooses to abandon his or her right to resentment and retaliation, and instead offers mercy to the offender. North (1987) has stated that forgiveness occurs when the injured person is able to "view the wrongdoer with compassion, benevolence, and love while recognizing that he has willfully abandoned his right to them" (p. 502).

Inherent in this definition of genuine forgiveness are three points worth noting. First, the injured one is able to recognize an actual injustice. Second, the injured one chooses willingly and without coercion to respond with mercy rather than what could be justifiable retribution. Third, forgiveness is decidedly moral, concerned with the good of human interaction. These points may be helpful in ascertaining the differences between genuine forgiveness and other concepts sometimes confused with it, such as: *pardoning, condoning, excusing, forgetting*, and *denying*.

The notion of *pardoning* suggests that an offender be spared the legal penalties incurred by the offense; however, we may forgive another even while our judicial system enforces its penalties. *Condoning* implies that the injured person justifies the offense committed against himself or herself; in such a case, forgiveness would be a moot point (Kolnai, 1973–74). *Excusing* implies that the injured believes the offender has a defensible reason for committing the offense; again, forgiveness would not seem to be an issue if the offender is not guilty. As Veenstra (1992) has argued, "Overlooking, excusing, condoning are theoretically not really forms of forgiveness. In all of these the injuring person has done nothing wrong. There is no need for forgiveness if there has been no wrongdoing" (p. 166).

Forgiveness also is not to be confused with *forgetting*. Smedes (1984) fittingly has observed that "forgetting, in fact, may be a dangerous way to escape the inner surgery of the heart that we call forgiving" (p. 60). Similarly, *denying* may be used to avoid facing the pain of an injury as well as to avoid the effort involved in genuine forgiveness. Extreme denial may be evidenced in a reaction formation in which the injured person believes that he or she has forgiven, but, in fact, is unable to consciously recognize his or her own anger (Hunter, 1978). Genuine forgiveness cannot even begin to be considered until one recognizes the pain and consequences of the injury (Fitzgibbons, 1986).

Still another misunderstanding of forgiveness may occur when the one who claims to have forgiven does so with "the intention of proving and aggravating the beneficiary's wickedness" (Kolnai, 1973–74). A similar distortion has been recognized by Augsburger (1981) and Cunningham (1985), in which the injured one claims to have forgiven, but then holds himself or herself to be morally superior to the one forgiven.

Reconciliation also is not to be confused or equated with forgiveness (Enright & the Human Development Study Group, 1991a). One can forgive another and yet choose not to remain in a relationship with him or her. While forgiveness may open the door to reconciliation, the nature of the relationship may well depend more on the trustworthiness of the offender than on the desires of the injured.

Genuine forgiveness is voluntary and unconditional. Thus, it is not motivated by pressure from a third party, nor is it dependent on the apology or recognition of wrongdoing on the part of the offender. Genuine forgiveness constitutes an internal process that transforms the forgiver and also may transform the one forgiven, if he or she is able to receive the gift of forgiveness. More details on the construct of interpersonal forgiveness can be found in Enright and the Human Development Study Group (1991a).

PHILOSOPHICAL OBJECTIONS TO FORGIVENESS

The topic of forgiveness has been, and continues to be, controversial. Nietzsche (1887) claimed that forgiveness is an expression of weakness. However, a review of the distinction between genuine and pseudoforgiveness may counter this claim. North (1987) has said that forgiveness "should not be confused with timidity or moral feebleness" (p. 507). Genuine forgiveness requires strength and courage. There is nothing cowardly about recognizing a painful injury and choosing to respond lovingly to the one who caused it. Pseudoforgiveness, on the other hand, may occur as a result of fear and weakness. If the injured is unable to recognize the degree of injustice or is lacking in healthy self-esteem, then he or she may condone or excuse the offender.

Lewis (1980) has argued that forgiveness has the potential to hinder social justice by encouraging too lenient an attitude toward criminals. This argument seems to confuse pardon with forgiveness. One can forgive an offender even while the offender pays a legal price following a violation of the law. Lauritzen (1987) has expressed concern that forgiveness may hinder personal justice and even perpetuate injustice, and, in that regard, he concluded that forgiveness might be immoral. However, genuine forgiveness cannot occur unless the injured person first has an appreciation of justice and then recognizes that an injustice has been done. The one who chooses to forgive genuinely is not denying justice. Rather, he or she recognizes mercy as well. Genuine forgiveness is not the equivalent of, and does not demand, reconciliation. The one who chooses to forgive an offender may not choose to trust that individual.

Some have proposed that forgiveness may result in the offender's feeling inferior to the injured (Droll, 1984/1985; O'Shaughnessy, 1967). This criticism fails to recognize the motives operating in genuine forgiveness (i.e., compassion, benevolence, and love) and also defines the forgiveness in terms of the offender's response to it. As Enright and the Human Development Study Group (1991a) have observed, "A gift rejected does not detract from the fact that it is a gift given" (p. 133).

Haber (1991) contended that forgiveness demonstrates a lack of self-respect and that resentment would be a more appropriate and moral response to an injury. As we refer to our definition of genuine forgiveness, we can see that resentment and anger must be recognized before we can move beyond them to the point of forgiveness. In addition, clinicians (Brandsma, 1982; Fitzgibbons, 1986) have observed that it is not forgiveness, but rather unresolved anger, that hurts the self. One could argue then that both self-respect and respect for others motivate one to forgive. In sum, most objections to forgiveness revolve around the failure to distinguish among genuine forgiveness, pseudoforgiveness, and related but distinct constructs. Again, the reader is referred to Enright and the Human Development Study Group (1991a) for further discussion.

A PSYCHOLOGICAL PROCESS MODEL OF FORGIVENESS

Enright and the Human Development Study Group (1996) have developed a process model of forgiveness that is based on the previously described definition. The model includes 20 units or psychological variables and incorporates the cognitive, behavioral, and affective aspects of the forgiveness process. As study and research have progressed, the model has been refined. Referring to Table 1, the most recent change is the addition of Unit 15, which emphasizes the gift-like quality of forgiveness. The actual number of units remains the same, as Unit 13 now represents a combination of what previously were two separate units. Our intent in proposing this specific model in 1991 was to be as complete as possible in describing how people forgive, avoiding, as much as possible, reductionism and oversimplification (see Table 1).

Table 1. Processes of Forgiving Another*

UNITS	COGNITIVE, BEHAVIORAL, AND AFFECTIVE PHASES
	UNCOVERING PHASE
1.	Examination of psychological defenses (Kiel, 1986)
2.	Confrontation of anger; the point is to release, not harbor, the anger (Trainer, 1981/1984)
3.	Admittance of shame, when this is appropriate (Patton, 1985)
4.	Awareness of cathexis (Droll, 1984/1985)
5.	Awareness of cognitive rehearsal of the offense (Droll, 1984/1985)
6.	Insight that the injured party may be comparing oneself with the injurer (Kiel, 1986)
7.	Realization that oneself may be permanently and adversely changed by the injury (Close, 1970)
8.	Insight into a possibly altered "just world" view (Flanigan, 1987)
	DECISION PHASE
9.	A change of heart/conversion/new insights that old resolution strategies are not working (North, 1987)
10.	Willingness to consider forgiveness as an option
11.	Commitment to forgive the offender (Neblett, 1974)

* Note: This table is extrapolated from work by Enright and the Human Development Study Group (1991a). The references at the end of each unit are prototypical examples or discussions of that unit.

WORK PHASE

12.   Reframing, through role taking, of who the wrongdoer is by viewing him or her in context (Smith, 1981)

13.   Empathy and compassion toward the offender (Cunningham, 1985; Droll, 1984/1985)

14.   Acceptance/absorption of the pain (Bergin, 1988)

15.   Giving a moral gift to the offender (North, 1987)

DEEPENING PHASE

16.   Finding meaning for oneself and others in the suffering and in the forgiveness process (Frankl, 1959)

17.   Realization that oneself has needed others' forgiveness in the past (Cunningham, 1985)

18.   Insight that one is not alone (universality, support)

19.   Realization that oneself may have a new purpose in life because of the injury

20.   Awareness of decreased negative affect and, perhaps, increased positive affect, if this begins to emerge, toward the injurer; awareness of internal, emotional release (Smedes, 1984)

The entire process model will now be briefly discussed. The first unit represents the examination of defense mechanisms that the injured may have employed to protect himself or herself from the pain of the injury (Unit 1). Such examination may, in turn, lead to the confrontation of anger (Unit 2) and an awareness of shame and/or embarrassment (Unit 3). The injured also may become increasingly aware of how much energy has been spent as a result of the injury (Unit 4), and how often he or she engages in cognitive rehearsal of the event (Unit 5). As the injured one compares his or her situation with that of the offender (Unit 6), he or she may realize the permanent and adverse nature of the change caused by the injury (Unit 7). The injured may also recognize that his or her view of justice has been altered (Unit 8), causing increasing cynicism or bitterness.

As the injured becomes more aware of both the impact of the injury and his or her responses to it, he or she may seek some form of resolution (Unit 9). At this point, the injured person may consider forgiveness as a response option (Unit 10) and perhaps then make a commitment to forgive the offender (Unit 11). To carry out such a commitment, the injured person may engage in reframing by attempting to view the offender in a larger context than merely that of the injury (Unit 12). Reframing may be facilitated by asking the injured person the following questions regarding the offender:

1. What was it like for the person as he or she was growing up? Did the offender come from a home in which there was conflict or even abuse?

2. What was happening in the person's life at the time he or she hurt you?

3. Can you see the person as having worth simply by being a member of the human community?

The purpose of these questions is not to find excuses for the offender, but rather to help the injured person to view the offender as a vulnerable human being. This enlarged view of the offender, achieved through cognitive exercises, may lead to a new affective stance, including empathy and even compassion, toward the offender (Unit 13). As the injured person continues to work through the process of forgiveness, he or she may realize that forgiveness requires an acceptance or absorption of pain (Unit 14). This decision, to contain one's pain, serves to prevent the transmission of pain to both the offender and to innocent others. It is often useful to use a concrete analogy to foster understanding of this concept. The concept of a sponge absorbing water may be useful, as may asking the injured person to put the concept into his or her own words. The concept of absorbing the pain exemplifies the moral gift-like quality of forgiveness (Unit 15). The injured person, by deliberately containing the pain of the injury, is giving a gift to the offender by withholding punishment.

As the injured one continues the forgiveness journey, he or she discovers the paradoxical nature of the gift of forgiveness: As he or she for-give, he or she experiences healing. In other words, forgiveness is not a self-seeking activity, but one that focuses morally on the offending per-son. As the offended person begins to forgive, he or she may find new meaning in the hurtful event (Unit 16). For example, the injured per-son may find himself or herself becoming more compassionate toward others that have been similarly hurt. The injured person also may real-ize that he or she has needed forgiveness from others (Unit 17) and that he or she is not alone in the experience of suffering (Unit 18). The experience of Units 17 and 18 may increase the value ascribed to for-giveness and may strengthen the resolve to forgive. Those who choose to forgive also may discover a new purpose in life because of the injury (Unit 19). They may begin a counseling career or initiate a support group for others who have been injured.

Finally, as one nears the end of the forgiveness journey, he or she may become aware of a decrease in negative emotions and perhaps an increase in positive feelings toward the offender. The exchange of negative for positive emotion results in the experience of an internal, emotional release (Unit 20). Some might describe this experience as a lightening, or a feeling of freedom. Enright and the Human Development Study Group (1996) have cautioned that this model is not meant to be inter-preted as a rigid step-like sequence, but rather as a flexible set of processes with feedback and feed-forward loops, leaving room for much individ-ual variation within the model.

FORGIVENESS INTERVENTION RESEARCH

Four published studies using the process model have been done. The first, by Hebl and Enright (1993), focused on elderly females who suffered a wide variety of injustices, including overmedication, spousal conflict, and disappointment that their children made so few contacts with them. This study is important from an historical perspective because it was the first publication ever to show that, in fact, one can induce forgiveness with deliberate therapeutic goals to do so.

The second, by Al-Mabuk, Enright, and Cardis (1995), concerned college students whose parent or parents were emotionally absent as the participants were growing up. We manipulated the process model in two studies. In Study 1, we chose a brief intervention that brought the participants to a point of deciding to and committing to forgive (through Units 9–11). In Study 2, we brought the participants through the entire model. We found that in Study 1, deciding and committing to forgive were not sufficient to improve the participants' emotional health, whereas we found that the entire process in Study 2 was sufficient to cause improvement.

The third of our four studies, conducted by Freedman and Enright (1996), involved female incest survivors. This 14-month program was successful in helping the women improve their emotional health, and the benefits were maintained at 14-month follow-up.

The fourth study, by Coyle and Enright (1997), addressed the issue of forgiveness within the context of men hurt by the abortion decision of a partner. This study and Study 2 by Al-Mabuk, Enright, and Cardis (1995) are detailed below.

Forgiveness with College Students
Emotionally Hurt by a Parent

Al-Mabuk, Enright, and Cardis' (1995) Study 2 is an intervention with parentally love deprived college students. Love deprivation refers to a situation in which one parent was perceived as being emotionally absent as the participant was growing up. Only the second of the two studies is described here.

Participants included 45 college students from a midwestern university randomly selected from a larger sample of 120 students who evidenced a score of at least 1 standard deviation (SD) above the mean on a screening measure used to evaluate parental love deprivation.

Testing and Instruments. We administered six scales in a group format:

✦ The Coopersmith Self-Esteem Inventory (Coopersmith, 1981)

✦ The Beck Depression Inventory (Beck, Ward, Mendelson, Mock, & Erbaugh, 1961)

✦ The Spielberger State-Trait Anxiety Inventory (Spielberger, Gorsuch, Lushene, Vagg, & Jacobs, 1983)

✦ A Hope Scale, which assesses optimism toward the future

✦ An Attitude Toward Mother/Father Scale

✦ The Psychological Profile of Forgiveness Scale, which was developed by Enright and seven graduate students

The forgiveness measure is a 30-item scale that assesses forgiveness in terms of the absence of negative emotions, thoughts, and behaviors and the presence of positive emotions, thoughts, and behaviors specifically toward the person (in this case, a parent) who was deeply unfair to the participant. Each of these subscales is represented by five items, and each item is ranked on a 4-point Likert Scale. The potential range of scores is 30–120, with higher scores indicating greater forgiveness.

A separate pseudoforgiveness scale that assesses condonation and excusing was included to ensure that the absence of negative affect was due to genuine forgiveness and not to a related construct. The Attitude Toward Mother/Father Scale served to assess a change in the student's view of the parent who was perceived as having been emotionally distant; a low score represented a harmonious relationship as perceived by the participant, a high score the perception of high conflict with the parent. All measures were administered at both the pre- and posttest with the exception of the self-esteem and depression measures, which were given only at posttest. The test administrator was not aware of the research hypotheses.

Intervention Procedure. The participants were randomly assigned to either a treatment or a control group and stratified by gender. The experimental group included 18 females and 6 males, while the control group comprised 11 females and 10 males. The data from 3 control group participants were not included in the final analysis because of incomplete questionnaires. Each group met once per week for 6 consecutive weeks. The experimental group received the forgiveness intervention, which incorporated the 17 units of the original process model. The control group took part in a human relations program.

Experimental Sessions. The intervenor developed and used a manual to lead the experimental group sessions. As noted, the manual incorporated most (17) of the units of the entire process model. The manual was not distributed to the participants. In the first session, participants were given an overview of the intervention as well as a detailed description of forgiveness. The second session focused on anger and its possible complications. The third, fourth, and fifth sessions centered on the decision phase of the process and the beginning units of the work phase (i.e., reframing, empathy, and compassion toward the offending parent). These units were reviewed in the sixth session as a bridge to Unit 14, "Acceptance/absorption of the pain." At this time, the student participant was encouraged and aided in bearing his or her pain, thereby improving his or her family's functioning. Unit 17 was explored in an effort to increase each student's awareness of his or her own need for forgiveness and to motivate the forgiveness of parents. This last session concluded with an examination of the student's affective state and whether the student was moving toward forgiveness.

The control group, which was engaged in a human relations program, covered one topic each session. Topics included leadership skills, two-way communication, self-discovery, and person-perception skills. The control group did not discuss the topic of forgiveness.

Results and Discussion. Statistical significance was obtained on all but one of the measures administered. Compared with the control participants, those in the experimental group demonstrated significant gains on both the Psychological Profile of Forgiveness Scale and the Hope Scale. The experimental group also evidenced a significant improvement on the Attitude Toward Mother/Father Scale and a significant reduction in general anxiety compared with the control group. Only on the State Anxiety Inventory was no significant difference observed between the two groups. As for the two measures given only at posttest, the experimental group demonstrated significantly greater self-esteem than the control group, while no significant differences between the two groups were observed on the measure of depression. Among the 24 experimental participants, 23 chose to sign a commitment-to-forgive contract at posttest, while only 10 of the 21 control group members chose to do so.

These results provide evidence for the efficacy of a forgiveness intervention based on the process model previously described. The experimental group demonstrated movement toward psychological healing, particularly on the Attitude Toward Mother/Father Scale, the Hope Scale, and the Psychological Profile of Forgiveness Scale. The experimental group's posttest means on those measures were, respectively, 18.4 (range = 0–100, with a low score representing a harmonious relation and a high score representing a conflicting relation), 121 (range = 30–150), and 101.5 (range = 30–120). These means are quite strong relative to the potential range of scores for each measure.

While no significant differences were evident between the two groups on the measure of depression, it is noteworthy that neither group evidenced depression. The experimental group's posttest mean on the depression scale was 4.58, while that of the control group was 7.1. The potential range of scores on the Beck Depression Inventory is 0–63.

Forgiveness with Men Hurt
by the Abortion Decision of their Partner

Coyle and Enright (1997) used a forgiveness intervention with 10 adult males who described themselves as having been hurt by a personal abortion experience. Participants ranged in age from 21 to 43 years with a mean age of 28 years. All of the participants were single, and all were from the same midwestern city. One of the participants was biracial (Caucasian and African-American), 1 was Pakistani, and 8 were Caucasian. Six of the participants identified themselves as Christian, 2 as Muslim, and the rest as agnostic. The length of time elapsed since the abortion ranged from 6 months to 22 years, with the average length of time being 6 years. Half of the men were opposed to abortion from the time they learned of the pregnancies. One was supportive of abortion initially, and 1 was not even aware that an abortion had occurred until months after the procedure. The rest of the men described themselves as having felt confused or ambivalent at the time the decision to abort was made.

Instruments. A structured interview was used to validate that the participant perceived the abortion experience as painful and unjust and to ensure that the participant could identify one person, other than himself, that he blamed and felt anger toward. Four other measures were used to assess forgiveness, anger, anxiety, and grief.

The forgiveness measure used in this study was the Enright Forgiveness Inventory (EFI) (Subkoviak et al., 1992, 1995) and is a refinement of the Psychological Profile of Forgiveness Scale. This measure contains 60 items and has a scoring range of 60–360, with higher scores indicating greater forgiveness. The participants' level of anger and anxiety were assessed using the Spielberger State Anger Scale (1983) and the Spielberger State Anxiety Inventory (1983). Grief was measured using the short version of the Perinatal Grief Scale (Potvin, Lasker, & Toedter, 1989). A single-item question was used to evaluate self-forgiveness.

Design. Participants were randomly assigned to either the treatment or control group. Immediately after pretest, the experimental participants began the intervention program, while the control participants entered into a 12-week waiting period. Following the waiting period, the control participants were given the opportunity to take part in the intervention.

Testing Procedure. As in the Freedman and Enright (1995, 1996) study, participants were administered three rounds of pretests given at weekly intervals and presented in random order. Following this triple pretest administration, the experimental participants began the program, while the control participants began the 12-week waiting period. After the intervention program and/or the 12-week waiting period was completed, participants were given three rounds of posttest 1. Next, the control-turned-experimental participants received the intervention. After completing the program, they were administered three rounds of posttest 2. Posttest 2 was given to the experimental participants 12 weeks after they had completed the intervention, and this second posttest served as a follow-up of the first experimental group. At each of the testing periods, the three scores obtained for each measure were averaged to produce a single mean score for each measure at each testing time.

Intervention Procedure. The intervenor met with each participant on an individual basis once per week for a total of 12 weeks. Each session lasted 90 minutes. The intervention manual was based on the 20 units of the process model described above, and also incorporated five specific areas that have been identified as problematic for post-abortion men: anger, helplessness, guilt, relationships, and grief. The intervention addressed each of these areas individually and then related the problem to forgiveness.

Results and Discussion. Four comparisons were of interest in this study. The first looked at the change within the experimental group from pretest to posttest 1 (following the intervention program) versus that of the control group from pretest to posttest 1 (following the 12-week waiting period). As hypothesized, the experimental group demonstrated significant increases in self-forgiveness and forgiveness of another, as well as significant reductions in anger, anxiety, and grief. Only on the positive behavior subscale of the EFI was no significant difference between the two groups observed.

In the second comparison, the control group's mean change scores obtained from pretest to posttest 1 (before intervention) were compared with those obtained from posttest 1 to posttest 2 (after intervention). It was hypothesized that the control group would evidence significant and positive change toward psychological health following the intervention. In fact, the control group did demonstrate such change on all measures with the exception of the anger measure. The control-turned-experimental group demonstrated significant gains in self-forgiveness and forgiveness of another. Only on the positive and negative behavior subscales of the EFI were no significant differences observed. This group also evidenced significant reductions in anxiety and grief, but did not do so in terms of anger change scores. However, when anger mean scores, rather than mean change scores, were analyzed, a significant difference was found, indicating that the control group also benefited from a significant anger reduction after treatment.

The third comparison examined the mean change scores of the experimental group versus those of the control group after each had received the intervention. As both groups had experienced the same intervention, it was hypothesized that no significant differences would be observed. The hypothesis was supported, with no significant differences found on any of the dependent measures.

The fourth and last comparison looked at the experimental group's mean change from pretest to posttest 2 (12 weeks after treatment) versus that of the control group from posttest 1 to posttest 2 (immediately after treatment). No significant differences were found, indicating that the experimental participants maintained psychological benefits over at least 12 weeks.

These findings support the efficacy of this particular intervention with post-abortion men. Both groups demonstrated significant increases in forgiveness and significant reductions in anger, anxiety, and grief following the intervention. While neither group demonstrated a significant increase in positive behavior, it should be noted that none of the participants were still in a relationship with their partner, making the possibility of engaging in any behavior with them quite unlikely. These findings also confirm the general trends of other forgiveness intervention studies—that is, the decision to forgive and the practice of forgiveness to bring about psychological healing.

Overall Discussion

The above studies, taken as a whole, suggest that forgiveness may be taught and learned and that the outcomes can be quite favorable. In each of the four studies, because of the nature of the instruments used in the research, the participants could have potentially deteriorated or improved on psychological indicators. Across all of the studies, there was not one instance in which a group experiencing forgiveness education showed a decline in psychological health. In fact, statistically significant improvement in such variables as hope and self-esteem, as well as significant decreases in anxiety and depression, were more the rule than the exception.

In each case, the education was based on a model of forgiveness that is detailed and consistent with philosophers' and clinicians' views of what does and does not constitute forgiveness. Forgiveness education, in our view, should address: (a) the participants' accurate understanding of forgiveness, (b) their self-chosen commitment to try forgiveness,

(c) cognitive exercises to understand their offender, (d) affective exercises in which empathy and compassion are allowed to blossom, and (e) exercises that allow for the courageous act of absorbing or bearing the pain so that cycles of revenge and displacement cease.

As Professor Pargament (see Chapter 3) pointed out to us in his review of this chapter, all of us who do forgiveness interventions must avoid stereotyping either the people who participate or the interventions themselves. As he puts it, there is a danger in presuming that "one size fits all." We completely agree with this idea. In presenting our process model, we do not wish to imply that all people traverse the processes in the same way. Yes, we presume that forgiveness has certain essential components (see above paragraph), but each participant will experience these components in unique ways. The amount of time spent on a given unit (see Table 1), the difficulty in moving through that unit, and how often a person revisits that unit are idiosyncratic. We cannot at this point predict how a person will move through the units, regardless of the nature of the hurt or the person's individual characteristics, such as emotional health, religious beliefs, or cultural background.

We also believe that forgiveness education or therapy should not be isolated from the rest of a person's life. In other words, a person who learns forgiveness in a specific context of injustice might consider appropriating it in other areas of interpersonal difficulties. Forgiveness can be integrated with one's existing philosophies and religious beliefs in general. In fact, our experience is that people do not compartmentalize forgiveness, but naturally (without help or encouragement from us) synthesize what they learn from our programs into their own worldviews.

As we look toward the next century, we have no doubt that many researchers and practitioners will begin exploring the construct of forgiveness. In anticipation of this, we offer the following opinions that may be helpful, or at least challenging, to those entering the growing field of forgiveness education and therapy:

1. Anyone who enters the field of forgiveness studies as a researcher or practitioner should first start thinking like a philosopher. By this we mean that the person must deeply and broadly understand just what forgiveness is. The person will have to read extensively in philosophy,

in theology, and even in the ancient texts that first explicated the construct. We recommend the following: Brakenhielm (1993); Downie (1965); Enright, Gassin, and Wu (1992); Enright and the Human Development Study Group (1991a); Holmgren (1993); Horsbrugh (1974); Hughes (1975); Kolnai (1973–74); Lewis (1980); Neblett (1974); North (1987); Richards (1988); Smedes (1984); and Twambley (1976). This, of course, is not an exhaustive list, but only a beginning. Profound knowledge of the concept is essential.

2. We as social scientists must be absolutely diligent in avoiding reductionism in the multifaceted concept of forgiveness. This is our greatest concern, that well-meaning scientists and practitioners, without intending to do so, reduce the meaning of forgiveness to something so simple that the meaning becomes distorted, and in some cases wrong. For example, McGary (1989), in an intriguing essay, reduces forgiveness to only giving up resentment or any other negative attitude or feeling toward a wrongdoer. By leaving out the other half of the equation—adopting friendlier attitudes toward the offender—McGary creates problems for the construct. As an example, as Charles stops resenting Beth, he may do so with a cold, neutral indifference. Is Charles forgiving or merely "moving on," in the contemporary colloquialism? Is Charles doing this for himself or for Beth? Is forgiving in this sense a self-serving psychological strategy or a moral gift given to someone who does not necessarily deserve it? McGary's reductionism seems to distort the essence of forgiveness.

We are particularly concerned about reductionism because it already has happened in other areas of psychology where subtle constructs become unrecognizable across the research generations. An example is Erik Erikson's concept of adolescent ego identity. It took Erikson (1968) an entire book to distill his meaning; yet he knew that the psychological research community would define identity in a few sentences, thus distorting his original meaning. Consider his own words on the matter:

> Social scientists, on the other hand, sometimes attempt to achieve greater specificity by making such terms as "identity crisis," "self-

identity," or "sexual identity" fit whatever more measurable item they are investigating at a given time. For the sake of logical or experimental maneuverability (and in order to keep in good academic company) they try to treat these terms as matters of social roles, personal traits, or conscious self-images, shunning the less manageable and more sinister—which often also means the more vital—implications of the concept. Such usages have, in fact, become so indiscriminate that the other day a German reviewer of the book in which I first used the term in the context of psychoanalytic ego theory called it the pet subject of the *amerikanische Populaerpsychologie* (p. 16).

One cause for hope is the establishment in 1994 of the International Forgiveness Institute, dedicated to the dissemination and creation of knowledge on the topic of forgiveness (IFI address: P.O. BOX 6153, Madison, WI 53716). In our newsletter, *The World of Forgiveness*, we have reported on scientific works. We will have an open forum in the future for debate, criticism, rebuttal, and analysis of research articles. Perhaps this outlet will be one avenue for avoiding, or at least addressing, reductionistic thinking.

3. Those who wish to do forgiveness interventions must invest in the lives of the participants. Forgiveness never has been a "quick fix" and never will be. The one-hour forgiveness intervention is an oxymoron for healing long-lasting, deep-seated injustices and for substantially reducing psychological symptoms of a clinical nature. Recall that the brief intervention of Study 1 in Al-Mabuk, Enright, and Cardis (1995) was ineffective compared with the longer, more in-depth Study 2 intervention. Might the reductionism in the meaning of forgiveness become manifest in the interventions themselves? If so, we hope there are many voices of critique out there that will be heard.

4. We have maintained elsewhere that there probably are many intervention models that will prove effective (Enright, Freedman, & Rique, 1998). We suspect, however, that the models withstanding the test of time will be those based on a deep knowledge of forgiveness, that do not distort its meaning, and that invest in the participants' lives.

These are the best of times and the worst of times for forgiveness studies. But we must forge ahead because research is beginning to show that forgiveness can be a major factor in the fields of education and therapy. We will encounter, as the field of psychology has encountered for its entire one-hundred-year existence, those that will unwittingly make the concept brittle and smaller than it should be. The more enthusiasm and funding that are available, the more forgiveness will be threatened by serious error. At the same time, the enthusiasm and funding should lead to some seminal studies. Let us anticipate that, indeed, the errors already have begun and start reading, debating, and critiquing one another's work. By this process, the hurting people who wish to forgive will be served. The concept of forgiveness is too important to do otherwise.

REFERENCES

Al-Mabuk, R., Enright, R. D., & Cardis, P. (1995). Forgiveness education with parentally love-deprived college students. *Journal of Moral Education, 24,* 427–444.

Augsburger, D. (1981). *Caring enough to forgive: True forgiveness.* Chicago: Moody Press.

Beck, A.T., Ward, C.H., Mendelson, M., Mock, J., & Erbaugh, J. (1961). An inventory for measuring depression. *Archives of General Psychiatry, 4,* 561–571.

Bergin, A.E. (1988). Three contributions of a spiritual perspective to counseling, psychotherapy, and behavior change. *Counseling & Values, 33,* 21–31.

Brakenhielm, C.R. (1993). *Forgiveness.* Minneapolis, MN: Fortress Press.

Brandsma, J.M. (1982). Forgiveness: A dynamic, theological and theoretical analysis. *Pastoral Psychology, 3,* 40–50.

Close, H.T. (1970). Forgiveness and responsibility: A case study. *Pastoral Psychology, 21,* 19–25.

Coopersmith, S. (1981). *Self-esteem inventories.* Palo Alto, Ca: Consulting Psychologists, Inc.

Coyle, C.T., & Enright, R.D. (1997). Forgiveness intervention with post-abortion men. *Journal of Consulting and Clinical Psychology, 65,* 1042–1045.

Coyle, C.T., & Enright, R.D. (1988). Forgiveness education with adult learners. In M.C. Smith & T. Pourchot (Eds.), *Adult learning and development: Perspectives from educational psychology* (pp.219–238). Hillsdale, NJ: Erlbaum.

Cunningham, B.B. (1985). The will to forgive: A pastoral theological view of forgiving. *The Journal of Pastoral Care, 39*, 141–149.

Downie, R.S. (1965). Forgiveness. *Philosophical Quarterly, 15*, 128–134.

Droll, D.M. (1984/1985). Forgiveness: Theory and research (Doctoral dissertation, University of Nevada–Reno, 1984). *Dissertation Abstracts International –B, 45*, 2732.

Enright, R.D., Eastin, D.L., Golden, S., Sarinopoulos, I., & Freedman, S. (1992). Interpersonal forgiveness within the helping professions: An attempt to resolve differences of opinion. *Counseling and Values, 36*, 84–103.

Enright, R.D., Freedman, S.R., & Rique J. (1998). The psychology of interpersonal forgiveness. In R.D. Enright & J. North (Eds.). *Exploring forgiveness* (pp. 46–64). Madison: University of Wisconsin Press.

Enright, R.D., Gassin, E.A., & Wu, C. (1992). Forgiveness: A developmental view. *Journal of Moral Education, 21*, 99–114.

Enright, R.D. & the Human Development Study Group. (1991a). The moral development of forgiveness. In W. Kurtines & J. Gewirtz (Eds.), *Handbook of moral behavior and development* (Vol. 1, pp. 123–152). Hillsdale, NJ: Erlbaum.

Enright, R.D., & the Human Development Study Group (1991b). Five points on the construct of forgiveness within psychotherapy. *Psychotherapy, 28*, 493–496.

Enright R.D., & the Human Development Study Group (1996). Counseling within the forgiveness triad: On forgiving, receiving forgiveness, and self-forgiveness. *Counseling and Values, 40*, 107–126.

Enright, R.D., Santos, M.J.O., & Al-Mabuk, R. (1989). The adolescent as forgiver. *Journal of Adolescence, 12*, 95–110.

Erikson, E. (1968). *Identity: Youth and crisis*. New York: Norton.

Fitzgibbons, R.P. (1986). The cognitive and emotional uses of forgiveness in the treatment of anger. *Psychotherapy, 23*, 629–633.

Flanigan, B. (1987). Shame and forgiving in alcoholism. *Alcoholism Treatment Quarterly, 4*, 181–195.

Frankl, V.E. (1959). *The will to meaning: Foundations and applications of logotherapy.* NY: World Publishing House.

Freedman, S.R., & Enright, R.D. (1995, August). *Forgiveness as an educational intervention goal with incest survivors.* Paper presented at the annual meeting of the American Psychological Association, New York.

Freedman, S.R., & Enright, R.D. (1996). Forgiveness as an intervention goal with incest survivors. *Journal of Consulting and Clinical Psychology, 64*, 983–992.

Haber, J. (1991). *Forgiveness.* Savage, MD: Rowman & Littlefield.

Hebl, J.H., & Enright, R.D. (1993). Forgiveness as a psychotherapeutic goal with elderly females. *Psychotherapy, 30*, 658–667.

Hepp-Dax, S. (1996). *Forgiveness as an intervention goal with fifth grade inner city children.* Unpublished doctoral dissertation, Fordham University.

Holmgren, M.R. (1993). Forgiveness and the intrinsic value of persons. *American Philosophical Quarterly, 30*, 341–352.

Hope, D. (1987). The healing paradox of forgiveness. *Psychotherapy, 24*, 240–244.

Horsbrugh, H.J. (1974). Forgiveness. *Canadian Journal of Philosophy, 4*, 269–289.

Hughes, M. (1975). Forgiveness. *Analysis, 35*, 113–117.

Hunter, R.C.A. (1978). Forgiveness, retaliation, and paranoid reactions. *Canadian Psychiatric Association Journal, 23*, 167–173.

Kiel, D.V. (1986, February). I'm learning how to forgive. *Decisions*, 12–13.

Kolnai, A. (1973–74). Forgiveness. *Proceedings of the Aristotelian Society, 74*, 91–106.

Lauritzen, P. (1987). Forgiveness: Moral prerogative or religious duty? *Journal of Religious Ethics, 15*, 141–150.

Lewis, M. (1980). On forgiveness. *Philosophical Quarterly, 30*, 236–245.

Linn, D., & Linn, M. (1978). *Healing life's hurts: Healing memories through the five stages of forgiveness.* New York: Paulist Press.

McCullough, M.E., Worthington, E.L., Jr., & Rachal, K.C. (1997). Interpersonal forgiving in close relationships. *Journal of Personality and Social Psychology, 73*, 321–332.

McGary, H. (1989). Forgiveness. *American Philosophical Quarterly, 26*, 343–351.

Neblett, W. R. (1974). Forgiveness and ideals. *Mind, 83*, 269–275.

Nietzsche, F.W. (1887). *The genealogy of morals* (P. Watson, Trans.). London: S.P.C.K.

North, J. (1987). Wrongdoing and forgiveness. *Philosophy, 62*, 499–508.

O'Shaughnessy, R.J. (1967). Forgiveness. *Philosophy, 42*, 336–352.

Pargament, K.I., & Rye, M.S. (1998) Forgiveness as a method of religious coping. In E.L. Worthington, Jr. (Ed.), *Dimensions of forgiveness: Psychological research & theological perspectives* (pp. 59–78). Philadelphia, PA: Templeton Foundation Press.

Patton, J. (1985). *Is human forgiveness possible?* Nashville, TN: Abingdon.

Potvin, L., Lasker, J., & Toedter, L. (1989). Measuring grief: A short version of the perinatal grief scale. *Journal of Psychopathology and Behavioral Assessment, 11,* 29–45.

Richards, N. (1988). Forgiveness. *Ethics, 99,* 77–97.

Smedes, L.B. (1984). *Forgive and forget: Healing the hurts we don't deserve.* New York: Harper & Row.

Smith, M. (1981). The psychology of forgiveness. *The Month, 14,* 301–307.

Spielberger, C.D., Gorsuch, R.L., Lushene, R., Vagg, P., & Jacobs, G.A. (1983). *State-trait anxiety inventory (Form Y): Self-evaluation questionnaire.* Palo Alto, Ca: Consulting Psychologists Press, Inc.

Spielberger, C.D., Jacobs, G., Russell, S., & Craine, R. (1983). Assessment of anger: The state-trait anger scale. In J.N. Butcher & C.D. Spielberger (Eds.), *Advances in personality assessment* (Vol. 2). Hillsdale, NJ: Erlbaum.

Subkoviak, M.J., Enright, R.D., Wu, C., Gassin, E.A., Freedman, S., Olson, L.M., & Sarinopoulos, I.C. (1992, April). *Measuring interpersonal forgiveness.* Paper presented at the annual meeting of the American Educational Research Association, San Francisco.

Subkoviak, M.J., Enright, R.D., Wu, C., Gassin, E.A., Freedman, S., Olson, L.M., & Sarinopoulos, I.C. (1995). Measuring interpersonal forgiveness in late adolescence and middle adulthood. *Journal of Adolescence, 18,* 641–655.

Trainer, M.F. (1981/1984). Forgiveness: Intrinsic, role-expected, expedient, in the context of divorce (Doctoral dissertation, Boston University, 1981). *Dissertation Abstracts International–B, 45,* 1325.

Twambley, P. (1976). Mercy and forgiveness. *Analysis, 36,* 84-90.

Veenstra, G. (1992). Psychological concepts of forgiveness. *Journal of Psychology and Christianity, 11,* 160–169.

Worthington, E.L., & DiBlasio, F.A. (1990). Promoting mutual forgiveness within the fractured relationship. *Psychotherapy, 27,* 219–233.

CHAPTER 7

Science and Forgiveness Interventions: Reflections and Recommendations*

Carl E. Thoresen, Frederic Luskin, and Alex H.S. Harris

THIS CHAPTER OFFERS a scientific perspective on psychosocial interventions designed to foster forgiveness. We will comment on the evidence that people can learn to be more forgiving and that doing so can influence their health and well-being. The manner in which we try to help people learn to forgive and how we assess the impact of forgiveness on health depends, in part, on how we conceptualize forgiveness, which in turn depends on long-standing cultural factors. Therefore, we note briefly some historical and contemporary views on forgiveness. We then focus primarily on the scientific literature concerning interventions designed to foster forgiveness, offering recommendations to strengthen these methods.

As with other concepts, such as health, personality, and spirituality, forgiveness can be best thought of as a latent construct; that is, as a multidimensional, complex structure underlying a broad array of more or less

---

*The authors gratefully acknowledge the work of many colleagues whose studies have contributed to our thinking about this topic, especially Albert Bandura, David Barlow, Eknath Easwaran, Robert Enright (see Chapter 6), Meyer Friedman, Michael McCullough (see Chapter 8), Kenneth Pargament (see Chapter 3), Huston Smith, William Tiller, and Everett Worthington, Jr. (see Chapters 5 and 9). Note that many of the studies cited in this chapter are summarized in McCullough, Exline, and Sommer (Chapter 8).

observable phenomena (Miller & Thoresen, in press). Like an iceberg, only one-eighth of this structure lies above the surface, readily available for inspection. Context and perspective may powerfully influence how the iceberg is or should be viewed. For example, different cultures, marked by various religious traditions, may view forgiveness in very different ways. The number of facets or component dimensions of forgiveness remains an open question, the subject of discussion and debate (McCullough, Sandage, & Worthington, 1997).

In the present context, we look at forgiveness primarily from the perspective of psychosocial intervention, defining it broadly as the process of letting go of negative thoughts, feelings, and reactions toward the offender (and often toward oneself), as well as of seeking to gain a more compassionate understanding of the offender.

LEARNING TO FORGIVE
THROUGH RELIGION AND CULTURE

Learning to forgive someone who has hurt you may be one of life's most demanding, yet most meaningful, tasks. Forgiveness asks you to reappraise the hurt and its source and to go through a shift in how you think and feel about both the offender and yourself. As a goal commonly advocated by all of the world's long-standing religions, forgiveness can be a truly transforming experience that allows us to move beyond our often selfish desires and needs (Smith, 1989). The prayer of Saint Francis of Assisi captures the transforming power of forgiveness and love while noting the underlying anger and hurt:

> Where there is hatred, let me sow love; where there is injury, pardon.... For it is in giving that we receive; it is in pardoning that we are pardoned.... (Easwaran, 1991a, p.29)

In the Hindu tradition, the transforming power of forgiveness is found in writings from more than 2,500 years ago (RigVeda): "Forgive me all the mistakes I have committed ...O Lord of Love" (Easwaran, 1991a, p. 41). The Compassionate Buddha noted in the Dhammapada, an ancient collection of his earliest writings, how hatred and anger could never be ended with hatred and anger, but only with love and compassion: "For hatred can never put an end to hatred. Love alone can. This is an unalterable law" (Easwaran, p. 43).

Forgiveness has played a highly significant role in religion, often allowing people to reduce conflict, anger, fear, and estrangement. Compassion, mercy, humility, and service are mainstream religious concerns, and forgiveness remains central to them all. Many religious and cultural traditions address the value of forgiveness for the individual and the community; yet little specific instruction exists about how to forgive, outside of the admonition to pray or meditate. This may be because of the role played historically by healers, elders, priests, and other religious professionals who provided help in forgiveness; that is, people have commonly sought forgiveness for their offenses or sins from (or through) religious representatives, such as confession to a priest, rather than through their own actions. Note, however, that seeking forgiveness for one's perceived offenses is not the same process as forgiving another person who has offended you.

Some information about the effects of forgiveness is known anecdotally from testimony and tradition (e.g., Jones, 1995; Smedes, 1996 [also see Chapter 10]). Forgiveness has often been taught through prayer, ritual, instruction, meditation, and parable. In many ways, the practice of forgiveness in Western religions, especially Christianity, seems focused more on offenders asking God to forgive their sins or offenses, either directly or through a religious professional such as a priest. Marty suggests that Christianity, when compared with other religions from an historical perspective, can be characterized most distinctively by the term "forgiveness" (see Chapter 1). In Judaism, as Dorff notes, the obligation to forgive has been codified: For example, if steps of atonement are followed and the offended person still refuses to forgive, the offended may then be viewed as an offender (see Chapter 2).

In Samoan culture, forgiveness is called "ifoga" and is ritualized (Filoiali'i & Knowles, 1983). Beginning in the morning, those performing the ifoga cover their heads and bodies with fine mats and sit outside the main village house and remain there until the village council (or the offended family in urban settings) decides when to call the offenders inside so that they can ask for forgiveness. Forgiveness is always grant-ed and the punishment levied less severe than if the ifoga were not per-formed. *The Tibetan Book of Living and Dying* (Sogyal Rinpoche, 1992) offers advice for those seeking to forgive themselves: Remember the good things you have done, forgive everyone else in your life, and ask forgiveness from anyone you may have harmed.

The practice of forgiving those who have hurt or offended us has long been recognized. Jesus forgave many for their offenses, and in so doing he set the example for Christians to follow. As in the Prayer of Saint Francis of Assisi cited earlier, the Lord's Prayer (Matt. 6:9–13) requests forgiveness for those who have trespassed against us. Still, admonition, prayer, and parable may not suffice for most people to understand and use the processes and skills that forgiving others requires.

THE SECULAR EMERGENCE OF FORGIVENESS

More recently, the helping professions have taken an interest in forgive-ness as a healing agent (e.g., Richards & Bergin, 1997; Thoresen, 1998). The popularity of self-help books on managing shame, guilt, grief, depression, and anger suggests that people are seeking ways to forgive themselves and to forgive others (e.g., Bradshaw, 1988; Williams & Williams, 1993). One of the early advocates of forgiveness in the pop-ular press was Jampolsky (1981), who authored the widely read *Love Is Letting Go of Fear*. Forgiveness was presented as a major mechanism to living with more love and understanding. (This work is based on the popular *A Course in Miracles*, a book program originally published in 1975 that also focuses heavily on forgiveness.) Weil's (1997) best-selling *8 Weeks to Optimum Health* features one major spiritual health topic: the value of forgiveness. Significantly, however, Weil offers no instruction on how to forgive, other than developing patience and understanding.

Although large-scale health interventions have not labeled forgiveness as one of their psychosocial strategies, elements of forgiveness have been taught to patients. Strategies include being slower to take offense and letting go of anger and resentment. Intervention studies addressing coronary heart disease (e.g., Friedman et al., 1986; Ornish et al., 1990); breast cancer (e.g., Spiegel, Bloom, Kraemer, & Gottheil, 1989); and alcoholism (e.g., Nowinski, Baker, & Carroll, 1992) have often implicitly embedded forgiveness in their treatment protocols (see Bracke & Thoresen, 1996).

Because these interventions were multidimensional and not explicitly focused on forgiveness, the influence of forgiveness on improved health outcomes—such as reduced mortality and morbidity—remains unknown. Kaplan (1992), however, has argued persuasively that, based on anecdotal evidence, becoming more forgiving enhances processes that protect patients from having a fatal or nonfatal coronary event, citing the Friedman et al. (1986) intervention. His reasoning seems compelling: If chronic anger and hostility are coronary risk factors, and if forgiveness is one way of reducing anger and hostility, then learning to be more forgiving should reduce cardiac risks. Note, however, that the etiology of chronic anger and hostility, while still unclear, may emerge as maladaptive coping strategies in trying to manage basic fears and anxieties, especially core beliefs of unworthiness and personal insecurities (Friedman et al.; Thoresen & Powell, 1992; Williams & Williams, 1993).

Before we consider controlled intervention studies, we acknowledge that the offenses to be forgiven range widely in terms of their frequency, severity, and duration, as well as in the relationship between the person hurt and the offender (e.g., strangers in traffic; parents and children). Given this heterogeneity of possible offenses and of the types of forgiveness (e.g., forgiving another, seeking forgiveness, forgiving oneself), the relatively few controlled interventions conducted to date have not answered the many questions about what interventions work best with whom. We suspect that a few general factors may be involved in all effective forgiveness interventions, such as reducing anger and blame and understanding key beliefs, as well as demographic factors such as gender, age, and ethnicity. With that in mind, we will address some major issues about the design, conduct, and evaluation of intervention studies. We also acknowledge from an epistemological perspective that knowledge comes in many forms, including religious tradition and personal revelation. In addition, we are mindful that science at its best is still a human endeavor, always subject to error.

FORGIVENESS INTERVENTIONS

We located a total of seven intervention studies (Hebl & Enright, 1993; Al-Mabuk, Enright, & Cardis, 1995; McCullough & Worthington, 1995; Freedman & Enright, 1996; McCullough, Worthington, & Rachal, 1997; Luskin & Thoresen, 1997; Coyle & Enright, 1997). One empirically based, but not scientifically controlled, forgiveness intervention was found (Phillips & Osbourne, 1989) using a phenomenological strategy (i.e., qualitative). While not meeting the generally accepted standards of experimental research designs (e.g., Cook & Campbell, 1979), the study provides useful information about the ongoing processes and actual experiences of people trying to forgive (Fow, 1996), something commonly lacking in published studies.

What do these studies tell us about trying to foster forgiveness? Most provide some evidence that people may be able to reduce levels of felt hurt and perceived offense. In these studies, participants ranged from college students to elderly females; problems ranged from being hurt by a close friend or romantic partner to long-term sexual abuse; and interventions ranged from two brief sessions to about 60 individual sessions over 14 months. How the specific techniques were actually used in some of these interventions remains somewhat vague. All studies, however, emphasized personal and interpersonal factors, especially letting go of anger and resentment and developing greater empathic understanding of the offender. Most also focused on forgiving another person (or other persons), not on asking or seeking forgiveness or on forgiving oneself.

Finally, several studies used the Psychological Profile of Forgiveness Scale (see Enright & Coyle, Chapter 6) and/or the Willingness to Forgive Scale (Al-Mabuk, Enright, & Cardis, 1995), and some included measures of anxiety and depression. Only two studies assessed anger (Coyle & Enright, 1997; Luskin & Thoresen, 1997), and none measured hostility, coping styles, or various dispositional personality factors. Sample sizes in most studies were small, seldom more than 25 participants. Only one formally assessed any spiritual or religious beliefs or behaviors (Luskin & Thoresen). While almost all appeared to include the participants' spiritual or religious beliefs, practices, or experiences in their interventions, all could be construed as having provided an "ecumenical spiritual intervention" (Richards & Bergin, 1997), combining in varying degrees psychodynamic, behavioral, cognitive, and humanistic techniques.

Studies to date have worked with volunteers who have typically identified one or more hurtful offenses to work on and believed that they could conceivably forgive the offender. Participants have reported experiencing more forgiveness, less resentment, and, in some studies, improved mental health (e.g., lower self-reported depression or anxiety scores). Hebl and Enright (1993), for example, reported that 13 elderly female participants who received an explicit forgiveness intervention improved in terms of less negative affect and cognitions and more positive affect and behavior, as assessed by changes on the Psychological Profile of Forgiveness Scale. Commendably, evidence of the need to intervene specifically in forgiveness emerged in this study. The 11 control participants, who received a "traditional social support treatment," also improved on measures of anxiety and depression, but did not improve on measures of forgiveness.

Still lacking are data on a number of issues, especially gender, ethnic, and racial factors, as well as a broad range of interpersonal and intrapersonal problems deemed offensive. Evidence of the longer-term benefits of interventions is also modest, is often not available, or spans only a few weeks. Intervention studies in which data are gathered repeatedly over time (e.g., 1 month, 6 months, 12 months, and 24 months posttreatment) are needed to document the *pattern* of change over time. Such evidence could help reveal which types of offenses and what personal characteristics (e.g., gender, age, coping style) are associated with different types of interventions. Two studies to date (Freedman & Enright, 1996; Coyle & Enright, 1997) have, however, provided longer-term follow-up spanning several months.

Also missing are cost-benefit comparisons of forgiving another person (or other persons). Little information is available on how forgiveness has been influenced by other psychosocial (e.g., coping style, introversion), intellectual (e.g., cognitive complexity, literacy), and physiological (e.g., reactivity to stress, cortisone levels) factors over time. In addition, no controlled interventions were found that focused primarily on asking for and receiving forgiveness or on self-forgiveness.

Finally, the need to replicate studies, particularly by investigators other than those reporting findings, is vital. Such evidence, considered by many as the hallmark of scientific inquiry, will help clarify and correct inadvertent biases and errors that may exist in current findings.

Reflections on Intervention Models

Enright and his colleagues have provided the bulk of controlled intervention studies to date ($n = 4$). Their work at present serves as the only established research program focused on forgiveness. Such programmatic efforts have allowed them to benefit from several years of experience in creating a process model of forgiveness to guide their interventions. For example, Enright and Coyle's 20-step process model reflects four major phases of forgiveness—Uncovering, Decision, Work, and Deepening—and offers a comprehensive perspective focused on several variables (see Chapter 6). These include confrontation of anger and its release, awareness of cognitively rehearsing the past offense (replaying it again and again), insight about belief related to a "just world," and making the commitment to forgive the offender, as well as empathy, compassion, and understanding of the offender as a person. At issue, of course, is whether this forgiveness model (or *any* current model) provides the kind of framework to guide interventions in terms of overall costs and effects over time.

Worthington sees forgiveness primarily as a motivational experience based on developing empathy for the offender, with fear as a major underlying factor. He describes a five-step model represented by the acrostic REACH: Recall the hurt, Empathize with the one who hurt you, (offer the) Altruistic gift of forgiveness, (make a) Commitment to forgive, and Hold onto the forgiveness (see Chapter 5). Two studies based on this model have reported encouraging results (McCullough & Worthington, 1995; McCullough, Worthington, & Rachal, 1997).

Martin and Thoresen (1997) have proposed a six-step forgiveness model based on a cognitive-behavioral perspective highlighting beliefs, behaviors, emotions, and social contexts. Major steps include

1. exposure to the situation—this may involve "reexperiencing" the trauma along with a specific description of the situation;

2. acknowledging one's negative reactions and effects—for example, admitting bitterness, blame, anger, resentment, and so forth and recognizing the effects of these negative reactions;

3. the act of forgiveness—that is, making a conscious decision to forgive before experiencing the emotional desire to do so;

4. healing the hurt—a process that starts with the act of forgiveness, increases as negative emotions and actions decrease, and continues until the situation no longer elicits negative reactions;

5. approaching the offender—that is, considering the possibility of gaining closure through contact with the person and acting with love (reconciliation is not required, but is considered a possibility); and

6. reducing future hurt reactions—that is, learning to see and react to others with more empathy, compassion, and love when they act in potentially hurtful ways, thus raising one's hurt threshold.

Note that the last two steps (approaching the offender, reducing future hurt reactions) may not technically be considered part of forgiveness, but are its possible consequences or correlates.

All of these models overlap to some extent, and all appear to emphasize helping others to let go of hurt; reduce negative thoughts, feelings, and actions related to the offender; and experience more compassion and empathic understanding of the offender and his or her life situation. None of these models require the parties to reconcile or demand that the offender apologize or make restitution.

Consider the forgiveness intervention by Freedman and Enright (1996), which offered an average of 60 hourly sessions over 14 months for female incest survivors. This study demonstrated significant improvements in reducing hurt and offense and increased forgiveness of the offender. What is unknown, however, is whether all persons suffering from a history of chronic abuse, such as parental incest, are best served by 60 hours of individual therapy.

Conceivably, some incest survivors could benefit as much, or perhaps more, from a short-term small-group intervention, similar to the protocol used by Spiegel and his colleagues with breast cancer patients to deal with several personal issues, including forgiveness (Spiegel et al., 1989). Some may benefit from a short-term mix of individual and group treatments similar to the one being used with post-myocardial infarction women and men also suffering from depression and low social support (Thoresen, 1997).

Note also the brief, highly structured small-group intervention for young adults in Luskin and Thoresen's (1997) study. Do all young adults seeking help in forgiving someone who has recently hurt or offended them need six sessions of a self-management-focused cognitive-behavioral therapy? Some, in fact, may have benefited just as much from a protocol that featured only self-help materials (e.g., workbook, videotape, Internet "chat room"), while others may have needed a longer-term intervention. This and the Freedman and Enright (1996) study, using different conceptual perspectives and different treatment procedures, demonstrated significant results with very different populations. What we do not yet know, but need to examine, is: Who needs how much of what kinds of forgiveness interventions?

Could existing intervention models in the psychological (and especially psychotherapeutic) literature, such as cognitive therapy (Beck, 1995), existential psychotherapy (Yalom, 1980), and social cognitive theory (Bandura, 1995, 1998), provide useful frameworks for designing forgiveness interventions? We will comment on this question shortly.

Keep in mind that any of the forgiveness models may prove to be especially useful with *some* hurtful interpersonal situations, but not all. Kiesler (1966) and others (e.g., Goldfried & Wolfe, 1996) have warned repeatedly about the "uniformity myths" that have plagued clinical interventions. These myths concern clients, problems, treatments, and contexts. Too often, it is assumed—erroneously—that all persons with a particular problem (e.g., depression) need the same treatment delivered in the same fashion. Thus, women may receive a treatment based solely on studies of men; people of color may be given treatments based only on white, middle-class males; and children evidencing attention problems may all be prescribed the same type of medication.

Black and Coster (1996) have argued for a Stepped Approach Model (SAM) as one way to avoid these uniformity myths. They argue that various types of interventions can be offered: from short, inexpensive treatments with high reach or wide availability (e.g., reading materials, self-help manuals) to more expensive, intensive programs with more limited reach or availability (e.g., face-to-face group, individual therapy). Brownell and Wadden (1992) have illustrated the value of a stepped-care model in treating obesity-related problems, while Thoresen and Hoffman-Goldberg (1998) have discussed the value of this approach with cardiovascular health-related problems, such as smoking, depression, and hostility. It seems highly probable that those seeking help in dealing with resentments, grudges, hurts, and abuses of varying severity may need different mixes and amounts of forgiveness training, even for all those suffering from a particular kind of hurt or abuse.

Forgiveness Training for Young Adults

As descriptions of published intervention studies are available elsewhere in this volume (see McCullough et al., Chapter 8), we describe a recently completed unpublished study here, in part to illustrate the possible value of a cognitive-behavioral model.

Luskin and Thoresen (1997) explored the following question: Could a brief psychoeducational program teach forgiveness skills to reasonably healthy young adults who had recently been hurt by another person with whom they were currently in contact? Interpersonal injuries involving physical and sexual abuse were excluded. Participants ($n = 55$) also had to affirm that they could at least imagine being able to forgive the offender. Ages ranged from 18 to 30 years (mean = 22 years); females composed 77% of the sample.

A total of 28 participants were randomized to the treatment group and 27 to the assessment control condition. Each completed assessments at baseline, posttreatment, and 10-week follow-up. These included the State-Trait Anger Expression Inventory (Spielberger, 1994); Willingness to Forgive Scale; Degree of Hurt (1-ITEM, 10-point scale re offender); Interpersonal Distance Scale; Focus on the Future Scale; Principles of Living Scale (selected spiritual and religious behaviors and beliefs); Interpersonal Hurt Vignette, a generalization measure designed for this study to be assessed at follow-up only; and several self-efficacy scales focused on the forgiveness process (Luskin & Thoresen, 1997).

The intervention consisted of six highly structured 1-hour sessions. Three themes guided the intervention: taking less offense, reducing the blaming of others, and gaining more empathy and understanding of offenders. Participants received workbooks describing each session with worksheets for practicing techniques and for homework assignments. They were also asked to keep personal journals to track their experiences over the 16 weeks of the study. Major emphasis was placed on changing cognitive and affective processes using cognitive therapy based on Rational Emotive Therapy (Ellis & Dryden, 1997) to alter unreasonable beliefs and behaviors. Heart Math techniques (e.g., McCraty, Atkinson, Tiller, Rein, & Watkins, 1995), particularly the "freeze-frame" procedure, were used to promote positive emotions, such as feeling appreciation, love, and gratitude for others. Participants were taught the use of these techniques immediately when they felt negative emotions, such as anger or sadness, in order to transform or shift their perceptions of the hurt and of the offender. Each group session included practicing shifting perceptions of specific situations that could be hurtful.

Results were encouraging. In almost all cases, estimated effect sizes (ES), assessed as the reduction from baseline level for the experimental group minus reduction in the control group over pooled standard deviations of both groups (Kraemer, personal communication, May 14, 1997), were noteworthy, typically in the 0.30 to 1.0 range. For example, self-efficacy (a perceived level of confidence to act successfully) improved in four contexts: (1) toward the offender identified at baseline, (2) toward offending people in general, (3) in situations similar to the initial hurt, and (4) being able to increase the threshold level of experiencing hurt or offense in general. Those treated showed a 36% increase (ES = 1.0) that was maintained at 10-week follow-up (ES = 0.90). By contrast, wait-listed control participants showed a 2% improvement from baseline to posttreatment and follow-up. From a clinical perspective, this magnitude of change can be seen as noteworthy (Bandura, 1995).

Trait Anger showed a 13% reduction (ES = 0.70), which was maintained at follow-up. Control participants showed no change. On the Willingness to Forgive Scale, those receiving forgiveness training were found to prefer the forgiveness option (out of 10 possible options) more frequently in various situations (ES = 0.9), at posttest (6.8 versus 3.7), and at follow-up (ES = 0.5). But when asked whether they would actually choose the forgiveness option in those same situations, the differences between groups, while still significant, were lower.

To assess generalization at follow-up, participants were asked to describe in writing how they would handle a hypothetical offense involving the sexual infidelity of a partner, a topic not discussed or assessed in the treatments. Written descriptions were assessed by two independent raters masked to each person's treatment status on the following: degree of offense taken, level of blame, use of self-management skills, evidence of planning to use cognitive coping skills, and degree of forgiveness (preferred and actual) of the hypothetical offender. Interrater reliability of ratings (%) ranged from 76 to 86. Participants also completed self-efficacy scales on their confidence in successfully using forgiveness-related, self-management skills in that situation and actually being able to forgive the person. On almost all of these generalization measures, those treated scored significantly higher than the control subjects. For example, on perceived self-efficacy to forgive in the hypothetical situation (100-point scale), the average level was 64.1 for those treated, significantly higher than the 47.8 level for control participants.

The study has its shortcomings, similar to those shared by almost all studies to date. These include almost sole reliance on self-report measures, as well as the lack of process data gathered during and after the intervention on just how participants were experiencing forgiveness-related events. Furthermore, little individualization of the intervention occurred. In addition, this study did not involve participants' spiritual or religious beliefs or practices as part of the intervention in any planned or systematic manner. (It did, however, assess changes in selected spiritual and religious factors.)

Given that forgiveness ranks high as an important religious and spiritual issue, especially as a way of coping with life's major problems (e.g., Pargament, 1997), and that some data support the effectiveness of interventions that include a religious or spiritual facet (Worthington, Kurusu, McCullough, & Sandage, 1996), this omission deserves careful consideration in future studies.

What this study and others suggest is the lack among people in general of any kind of systematic preparation in the basics of forgiveness as a way to cope with interpersonal problems. Most participants may have known about forgiveness, but did not seem to understand that several processes were involved, including some basic life issues (e.g., managing anger, using empathy to reframe the hurt and the offender, forgiving even when the offender was not contrite or even aware of the offense). Clearly, a role exists for primary prevention studies that assess the effects of teaching forgiveness processes, optimally starting with children. Conceivably, educating the young in how to forgive could foster the kind of spiritual health and social competence that is instrumental in an enhanced quality of life (Damon, 1995). The obvious link between social violence, physical aggression, and conflict resolution on the one hand, and competence in forgiveness on the other hand, also deserves consideration.

IMPROVING INTERVENTION RESEARCH

Keeping in mind the relatively few intervention studies conducted to date, what steps might improve the overall quality of future studies? The work of the Enright and the Human Development Study Group (see Chapter 6) reminds us of the need to think deeply and act carefully in helping people forgive. The basic beliefs and core values involved, along with the genuine grief and suffering people experience, require us to avoid trivializing hurtful experiences with superficial, quick-fix interventions (see Enright & Coyle, Chapter 6). McCullough, Sandage, and Worthington (1997) and Worthington (see Chapter 5) have offered several issues and concerns to consider, such as the centrality of empathy, the dangers of isolated interventions that fail to recognize the role of personal and social contexts, and the theoretical work and research findings from a variety of psychosocial intervention studies, including different research methodologies.

Lessons from Psychotherapy Research

We can greatly benefit by heeding the experience of psychotherapy research with interventions over the past three decades (e.g., Goldfried & Wolfe, 1996; Vanden Bos, 1996). Several major points relevant to forgiveness interventions emerge from the theoretical and research experience in psychotherapy outcome research. Some points follow.

1. cognitive-behavioral and interpersonal therapy approaches appear to be more effective with a range of depression, anxiety, anger, and marital problems (e.g., Barlow & Lehman, 1996; Chambless et al., 1996; Frank & Spanier, 1995), but not with all problems (Goldfried & Wolfe, 1996), compared with other approaches. Note, however, that Wampold et al. (1997) have argued that all well-established psychotherapies may be equally effective. We believe, however, that the evidence supporting the effectiveness of cognitive-behavioral and interpersonal interventions for reducing anxiety, depression, and anger/hostility is highly relevant to consider, given these issues in promoting forgiveness and its consequences.

2. Clinical trial methodology, when used exclusively, is not well suited to create effective interventions for the diversity of people suffering from a particular problem, such as needing to forgive (e.g., Persons, 1991; Goldfried & Wolfe, 1996). The major issue remains one of clinical validity or effectiveness (compared with efficacy) and the need to balance the internal validity of clinical trials with studies that satisfy external or clinical validity (generalizability) involving a variety of differing factors (e.g., gender, age, ethnicity, spiritual orientation).

3. Process-oriented studies (often termed "phenomenological" or "qualitative" studies) using more intensive methods, such as in-depth interviews, narratives or stories, journalizing, and self-observation ratings, have been sadly lacking. This deficiency has deprived researchers of data about people's ongoing experiences (e.g., feelings, beliefs, expectations, attributions). Such data are needed to develop interventions that can be more tailored to fit particular individuals, such as variations of a treatment focused on forgiving intimate partners (see Folkman, 1997; Folkman & Stein, 1997; Fow, 1996; Phillips & Osbourne, 1989). Goldfried and Wolfe (1996) commented that when psychotherapy research abandoned a mix of process and smaller n group study designs a decade ago in favor of only large-scale clinical trials, invaluable data (e.g., behaviors, "meaning" experiences, changing

attitudes) were lost that could clarify changes and provide evidence of the ecological validity of treatments and their clinical utility. Treatment or intervention manuals used in clinical trials are no substitute for careful documentation of the treatment process, especially as experienced by those being treated. The process study of those going through the forgiveness experience, as reported by Phillips and Osbourne, illustrates the value of process-related research. The current trend in psychotherapy research to reintroduce process studies has been noted (Goldfried & Wolfe). McAdams (1993) also offers an intriguing approach that documents stories about major events and key episodes that often shape basic beliefs and perceptual experience.

4. The need for a variety of research designs used in combination has been recognized to provide ecological and external validity, as well as improved internal validity (Barlow, 1996; Goldfried & Wolfe, 1996). A strong case exists in particular for combining the use of experimental group designs with the process-focused designs cited above. In this way, the ongoing experiences of subsamples of those in different experimental group conditions can be assessed in greater depth (e.g., series of interviews, self-monitoring, brief repeated questionnaires) than is possible with only pre- and posttest questionnaires. In addition, rigorous single-case experimental designs (intraindividual, own-control designs) have been advocated because they can offer valuable insights that bear on several issues of theory, assessment, change processes, and outcomes assessed over time (Hilliard, 1993).

We acknowledge that intervention studies must use well-established experimental design and analysis procedures. Publication of forgiveness interventions in major journals, for example, mandates that studies offer evidence of internal and external validity, reliability and validity of measures, and sufficient statistical power. Koenig and Futterman (1995) provided an excellent illustration of basic research design features in evaluating studies on religiousness and the physical health in the elderly. Information on basic experimental designs is readily available. See for example Campbell and Stanley (1963), Cook and Campbell (1979), and especially Cook (1985) on postpositivist criticial theory and assessment.

Table 1, adapted from Barlow (1996), offers a useful framework for developing intervention guidelines in forgiveness research. Note the attempt to blend issues of rigorous research designs with clinical utility (i.e., external validity), which is divided into issues of feasibility, generalizability, and the costs/benefits of interventions.

Table 1. Guidelines for Developing More Effective Psychological Interventions	
INTERNAL VALIDITY OR EFFICACY (RANK-ORDERED)	EXTERNAL VALIDITY, EFFECTIVENESS, OR CLINICAL UTILITY

1. Better than alternative control treatment (randomized controlled trials [RCTs])
 	
2. Better than nonspecific therapy (RCTs)
 	
3. Better than no therapy (RCTs)
 	
4. Quantified clinical observations
 	
5. Strongly positive clinical consensus
 	
6. Mixed clinical consensus
 	
7. Strongly negative clinical consensus
 	
8. Contradictory evidence
	1. Feasibility
	
	✦ Patient acceptability (cost, pain, duration, side effects, etc.)
	
	✦ Patient choice in face of relatively equal efficacy
	
	✦ Probability of compliance
	
	✦ Ease of disseminability— e.g., number of practitioners with competence, requirements for costly technologies or additional support personnel, etc.
	
	2. Generalizability
	
	✦ Patient characteristics
	
	  ✦ Cultural background issues
	
	  ✦ Gender issues
	
	  ✦ Developmental issues
	
	  ✦ Other relevant patient characteristics

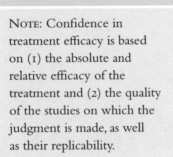

+ Therapist characteristics

+ Issues of robustness when applied in practice settings with different time frames, etc.

+ Contextual factors regarding setting in which treatment is delivered

3. Costs and Benefits

+ Costs of delivering intervention to individual and society

+ Costs of withholding intervention to individual and society

NOTE: Confidence in treatment efficacy is based on (1) the absolute and relative efficacy of the treatment and (2) the quality of the studies on which the judgment is made, as well as their replicability.

NOTE: Confidence reflected in these three dimensions should be based on systematic and objective methods and strategies for assessing these characteristics of treatment as they are applied in actual practice. In some cases, RCTs exist. More often, data are in the form of quantified clinical observations (clinical replication series) or other strategies, such as health economic calculations.

Adapted with permission from Barlow (1996). Originally from "Template for Developing Guidelines: Interventions for Mental Disorders and Psychosocial Aspects of Physical Disorders," by American Psychological Association Board of Professional Affairs Task Force on Psychological Intervention Guidelines, 1995. Approved by the APA Council of Representatives, February 1995, Washington, D.C. © 1995 by the American Psychological Association.

SOME RECOMMENDATIONS

We now turn to what we see as priority issues and recommendations, elaborating in some cases on topics already briefly mentioned. They include (1) reducing the abuse and misuse of statistical null hypothesis testing, (2) the value of the cognitive therapy model for interventions, (3) the need to focus on anger and hostility in small groups, (4) the practical value of self-efficacy theory and assessment, (5) the need to assess spiritual and religious factors in forgiveness intervention, and (6) the possible value of a forgiveness intervention within broader treatment programs designed to improve overall quality of life and reduce disease.

Abusing and Misusing Null Hypothesis Testing

The serious limitations of relying primarily on "not accepting the H0" has long been recognized, but seldom rectified (Cohen, 1990). Little can be learned if researchers report only whether differences or changes are probably not due to random fluctuations. Recently, Cohen (1994) again reminded researchers of the serious misinterpretations of null hypothesis testing: "...near universal misinterpretations of p [values] as the probability that H0 is false, the misinterpretation that its complement is the probability of a successful replication, and the mistaken assumption that if one rejects H0, one thereby affirms the theory that led to the test" (p. 997). While the value of H0 testing still has its defenders (e.g., Hagen, 1997), much more can be gained by estimating effect sizes with confidence intervals, exploratory data analysis (e.g., using visual graphing), studying patterns of change over time, judging successful interventions with clinically justified levels or bands of change, and emphasizing power analysis. Clarifying just how big a change needs to be (not whether results differ from chance) will move forgiveness interventions research well beyond $p < .05$ (Jacobson & Truax, 1991). Optimally, we need to begin considering what may constitute at least an adequate understanding of the forgiveness process and what are sufficient skills in being able to use the forgiveness process when hurt or offended. Having a clearer idea of this could allow researchers to have a set of criteria in mind (i.e., a norm) when assessing forgiveness, especially as a coping skill.

The Value of a Cognitive Therapy Model

As one of the most evidence-based clinical interventions, we believe that cognitive therapy (CT) offers one approach deserving consideration (e.g., Beck, 1995). As already noted, its success with issues of depression, anxiety, and anger (Chambless et al., 1996) has been impressive. Variations of the model have also proven successful with other problems, such as character disorders (e.g., Linehan, Armstrong, Suarez, Allmon, & Heard, 1991). For example, CT currently serves as the basic treatment strategy, coupled with social and perceived emotional support training, of a large-scale clinical trial ($n = 3,000$) of post-myocardial infarction patients suffering from perceived low social support, depression, and related problems, such as anxiety, anger, and the inability to express positive emotions (Thoresen, 1997). What seems most promising about the CT model for forgiveness is its focus on helping people learn how to become aware of their cognitions (e.g., "automatic thoughts") that can promote negative reactions (e.g., angry feelings about an offender) and their consequences (e.g., fearful behaviors and feelings), as well as how to alter these automatic thoughts and revise beliefs, and therefore consequences.

Anger/Hostility and Small Groups

The centrality of anger and, to a lesser degree, hostile cognitions in helping people forgive has long been recognized (e.g., Fitzgibbons, 1986; Kaplan, 1992); yet, with few exceptions, intervention studies have not included any assessment and evaluation of anger and hostility. Much has been learned about ways to reduce chronic and excessive episodes of anger and about altering hostile schema and ideation in the past two decades (e.g., Thoresen & Powell, 1992; Williams & Williams, 1993). Chronic hostility has been shown to be a significant risk factor for all-cause mortality (e.g., Miller, Smith, Turner, Guijarro, & Halett, 1996). Small-group-based interventions using variations of cognitive-behavioral and interpersonal treatments (e.g., Bracke & Thoresen, 1996) have proven effective in helping post-coronary patients reduce mortality and morbidity (e.g., Blumenthal, et al., 1997; Friedman, et al., 1986). Given the intimate relationship between anger and hostility and forgiveness, as well as with empathic understanding, interventions, at a minimum, need to assess changes in anger and hostility and, optimally, reduce the chronicity of these emotions as a way of coping with hurt and offense.

Self-Efficacy Theory and Assessment

Truly impressive is the body of evidence that a person's confidence level to perform a particular activity (self-efficacy) powerfully influences the actual performance of that activity. Bandura (1995, 1998) has reviewed this evidence for self-efficacy effects across a broad spectrum of social, physical, and psychological problems and issues. A self-efficacy level often predicts future success in being able to do something more than a person's own past performance of that activity. Forgiveness interventions can use self-efficacy ratings not only as a baseline screening measure (e.g., if too low, the person may need a different intervention) and as a predictor of treatment outcomes, but also, importantly, as an ongoing process measure to gauge progress in treatment concerning a variety of tasks and goals (Luskin & Thoresen, 1997). Social systems can also influence a person's self-efficacy to forgive. Community institutions, such as schools, civic and business organizations, and adult education programs, can alter policies and practices to promote greater "collective efficacy" in people's beliefs about using forgiveness as a viable way of dealing with a variety of offenses (Bandura, 1995). Given the scientific evidence about the effects of self-efficacy, its inclusion in forgiveness interventions seems highly justified.

Spiritual and Religious Factors

The origins of forgiveness and its allied qualities and characteristics, such as humility, love, compassion, and service to others, seem to have emerged early in almost all major religions (Smith, 1989). Pargament speaks to the role of forgiveness in religion (see Chapter 3). Do those who are more spiritually focused or religiously active engage in more forgiveness? Some survey data suggest that they do (Richards & Bergin, 1997). Yet interventions on forgiveness have not, in general, assessed spiritual and religious factors and related them to outcomes. Forgiveness interventions need to measure selected spiritual and religious factors at baseline and, if possible, on a repeated-measures basis (e.g., pre- and posttest and at follow-up). As noted earlier, more religiously or spiritually minded people may profit more from a forgiveness intervention adapted to include religious beliefs and practices (Worthington et al., 1996). Christians, for example, may benefit from having forgiveness framed in part as following the practices of Jesus. The prayer of Saint Francis could be used as a daily meditation or prayer to foster forgiveness (Easwaran, 1991b). Indeed, we suspect an ecumenical blend of spiritual concepts and stories focused on forgiveness from across the world's major religions might be well received by many people. If a person is not actively religious or spiritually focused, then forgiveness could be couched in a more "philosophy of life" perspective, related to historical wisdom across world cultures (Smith, 1989; Thoresen, 1998).

The Value of Broader Treatment Programs

Worth exploring is the possible value of a forgiveness intervention within broader treatment programs designed to improve overall quality of life, such as Weil's (1997) optimum health program, with a focus on ways to slow down, feel less distracted and more focused, put others first more often, increase dispositional levels, and experience more joy and enthusiasm in daily living. (Also see Easwaran's [1991b] eight-point program for spiritual growth.) The question is: Would forgiveness interventions prove more successful in terms of producing lasting change for some people if offered within a larger context, such as a "healthy living" program or a spiritually based lifestyle program, as compared with an intervention focused only on forgiveness? While a more comprehensive program would be more costly, such a program could prove to be more cost effective in terms of having greater long-term effects on health-related outcomes.

CLOSING WORDS

A small but impressive beginning has been made in intervention studies that meet fairly rigorous scientific standards. Results to date have been encouraging and provide what we believe is justification for programmatic research in this area. We have come to appreciate the pervasive neglect of and poverty of knowledge about forgiveness in our social and cultural institutions. Why are children and youth almost never provided the basics of forgiveness as a coping skill? Why is it absent even in most moral or character education programs, which are in themselves rare? We know from clinical experience, anecdotal data, and controlled studies that many people harbor a great deal of hostility and resentment, and as a result are living more diminished and unhealthy lives. We also know that many do not know, or understand, how to forgive—or realize how doing so can benefit themselves and others, especially in the long term. Many feel that much seems missing in their lives, including how to mend estranged relationships and how to release long-held fears and resentments.

We hope that efforts in developing more effective forgiveness-related interventions will provide the kind of persuasive evidence that could convince policy makers to increase the availability of forgiveness training in different social institutions, such as schools, colleges, youth agencies, and senior centers. Many can greatly benefit by living with more forgiveness, and thus with more love, in their lives.

REFERENCES

Al-Mabuk, R.H., Enright, R.D., & Cardis, P.A. (1995). Forgiveness education and parentally love-deprived college students. *Journal of Moral Education, 24,* 427–444.

Bandura, A. (1995). *Self-efficacy in changing societies.* New York: Cambridge University Press.

Bandura, A. (1998). Health promotion from the perspective of social cognitive theory. *Psychology and Health, 14,* 1–27.

Barlow, D. (1996). Health care policy, psychotherapy research, and the future of psychotherapy. *American Psychologist, 51,* 1050–1058.

Barlow, D.H., & Lehman, C. (1996). Advances in the psychosocial treatment of anxiety disorders: Implications for natural health care. *Archives of General Psychiatry, 53,* 727–735.

Beck, J.S. (1995). *Cognitive therapy: Basics and beyond*. New York: Guilford Press.

Black, D.R., & Coster, D.C. (1996). Interest in a Stepped Approach Model (SAM): Identification recruitment strategy for university alcohol programs. *Health Education Quarterly, 24*, 348–356.

Blumenthal, J., Jiang, W., Babyak, M.A., Krantz, D.S., Frid, D.J., Cokman, R.E., Waugh, R., Hanson, M., Appelbaum, M., & O'Conner, C. (1997). Stress management and exercise training in cardiac patients with myocardial ischemia. *Archives of Internal Medicine, 157*, 2213–2223.

Bracke, P., & Thoresen, C.E. (1996). Reducing Type A behavior patterns: A structured group approach. In R. Allan & S. Scheidt (Eds.), *Heart and mind* (pp. 255–290). Washington, D.C.: American Psychological Association.

Bradshaw, J. (1988). *Healing the shame that binds you*. Deerfield Beach, FL: Health Communications.

Brownell, K.D., & Wadden, T.A. (1992). Etiology and treatment of obesity. *Journal of Consulting and Clinical Psychology, 60*, 505–517.

Campbell, D., & Stanley, J. (1963). *Experimental and quasi-experimental designs for research*. Chicago: Rand McNally.

Chambless, D.L., Sanderson, W.C., Shovam, V., Johnson, S.B., Pope, K.S., Crits-Chrestoph, P., Baker, M., Johnson, B., Woody, S.R., Sue, S., Beutler, L., Williams, D.A., & McCurry, S. (1996). An update on empirically validated therapies. *The Clinical Psychologist, 49*, 5–18.

Cohen, J. (1990). Things I have learned (so far). *American Psychologist, 45*, 1304–1312.

Cohen, J. (1994). The earth is round ($p <.05$). *American Psychologist, 49*, 997–1003.

Cook, T.D. (1985). Postpositivist critical multiplism. In R.L. Shotland & M.M. Mark (Eds). *Social science and policy* (pp. 21–62). Beverly Hills, CA: Sage.

Cook, T., & Campbell, D. (1979). *Quasi-experimentation*. Chicago: Rand McNally.

A course in miracles (1975). Mill Valley, CA: Foundation for Inner Peace.

Coyle, C.T., & Enright, R.D. (1997). Forgiveness intervention with post-abortion men. *Journal of Consulting and Clinical Psychology, 65*, 1042–1046.

Damon, W. (1995). *Greater expectations*. New York: Free Press.

Dorff, E.N. (1998). The elements of forgiveness: A Jewish approach. In E.L. Worthington, Jr. (Ed.), *Dimensions of forgiveness: Psychological research & theological perspectives* (pp. 29–55). Philadelphia, PA: Templeton Foundation Press

Easwaran, E. (1991a). *God makes the rivers to flow*. Tomales, CA: Nilgiri Press.

Easwaran, E. (1991b). *Meditation.* Tomales, CA: Nilgiri Press.

Ellis, A., & Dryden, W. (1997). *The practice of rational-emotive therapy* (2nd ed.). New York: Springer.

Enright, R.D., & Coyle, C.T. (1998). Researching the process model of forgiveness within psychological interventions. In E.L. Worthington, Jr. (Ed.), *Dimensions of forgiveness: Psychological research & theological perspectives* (pp. 139–161). Philadelphia, PA: Templeton Foundation Press.

Filoiali'i, L.A., & Knowles, L. (1983). Ifoga: The Samoan practice of seeking forgiveness for criminal behavior. *Oceania, 53,* 384–388.

Fitzsgibbons, R.P. (1986). The cognitive and emotive uses of forgiveness in the treatment of anger. *Psychotherapy, 23,* 629–633.

Folkman, S. (1997). Positive psychological states and coping with severe stress. *Social Science and Medicine, 45,* 1207–1221.

Folkman, S., & Stein, N.L. (1997). A goal-process approach to analyzing narrative memories for AIDS related stressful events. In N.L. Stein, P.A. Ornstein, B. Tversky, & C. Brainerd (Eds.), *Memory for everyday and emotional events* (pp. 113–137). Mahway, NJ: Erlbaum.

Fow, N.R. (1996). The phenomenology of forgiveness and reconciliation. *Journal of Phenomenological Psychology, 27,* 219–233.

Frank, E., & Spanier, C. (1995). Interpersonal psychotherapy for depression: Overview, clinical efficacy, and future directions. *Clinical Psychology: Science and Practice, 2,* 349–369.

Freedman, S.R., & Enright, R.D. (1996). Forgiveness as an intervention goal with incest survivors. *Journal of Consulting and Clinical Psychology, 64,* 983–992.

Friedman, M., Thoresen, C.E., Gill, J., Ulmer, D., Powell, L.H., Price, V.A., Brown, B., Thompson, L., Rabin, D., Breall, W.S., Bourg, W., Levy, R., & Dixon, T. (1986). Alteration of Type A behavior and its effect on cardiac recurrences on post-myocardial infarction patients: Summary results of the Recurrent Coronary Prevention Project. *American Heart Journal, 112,* 653–665.

Goldfried, M.R., & Wolfe, B.E. (1996). Psychotherapy practice and research: Repairing a strained alliance. *American Psychologist, 51,* 1007–1016.

Hagen, R.L. (1997). In praise of the null hypothesis statistical test. *American Psychologist, 52,* 15–24.

Hebl, J., & Enright, R.D. (1993). Forgiveness as a psychotherapeutic goal with elderly females. *Psychotherapy, 30,* 658–667.

Hilliard, R.B. (1993). Single-case methodology in psychotherapy process and outcome research. *Journal of Consulting and Clinical Psychology, 61,* 373–380.

Jacobson, N.S., & Truax, P. (1991). Clinical significance: A statistical approach to defining meaningful change in psychotherapy research. *Journal of Consulting and Clinical Psychology, 59*, 12–19.

Jampolsky, G.G. (1981). *Love is letting go of fear.* New York: Bantam.

Jones, L.G. (1995). *Embodying forgiveness.* Grand Rapids, MI: William Eerdmans.

Kaplan, B.H. (1992). Social health and the forgiving heart: The Type B story. *Journal of Behavioral Medicine, 15*, 3–14.

Kiesler, D. (1966). Some myths of psychotherapy research and the search for a paradigm. *Psychological Bulletin, 65*, 110–30.

Koenig, H.G., & Futterman, A. (1995, March 15). *Religion and health outcomes: A review and synthesis of the literature.* Presented at the National Institute of Aging Conference on Spiritual and Religious Factors in Health, Durham, NC.

Lasch, C. (1978). *The culture of narcissism.* New York: Norton.

Linehan, M.A., Armstrong, H.E., Suarez, A., Allmon, D., & Heard, H.C. (1991). Cognitive-behavioral treatment of chronically parasuicidal borderline patients. *Archives of General Psychiatry, 48*, 1060–1064.

Luskin, F., & Thoresen, C.E. (1997). *The effects of forgiveness training on psychosocial factors in college age adults.* Unpublished manuscript, Stanford University.

Martin, J., & Thoresen, C.E. (1997). *A cognitive-behavioral intervention model of forgiveness.* Unpublished manuscript, Stanford University.

Marty, M.E. (1998). The ethos of Christian forgiveness. In E.L. Worthington, Jr. (Ed.), *Dimensions of forgiveness: Psychological research & theological perspectives* (pp. 9–28). Philadelphia, PA: Templeton Foundation Press.

McAdams, D.P. (1993). *The stories we live by.* NY: Guilford.

McCraty, R., Atkinson, M., Tiller, W.A., Rein, G., & Watkins, A. (1995). The effects of emotions on short term heart rate vulnerability using power spectrum analysis. *American Journal of Cardiology, 76*, 1089–1093.

McCullough, M.E., Exline, J.J., & Baumeister, R.F. (1998). An annotated bibliography of research on forgiveness and related concepts. In E.L. Worthington, Jr. (Ed.), *Dimensions of forgiveness: Psychological research & theological perspectives* (pp. 193–317). Philadelphia, PA: Templeton Foundation Press.

McCullough, M.E., Sandage, S.J., & Worthington, E.L. (1997). *To forgive is human.* Downers Grove, IL: Inter-Varsity Press.

McCullough, M.E., & Worthington, E.L. (1995). Promoting forgiveness: The comparison of two brief psychoeducational interventions with a waiting-list control. *Counseling and Values, 40*, 55–68.

McCullough, M.E., Worthington, E.L., & Rachal, K.C. (1997). Interpersonal forgiving in close relationships. *Journal of Personality and Social Psychology, 73,* 321–336.

Miller, W., & Thoresen, C.E. (in press). Spirituality and health. In W. Miller (Ed.), *Integrating spirituality into treatment.* Washington, D.C.: American Psychological Association.

Miller, T.Q., Smith, T.W., Turner, C.W., Guijarro, M.L., & Halett, A.J. (1996). A meta-analytic review of research on hostility and physical health. *Psychological Bulletin, 119,* 322–348.

Nowinski, J., Baker, S., & Carroll, K. (1992). *Twelve-step facilitation therapy manual: A clinical research guide for therapists treating individuals with alcohol abuse and dependence* (Vol. 1, Project MATCH Monograph Series). Rockville, MD: National Institute on Alcohol Abuse and Alcoholism.

Ornish, D., Brown, S.E., Scherwitz, L.W., Billings, J.H., Armstrong, W.T., & Ports, T.A. (1990). Can coronary artery disease be reversed? *Lancet, 336,* 129–133.

Pargament, K.I. (1997). Religious methods of coping: Resources for the conservation and transformation of significance. In E. Shafranske (Ed.), *Religion and the clinical practice of psychology* (pp. 215–239). Washington, D.C: American Psychological Association.

Pargament, K.I., & Rye, M.S. (1997). Forgiveness as a method of religious coping. In E.L. Worthington, Jr. (Ed.), *Dimensions of forgiveness: Psychological research & theological perspectives* (pp. 59–78). Philadelphia, PA: Templeton Foundation Press.

Persons, J.B. (1991). Psychotherapy outcome studies do not accurately represent current models of psychotherapy. *American Psychologist, 46,* 99–106.

Phillips, L.J., & Osbourne, J.W. (1989). Cancer patients' experiences of forgiveness therapy. *Canadian Journal of Counseling, 23,* 236–251.

Richards, P.S., & Bergin, A.E. (1997). *A spiritual strategy for counseling and psychotherapy.* Washington, D.C.: American Psychological Association.

Smedes, L.B. (1996). *The art of forgiving.* New York: Ballantine Books.

Smedes, L.B. (1998). Stations on the journey from forgiveness to hope. In E.L. Worthington, Jr. (Ed.), *Dimensions of forgiveness: Psychological research & theological perspectives* (pp. 341–354). Philadelphia, PA: Templeton Foundation Press

Smith, H. (1989). *The world's religions.* San Francisco, CA: Harper Collins.

Sogyal Rinpoche. (1992). *The Tibetan book of living and dying.* New York: Harper Collins.

Spiegel, D., Bloom, J.R., Kraemer, H.C., & Gottheil, E. (1989). Effects of psychosocial treatment on survival of patients with metastatic breast cancer. *Lancet, 14,* 888–891.

Spielberger, C.D. (1994). State-Trait Anger Expression Inventory, Research Edition. Psychological Assessment Resources, Inc.

Thoresen, C. (1997, March). Reducing depression and increasing social support: Overview of intervention. In N. Schneidermann (Chair), *ENRICHD: the NHLBI multicenter trial for enhancing recovery in ischemic coronary heart disease.* Symposium conducted at the meeting of the Society of Behavioral Medicine, San Francisco.

Thoresen, C.E. (1998). Spirituality, health, and science: The coming revival? In S. Roth-Roemer, S. Kurpius Robinson, & C. Carmin (Eds.), *The emerging role of counseling psychology in health care* (pp. 409–431). New York: Norton.

Thoresen, C.E., & Hoffman-Goldberg, J. (1998). Coronary heart disease: A psychosocial perspective on assessment and intervention. In S. Roth-Roemer, S. Kurpius Robinson, & C. Carmin (Eds.), *The emerging role of counseling psychology in health care* (pp. 94–136). New York: Norton.

Thoresen, C.E., & Powell, L.H. (1992). Type A behavior pattern: New perspectives on theory, assessment, and intervention. *Journal of Consulting and Clinical Psychology, 60*, 595–604.

Vanden Bos, G.R (1996). Outcome assessment of psychotherapy. *American Psychologist, 51*, 1005–1006.

Wampold, B.E., Monden, G.W., Moody, M., Stick, F., Beuson, K., & Ahm, H. (1997). A meta-analysis of outcomes studies comparing bonafide psychotherapies: Empirically, "All Must Have Prizes." *Psychological Bulletin, 122*, 203–215.

Weil, A. (1997). *8 weeks to optimum health.* New York: Knopf.

Williams, R., & Williams, V. (1993). *Anger kills.* New York: Random House.

Worthington, E.L. (1998). The Pyramid Model of forgiveness: Some interdisciplinary speculations about unforgiveness and the promotion of forgiveness. In E.L. Worthington, Jr. (Ed.), *Dimensions of forgiveness: Psychological research & theological perspectives* (pp. 107–137). Philadelphia, PA: Templeton Foundation Press.

Worthington, E.L. (1998). Empirical research in forgiveness: Looking backward, looking forward. In E.L. Worthington, Jr. (Ed.), *Dimensions of forgiveness: Psychological research & theological perspectives* (pp. 321–339). Philadelphia, PA: Templeton Foundation Press.

Worthington, E.L., Kurusu, T.A., McCullough, M.E., & Sandage, S.J. (1996). Empirical research on religion and psychotherapeutic processes and outcomes: A 10-year review and research prospectus. *Psychological Bulletin, 119*, 448–487.

Yalom, I.D. (1980). *Existential psychotherapy.* New York: Basic.

PART IV

✦

Forgiveness in Published Research

CHAPTER 8

An Annotated Bibliography of Research on Forgiveness and Related Concepts

Michael E. McCullough, Julie Juola Exline,
and Roy F. Baumeister

D
ESPITE THE IMMENSE IMPORTANCE of the concept of forgiveness in religion, theology, and philosophy, very little explicit attention has been paid to forgiveness by scientists in the social, behavioral, and medical sciences. This neglect is especially remarkable in light of the fact that forgiveness has also been held as an important virtue by most societies throughout history and around the world. Interestingly, there is no real evidence that the social sciences had any particular disdain for the concept of forgiveness; rather, the concept simply seems to have been viewed as not sufficiently relevant or amenable to scientific investigation.

The benign neglect of the concept of forgiveness within the sciences continued through most of the 1980s. Beginning at the end of that decade, however, a few researchers in the social and behavioral sciences began to develop theories and collect data that would help to shed light on the phenomenon of forgiveness.

Given the centrality of the concept of forgiveness to Sir John M. Templeton's *Worldwide Laws of Life*, which he published in 1997, the John Templeton Foundation made a commitment to fostering a significant expansion of high-quality scientific research on forgiveness. To promote this initiative, the Foundation thought it wise to survey the current state of the empirical literature that could be marshaled to develop a scientific understanding of forgiveness. As a result of the Foundation's initiative, we were commissioned to conduct a thorough review of the published research within the social sciences to retrieve the available scientific knowledge on forgiveness and related concepts.

While we found many studies that directly addressed the concept of forgiveness, we also found some interesting and potentially applicable research on revenge, blame, apologies, and confession that seemed directly relevant to the concept of forgiveness. The studies that we uncovered employed a wide range of scientific methodologies, from gaming studies and deception-based laboratory experiments to field interventions. The studies that we found are summarized in a standardized, annotated bibliography format in this chapter.* To facilitate easy use of this annotated bibliography, we have developed a subject index of more than 20 terms by which we categorized each study.

Our existing scientific understanding of the concept of forgiveness is quite limited. As a result of the John Templeton Foundation's Program to Encourage Scientific Research on Forgiveness, we hope to see a proliferation of scientific research in the years to come on this important, currently understudied, aspect of human nature.

---

*This annotated bibliography is a condensed version of the original, which is located on the John Templeton Foundation website (http://www.templeton.org, Grant Opportunities, Forgiveness RFP [1997]).

Al-Mabuk, R.H., Enright, R.D., & Cardis, P.A. (1995)

FORGIVENESS EDUCATION WITH PARENTALLY LOVE-DEPRIVED LATE ADOLESCENTS

Journal of Moral Education 24, 427–444

OBJECTIVE: To describe and evaluate the efficacy of an intervention to help adolescents who felt inadequately loved by their parents to forgive their parents.

DESIGN: Two controlled, randomized experiments blocking on gender. Study 1 included only a partial intervention (four sessions over a 2-week period) designed to facilitate insight and a commitment to forgive. Study 2 included a more complete intervention (six sessions over a 6-week period), including greater education on the specific steps necessary to forgive.

SETTING: Two public universities in the midwestern U.S.

PARTICIPANTS: College students (average age 20 years) who indicated on a screening questionnaire that they had experienced love deprivation from their parents. Study 1 included 48 students (37 females, 11 males). Study 2 included 45 students (29 females, 16 males).

INTERVENTION: Participants were randomly assigned to either the forgiveness education program or a human relations program. Both groups were led by the same male graduate student, who had training in both topics.

ASSESSMENT OF OUTCOME VARIABLES: At pretest, participants completed: (a) the Willingness-to-Forgive Scale, a 12-item measure of willingness to choose forgiveness as a problem-solving strategy; (b) 25 items measuring attitudes toward one's mother and father (Hudson, 1976); (c) the Hope Scale, a 30-item measure developed for this study, which assesses optimism about the future of one's relationship with one's parents; and

(d) the Spielberger State-Trait Anxiety Inventory (Spielberger, Gorsuch, Lushene,Vagg, & Jacobs, 1983). At posttest (directly after the final intervention), each of these measures was administered again, with the addition of the following: (a) the Psychological Profile of Forgiveness (Hebl & Enright, 1993), a 30-item measure of the degree to which one person has forgiven another; (b) the Beck Depression Inventory (Beck, Ward, Mendelson, Mock, & Erbaugh, 1961); and (c) the Coopersmith Self-Esteem Inventory (Coopersmith, 1981).

MAIN RESULTS: Study 1: At posttest, the forgiveness group reported higher levels of hope and willingness to forgive than the human relations group. However, there were no differences in actual forgiveness of the parent as measured by the Psychological Profile of Forgiveness.

Study 2: After receiving the more thorough intervention used in this study, virtually all measures favored the forgiveness group. Anxiety and depression did not differ between the groups. In both studies, greater self-reported forgiveness was associated with lower levels of anxiety and depression, higher self-esteem, and more positive views of the parents.

CONCLUSION: The first, less comprehensive intervention may have increased participants' awareness of forgiveness issues and their potential to engage in forgiveness; however, the more comprehensive intervention appears to have been necessary to facilitate actual forgiveness. In both studies, forgiveness was associated with positive psychological outcomes: reduced anxiety and depression and higher self-esteem.

COMMENTARY: This study provides some interesting initial evidence that educational approaches to forgiving, as well as psychotherapeutic ones, can be effective in helping target populations to forgive people who have hurt them. The success of these interventions in group settings also provides encouragement that forgiveness interventions can be successfully administered to groups, and not simply to individuals. As is the case in most of the literature on the effects of educational and therapeutic interventions, both treatments led to reductions in psychological symptoms. Because the relationship between reductions in psychological symptoms and improvements in forgiveness seemed to occur regardless of whether participants completed the forgiveness treatment or the control treatment, the therapeutic effects of psychoeducational interventions—designed to encourage forgiveness on psychological symptoms—might not be solely related to the forgiveness-related content of the interventions *per se*, but also to other elements of the treatment program that it shares in common with other psychoeducational approaches.

CORRESPONDENCE: Dr. Radhi H. Al-Mabuk, Department of Educational Psychology, University of Northern Iowa, Cedar Falls, Iowa.

Axelrod, R. (1980a)

EFFECTIVE CHOICE IN THE PRISONER'S DILEMMA

Journal of Conflict Resolution, 24, 3–25

OBJECTIVE: To compare the effectiveness of various strategies in the Prisoner's Dilemma Game (PDG), a tool used to simulate conflict situations in the laboratory.

DESIGN: Round-robin tournament in which various computer-simulated strategies were pitted against one another.

SETTING: Entries were submitted from three countries and five scholarly disciplines.

PARTICIPANTS: Fourteen computer programs were submitted.

ASSESSMENT OF PREDICTOR VARIABLES: In the PDG, two players are repeatedly faced with the choice of choosing a cooperative or a competitive strategy. The object is to win as many points as possible. If both cooperate, they each win 3 points. If one defects while the other cooperates, the defector wins 5 points while the cooperator receives 0 points. If both defect, both win 1 point.

Each submitted strategy was pitted against the other entries, a "twin" copy of itself, and RANDOM, a program that randomly cooperated and defected with equal probability. Submitted programs varied in the degree to which they incorporated strategies that were "nice" (i.e., never the first to defect) and "forgiving" (i.e., cooperating after receiving a defection from the other player).

ASSESSMENT OF OUTCOME VARIABLES: For each submitted strategy, the average number of points won per game was computed. These average scores were compared across strategies to determine which were most effective.

MAIN RESULTS: Each of the top eight ranking entries were nice in that they did not initiate a competitive move. The winning strategy overall, TIT FOR TAT, was only moderately forgiving: It started with a cooperative choice and thereafter did whatever the other player did on the previous move. In other words, if faced with a defection it would retaliate once, but by the time of the next move it had "forgotten" the earlier defection. Less successful strategies attempted to occasionally exploit the other player. The second and third most effective strategies were also moderately forgiving: They would punish defections but would occasionally give the other player "a fresh start" by risking cooperation. Destructive patterns of mutual defection could thus be broken. Among the nice rules, the least forgiving did the least well.

TIT FOR TWO TATS, a more forgiving version of TIT FOR TAT proposed by the author (although not submitted by any of the contestants), defected only after two defections by the other player. It was found to be even more successful than TIT FOR TAT and would have won the tournament if submitted.

CONCLUSION: Even in terms of purely pragmatic interpersonal strategies (i.e., independent of emotional effects), behavior that is nice and moderately forgiving appears to bring more benefits for the self than hostile or unforgiving behavior. Yet the most pragmatic strategy submitted— TIT FOR TAT—was not based on a pure "turn-the-other-cheek" strategy, but rather on immediate reciprocity followed by subsequent forgiveness.

It protected itself, but did not amplify the effects of defection by the other player. The superior performance of TIT FOR TWO TATS, a more forgiving strategy proposed by the author, suggests that strategists often make a major tactical error: They assume that they can get more by becoming slightly less forgiving, whereas becoming slightly more forgiving might actually be more beneficial in many situations.

COMMENTARY: This study is an example of the possible uses of a game-theory approach to understanding forgiveness. The term "forgiving," when used in this context, differs markedly from how the term is typically used in the social sciences; however, the commonality is that both probably involve the refraining of one's impulses to respond in kind to aversive behavior from one's partner. In this way, "forgiving" in the PDG might actually have more in common with Rusbult's (1991) notion of "accommodation" than with forgiveness, although obvious commonalities exist among all three concepts. The discovery in the present study that becoming more, rather than less, forgiving in mixed-motive situations can actually be to one's long-term benefit is a surprising and provocative insight that should be investigated in studies involving human subjects.

CORRESPONDENCE: Robert Axelrod, Institute of Public Policy Studies, University of Michigan, Ann Arbor, Michigan.

Axelrod, R. (1980b)

MORE EFFECTIVE CHOICE IN THE PRISONER'S DILEMMA

Journal of Conflict Resolution, 24, 379–403

OBJECTIVE: To compare the effectiveness of various strategies in the Prisoner's Dilemma Game (PDG), a tool used to simulate conflict situations in the laboratory. This article explains the second round of the tournament described in Axelrod (1980a).

DESIGN: Second round of a round-robin tournament in which various computer-simulated strategies were pitted against each other.

SETTING: Entries were submitted from six countries and a wide variety of disciplines.

PARTICIPANTS: Sixty-two computer programs were submitted. Participants, who ranged from a 10-year-old computer hobbyist to university professors, were recruited largely through advertisements in journals for users of small computers. All entrants were first given a detailed analysis of the first round (Axelrod, 1980a), which they could use in designing their strategies.

ASSESSMENT OF PREDICTOR VARIABLES: In the PDG, two players are repeatedly faced with the choice of choosing a cooperative or a competitive strategy. The object is to win as many points as possible. If both cooperate, they each win 3 points. If one defects while the other cooperates, the defector wins 5 points while the cooperator receives 0 points. If both defect, both win 1 point.

Each submitted strategy was pitted against the other entries, a "twin" copy of itself, and RANDOM, a program that randomly cooperated and defected with equal probability. Submitted programs varied in the degree to which they incorporated strategies that were nice (i.e., never the first to defect) and forgiving (i.e., cooperating after receiving a defection from the other player).

ASSESSMENT OF OUTCOME VARIABLES: For each submitted strategy, the average number of points won per game was computed. These average scores were compared across strategies to determine which were most effective.

MAIN RESULTS: As in round one (Axelrod, 1980a), TIT FOR TAT emerged as the winner. This was a nice and moderately forgiving strategy, starting with a cooperative choice and thereafter doing whatever the other player did on the previous move. Nice strategies generally fared better than more competitive ones. When playing against strategies that favored testing limits and occasionally exploiting one's partner, highly forgiving strategies (e.g., TIT FOR TWO TATS, which defects only after two defections by the other player) left themselves open to attack. Strategies that were nice and moderately forgiving but more "provocable"—that is, they defected after an uncalled-for defection by the other—fared better against these exploitative players.

CONCLUSION: This tournament reaffirmed the benefits of being moderately forgiving and cooperative. However, it also suggested some dangers of behaving in a manner that is "too forgiving" when dealing with someone dedicated to testing the limits or exploitation. In short, behaving in a forgiving manner can entail risks for the self when the other person cannot be trusted to respond in kind.

COMMENTARY: This study illustrates some of the interesting and immensely practical insights that can be gained from the study of mixed-motive simulations such as the PDG. The findings that the most forgiving strategies are effective with less exploitative relationship partners, and that slightly less forgiving strategies are most effective with more exploitative partners, are fascinating and should be investigated further using samples of human subjects. Hypotheses generated from these findings would be especially interesting to study in the context of ongoing relationships, such as work, family, and romantic relationships.

CORRESPONDENCE: Robert Axelrod, Institute of Public Policy Studies, University of Michigan, Ann Arbor, Michigan.

Baumeister, R.F., Stillwell, A.M., & Heatherton, T.F. (1995)

PERSONAL NARRATIVES ABOUT GUILT: ROLE IN ACTION
CONTROL AND INTERPERSONAL RELATIONSHIPS

Basic and Applied Social Psychology, 17, 173–198.

OBJECTIVE: To examine the interpersonal and action–control aspects of guilt. (The action–control view of guilt proposes that guilt can influence subsequent behavior, such as by "teaching someone a lesson" and causing subsequent behavior change.)

DESIGN: Two cross-sectional studies using an autobiographical essay format: The first study focused on the presence or absence of guilt, whereas the second focused on interpersonal induction of guilt.

SETTING: Private university in Ohio.

PARTICIPANTS: Study 1: Forty-seven undergraduates from upper-level psychology courses received extra credit for participation. Study 2: The sample was composed of visitors to the Ontario Science Centre and undergraduates from upper-level courses. A total of 104 persons participated, with ages ranging from 19 to 65 years.

MANIPULATED VARIABLES: Study 1: Participants were asked to write two descriptions of incidents in which they angered someone: one in which they felt guilty/regretful (guilt condition) and one in which they did not feel guilty/regretful (no guilt condition). They were asked to be as thorough as possible, describing the background, the incident itself, and the consequences. Order was counterbalanced.

Study 2: Participants each wrote a description of one incident. They were asked to recall a time in which they made someone feel guilty (guilt-inducer condition) or in which someone else made them feel guilty (target condition). They were asked for as much detail as possible, as in Study 1.

ASSESSMENT OF OUTCOME VARIABLES: Study 1: A single coder rated each story for the presence versus the absence of seven features: transgressor learned a lesson, transgressor changed behavior, apology was given, transgressor confessed misdeed, relationship was communal, transgressor regarded victim highly, and transgressor was selfish.

Study 2: Two persons coded the stories for the presence versus the absence of six features: offense was interpersonal neglect, target resented being manipulated, guilt inducer felt metaguilt (guilt about inducing guilt), inducer felt better afterward, reference was made to other's standards, and differing expectations were mentioned as a cause of conflict. Initial interrater agreement was above 80% on all dimensions. Differences were resolved by conferring.

MAIN RESULTS: Study 1: Relative to stories not involving guilt, those involving guilt showed higher levels of: (a) having learned a lesson, (b) subsequent behavior change, (c) apologies offered, (d) confessions offered, (e) occurrence within communal relationships, (f) high regard or esteem for the victim, and (g) indications of one's own selfishness. Not-guilty stories, relative to guilty stories, showed higher levels of: (a) references to mitigating circumstances, (b) blaming the victim, (c) self-justification, and (d) indication that the transgressor could foresee the outcome of his or her actions.

Study 2: Experiences of guilt induction were drawn almost exclusively from within close relationships. The largest category of offenses involved interpersonal neglect—failing to spend enough time with one's partner or to pay sufficient attention to him or her. More than a third of the targets indicated resentment over the other's manipulation of their guilty feelings, whereas inducers' references to resentment by the target were much less common (2%). A sizable minority of guilt inducers reported metaguilt, whereas none of the targets reported metaguilt. Inducers, relative to targets, were more likely to mention feeling better about successful guilt induction; however, they were also more likely to report that the guilt induction involved exaggeration, lies, or manipulation. Targets were more likely than inducers to refer to differing standards or expectations and to make reference to the other person's standards. Targets, relative to inducers, were also more likely to depict the inducer as having overreacted to the problem.

CONCLUSION: These findings provide support for the view that guilt can facilitate improvements within close relationships (cf. Baumeister, Stillwell, & Heatherton, 1994). People who feel guilty are more likely to take corrective action. However, the induction of guilt is often viewed with ambivalence: Although it can foster reparations and restore some equity to the victim, it is often perceived as manipulative or as an overreaction to the problem at hand.

COMMENTARY: The power of guilt, in part, lies in its efficacy in shaping our future behavior toward other people. When we feel guilty, we become less likely to repeat our hurtful behaviors in the future and are more likely to confess and apologize. Moreover, most people appear to be aware that guilt can be used in social settings to achieve such changes in one's perpetrator. Given these potentially valuable (yet sometimes counterproductive) social functions of guilt, therapeutic strategies that seek to relieve people's guilt without attention to the positive effects of guilt on maintaining healthy relationships fail to appreciate that not all guilt is bad. Indeed, guilt might be a major motivator to seeking forgiveness when we have hurt others. Understandings of guilt should be incorporated into future work on the study of how people seek forgiveness when they have hurt others.

CORRESPONDENCE: Roy F. Baumeister, Department of Psychology, Case Western Reserve University, Cleveland, Ohio.

Baumeister, R.F., & Stillwell, A.M., & Wotman, S.R. (1990)

VICTIM AND PERPETRATOR ACCOUNTS OF INTERPERSONAL CONFLICT: AUTOBIOGRAPHICAL NARRATIVES ABOUT ANGER

Journal of Personality and Social Psychology, 59, 994–1005

OBJECTIVE: To compare people's recollections of two types of transgression incidents: those in which they were the victim and those in which they were the perpetrator.

DESIGN: Within-subjects experiment.

SETTING: Private university in northeast Ohio.

PARTICIPANTS: Sixty-three undergraduates enrolled in various psychology classes.

MANIPULATED VARIABLES: Each participant was asked to write a detailed, story-format account of two real-life incidents: one in which he or she was angered by someone else (victim account) and one in which he or she angered someone else (perpetrator account). By random assignment, half the participants wrote the victim account first, while the other half wrote the perpetrator account first.

ASSESSMENT OF OUTCOME VARIABLES: Victim and perpetrator accounts were coded as to the presence versus absence of approximately 26 features (e.g., whether the perpetrator apologized, description of perpetrator's intentions as arbitrary, portrayal of victim's response as an overreaction). The percentages of victims versus perpetrators coded positively for each item were compared.

MAIN RESULTS: Victim accounts referred to lasting negative consequences, continuing anger, and long-term relationship damage, whereas perpetrator accounts were more likely to deny negative consequences and to feature apologies and happy endings. Victims were much more likely than perpetrators to describe the perpetrators' motives and actions as incomprehensible, arbitrary, contradictory, senseless, unjustified, immoral, and deliberately cruel or harmful. Perpetrators, in contrast, were more likely to describe their motives as impulsive, uncontrollable, justifiable, or due to mitigating circumstances. They also tended to see any expressions of anger by the victims as overreactions. A substantial number of perpetrators also reported regret; however, almost none of the victim accounts acknowledged any possible regret by the perpetrator. Victim accounts were more likely than perpetrator accounts to refer to multiple, accumulating provocations.

CONCLUSION: Victims and perpetrators interpret transgressions in different and possibly distorted ways, and these differing views are likely to precipitate continued misunderstanding and conflict. For example, victims tend to place the incident in a broader time frame and to focus on the damage caused. They also tend to ascribe malevolent motives to the perpetrators. Perpetrators, in contrast, tend to encapsulate the incident and downplay its negative effects, and they often view their own actions as justifiable while seeing the victim's response as an overreaction.

COMMENTARY: These studies provide some important insights into the differences in how victims and perpetrators view interpersonal transgressions. Because of their limited perspective on the victims' perceptions, perpetrators tend to view their actions as less serious, more justifiable, and accompanied by more contrition—that is, imminently more forgivable—than do victims. Conversely, because of their limited perspective on the perpetrators' perceptions, victims tend to view perpetrators using the same attributional style that other researchers (e.g., Boon & Sulsky, 1997; Darby & Schlenker, 1982; Weiner, Graham, Peter, & Zmuidinas, 1991) have identified as contributing to difficulty in forgiving. This wide gap in victims' and perpetrators' construals of their relationship partners, the interpersonal transgressions that occur between them, and the psychological and interpersonal effects of those transgressions help to explain why interpersonal forgiveness might be difficult to negotiate in ongoing relationships.

CORRESPONDENCE : Roy F. Baumeister, Department of Psychology, Case Western Reserve University, Cleveland, Ohio.

Bendor, J., Kramer, R.M., & Stout, S. (1991)

WHEN IN DOUBT...COOPERATION IN A NOISY PRISONER'S DILEMMA

Journal of Conflict Resolution, 35, 691–719

OBJECTIVE: To determine whether alternative strategies for the Prisoner's Dilemma Game (PDG) work better than the reciprocity-based TIT FOR TAT (cf. Axelrod, 1980a, 1980b) within noisy environments. (Noisy environments are those in which people sometimes draw incorrect inferences because they lack perfect information about the actions of others.)

DESIGN: Round-robin tournament in which various computer-simulated strategies were pitted against each other. The overall strategy was based on that of Axelrod (1980a, 1980b).

SETTING: Stanford University.

PARTICIPANTS: Thirteen strategies were submitted. Participants were recruited from several departments across the university and from a university seminar.

ASSESSMENT OF PREDICTOR VARIABLES: In the PDG, two participants are repeatedly faced with the decision to choose a cooperative or a competitive strategy. The object is to win as many points as possible. Participants win a moderate number of points if they both cooperate. If one defects while the other cooperates, the defector wins a large sum while the cooperator receives nothing. If both defect, both win a small sum. In this version, noise was created as follows: Each player's cooperation level was obscured by adding a small amount of random variation during each period of play.

Each strategy was pitted against all other strategies and against a copy of itself. Play continued for a random number of periods with a probability of .0067 of stopping after any given period. A monetary reward structure was devised in which the reward depended only on one's own performance and was not diminished by someone else's good performance. Submitted strategies varied in the degree to which they were nice (never the first to defect) and generous/forgiving (returning more cooperation than one receives).

ASSESSMENT OF OUTCOME VARIABLES: For each submitted strategy, the average number of points won per game was computed. These average scores were compared across strategies to determine which were most effective.

MAIN RESULTS: TIT FOR TAT, the nice but only moderately forgiving strategy that won the noiseless-environment tournaments (Axelrod, 1980a, 1980b), placed 8th out of 13. Given occasional noise, its tendency to reciprocate defections made it a poor performer when paired with other nice but provocable strategies. This tournament's winner, NICE AND FORGIVING, was a more generous strategy than TIT FOR TAT: First, as long as its partner's cooperation level exceeded a certain threshold (80 out of a possible 100), NICE would continue to play a strategy of maximal cooperation. Second, although NICE would retaliate if its partner's cooperation level fell below 80, it was willing to risk full cooperation before its partner did, as long as the partner met certain thresholds of cooperation. Both features deterred unintentional "vendettas" to which TIT FOR TAT was susceptible in the noisy environment. Other successful strategies in this tournament were also generous.

CONCLUSION: In a "noisy" environment characterized by uncertainty, miscommunication, and mistaken inferences, generous strategies fare better than purely reciprocal strategies. Generous strategies help to avoid overreaction to (unintended) slights and consequent escalation of conflict.

COMMENTARY: This study is one of the more interesting of the PDG studies included in this annotated bibliography because of its attempts to model the process of uncertainty in interpersonal relations. In relationships generally characterized by goodwill (with occasional defections), people's outcomes appear to be maximized by becoming more forgiving rather than less forgiving when occasional defections do occur. As hurtful behavior occurs even in ongoing relationships that are generally characterized by trust and positive behavior, these data suggest that the appropriate way to maximize gains in such relationships is to absorb a certain level of such hurts before responding in kind. Whether such a principle would bear out in ongoing interpersonal relationships in research with human subjects would be an interesting and important line of research.

CORRESPONDENCE : No mailing address listed. All authors were affiliated with Stanford University at the time of this writing.

Boon, S.D., & Sulsky, L.M. (1997)

ATTRIBUTIONS OF BLAME AND FORGIVENESS IN ROMANTIC RELATIONSHIPS: A POLICY-CAPTURING STUDY

Journal of Social Behavior and Personality, 12, 19–44

OBJECTIVE: To examine how people weight various criteria in drawing conclusions about blame and their own willingness to forgive.

DESIGN: Experiment using the policy-capturing method (Slovic & Lichtenstein, 1971).

SETTING: University in western Canada.

PARTICIPANTS: Fifty-six undergraduates (38 females, 18 males). Age range: 18 to 36 years, average age 23.2 years. A total of 62.5% were involved in ongoing heterosexual relationships at the time of the study. Ethnicity: 67.9% white, 21.4% Asian, remainder from other ethnic backgrounds.

MANIPULATED VARIABLES: Each participant read 40 counterbalanced profiles about a transgression incident within a romantic relationship. Each profile described an incident in which a person violated the trust of a romantic partner by telling a mutual friend very private details about the partner's past. Participants were asked to imagine themselves as the romantic partner whose trust had been violated. Three pieces of background information were varied: offense severity, avoidability (the extent to which the violation of trust was avoidable), and partner intent (the extent to which the violation was intentional). Five levels of offense severity and avoidability were included, varying from not at all severe (or avoidable) to entirely severe (or avoidable). Two levels of intentionality were included (intentional versus unintentional). Thirty of the profiles contained unique combinations of values for the 3 cues, while the remaining 10 contained duplicates to determine whether participants responded in a consistent fashion.

ASSESSMENT OF OUTCOME VARIABLES: Immediately following each profile were two questions, appearing in counterbalanced order: "How blameworthy were your partner's actions in this incident?" and "How likely would you be to forgive your partner for his/her hurtful actions?" Participants responded using 7-point Likert scales.

MAIN RESULTS: Within-subjects regression analyses were performed, followed by a between-subjects analysis of beta weights. Severity, intentionality, and avoidability of an offense were positively related to blame and negatively related to willingness to forgive. For judgments of blame, intent was given more weight than either offense severity or avoidability. Avoidability, in turn, was given more weight than offense severity. In contrast, for judgments of willingness to forgive, participants assigned more weight to both intentionality and severity than to avoidability. Complex interactions and nonlinear trends in the data also suggested that the strategies people use in making such judgments are more complicated than previously assumed.

CONCLUSION: This study demonstrates that the severity, intentionality, and avoidability of an offense can influence judgments about blame and willingness to forgive. However, people appear to weigh contextual factors differently when assessing blame than when rating their own willingness to forgive, and the strategies they use to make these judgments appear to be complex.

COMMENTARY: The results from this study form an important bridge between two areas of inquiry that have been unfortunately separated in discussions of interpersonal forgiveness to date: (a) the social-cognitive mechanisms that control forgiveness and (b) the role of forgiveness in close relationships. These findings suggest that people's understandings of forgiveness in romantic relationships are under the control of the same social-psychological factors that controls people's tendencies to forgive in less intimate relationships (e.g., see Darby & Schlenker, 1982; Weiner et al., 1991). Interestingly, these findings suggest that the processes controlling blame are similar, but not identical, to the processes controlling forgiveness (see also Weinberg, 1994).

CORRESPONDENCE: S.D. Boon, University of Calgary, Calgary, Alberta, Canada.

Brown, B.R. (1968)

THE EFFECTS OF NEED TO MAINTAIN FACE
ON INTERPERSONAL BARGAINING

Journal of Experimental Social Psychology, 4, 107–122

OBJECTIVE: To investigate the conditions under which people will act in a vengeful manner even at substantial cost to the self.

DESIGN: Laboratory experiment.

SETTING: New York City public high schools.

PARTICIPANTS: The sample consisted of 60 males ranging from age 15 to 17.5 years.

MANIPULATED VARIABLES: Participants were told that they would be observed and evaluated by an audience of classmates from behind a one-way mirror while participating in a bargaining task. (There were actually no classmates behind the mirror; a tape recording was used for simulation.) Participants could not see the other participant (actually a programmed confederate or "stooge"). A modification of the two-person, non-zero-sum "trucking game" (Deutsch & Krauss, 1960) was used to create a conflict of interest for participants. In this game, participants must move their trucks as quickly as possible around an electronic track. If they choose the shortest, most direct route, they must share a portion of the track. When encountering each other on the shared stretch of track, they have the option of blocking each other's progress (at considerable time cost) or backing up to enable the other player to pass. In this version, tollgates were also used, which on any one turn were controlled by only one player. Players who refused to pay the tolls had to back out of the shared territory and take the longer route.

In all conditions, a drawing of lots ensured that the stooge "won" control of the tollgate for the first 10 trials, while the participant won control for the last 10. The stooge charged high tolls, causing a considerable loss for the participant. In the second 10 trials (when the participant controlled the gate), the stooge was programmed to travel the direct route and pay all tolls. If the participant tried to block, the stooge refused to yield for 30 seconds or until the participant backed up to let him pass.

Participants were encouraged to win as much as possible for themselves without consideration for the other person's earnings. They were also informed that they could keep their earnings at the end of the experiment.

Manipulated variables were as follows: There were three audience feedback conditions—positive, negative, and no feedback. In the positive and negative feedback conditions, both the stooge and the participant were handed several sheets that ostensibly indicated the audience's evaluations of them after the 10th trial. Negative-feedback participants were told that they looked weak or like "suckers," while positive-feedback participants were told that they were fair and looked good. A toll schedule was then handed to each participant. Although participants could exact tolls of $0.15 or less at no cost to themselves, they had to pay to charge more than $0.15 per toll, with their costs escalating as they chose higher tolls. A knowledge-of-costs manipulation was also performed in which the participant either was or was not led to believe that the other player had received a copy of the participant's toll schedule.

ASSESSMENT OF OUTCOME VARIABLES: The primary dependent variables were: (a) the number of trials in which participants charged tolls of more than $0.15 and (b) the amount they spent in order to charge these tolls. As indices of bargaining efficiency, total earnings gained and time spent were also examined. Participants were also asked to rate the extent to which they tried to "appear strong" in the second half of the experiment.

MAIN RESULTS: Relative to participants given favorable audience feedback, those given derogatory feedback (a) were more likely to charge more than $0.15; (b) expended more of their own money to charge high tolls; (c) earned significantly less than those given positive feedback; (d) were more likely to obstruct the stooge and wait for him to "back down," even at considerable time cost; and (e) reported greater concern about "appearing strong" to the other player. Retaliation (as measured by toll charges and money expended) was less frequent when participants believed that the other person knew the toll schedule.

CONCLUSION: When the study participants believed that they appeared foolish, they were more likely to retaliate, even at substantial cost to themselves. Thus, retaliation appears to be, in part, a face-saving measure. In addition, the participants appeared less likely to retaliate when their strategies and costs were known by their rivals.

COMMENTARY: This study provides important insights into the basic motivations that may govern people's choices to retaliate or seek revenge. Typically, revenge is construed as something that involves costs to one's victim, but comes at little cost to the perpetrator. This study suggests that under some conditions (particularly, those in which the perpetrator has previously lost face or appeared weak or foolish), the perpetrator will retaliate or pursue revenge even at considerable cost to the self. This insight has not been well integrated in most discussions of revenge and points to exactly how powerful the motivation to retaliate or seek revenge can be.

CORRESPONDENCE: Bert R. Brown, Cornell University, School of Industrial and Labor Relations, Ithaca, New York.

Coyle, C.T., & Enright, R.D. (1997)

FORGIVENESS INTERVENTION WITH POST-ABORTION MEN

Journal of Consulting and Clinical Psychology, 65, 1042–1045.

OBJECTIVE: To test the efficacy of a forgiveness intervention within a sample of post-abortion men (men who identified themselves as being hurt by their female partner's decision to have an abortion).

DESIGN: Controlled field experiment.

SETTING: A midwestern city.

PARTICIPANTS: Ten adult males were recruited through an advertisement in a local newspaper. All identified themselves as hurt by the abortion decision of a partner. The time span between the abortion and study participation ranged from 6 months to 22 years with a mean of 5.9 years. Six identified themselves as Christian, one Muslim, and the rest agnostic. Five were always opposed to the abortion, 1 was supportive initially, 3 were ambivalent, and 1 was not told of the abortion until months after the procedure; 7 had experienced a single abortion, and 3 experienced two abortions.

INTERVENTION: Participants were randomly assigned to either the forgiveness intervention condition or a control condition involving a 12-week waiting period. The intervention consisted of 12 weekly, 90-minute sessions using individual, manualized treatment. Sessions were conducted by the first author, an M.S.N. in psychiatric nursing, under the supervision of the second author, a licensed psychologist. The intervention model was based on a model of forgiveness developed by Robert Enright (Enright & the Human Development Study Group, 1996).

ASSESSMENT OF OUTCOME VARIABLES: The following measures were given at pretest, at the first posttest (12 weeks after pretest, just after treatment for the intervention group and just before treatment for the control group), and at the second posttest (12 weeks after the first posttest, after the control group had completed its treatment): (a) the Enright Forgiveness Inventory, a 60-item, self-report measure of interpersonal forgiveness (participants were asked to think of the person they blamed most for the abortion); items are equally divided among six subscales: positive and negative affect, positive and negative behavior, and positive and negative cognition; (b) the State Anger Scale, a well-established, 10-item measure of current anger (Spielberger, Jacobs, Russell, & Crane, 1983); (c) the State Anxiety Scale, a well-established, 20-item measure of current anxiety (Spielberger, Gorsuch, Lushene, Vagg, & Jacobs, 1983); (d) the short version of the Perinatal Grief Scale (Potvin, Lasker, & Toedter, 1989), a symptom-based scale of 33 items with items equally divided among three subscales: active grief, difficulty coping, and despair; and (e) a single-item, self-forgiveness measure.

MAIN RESULTS: At the first posttest, experimental participants showed greater increases in forgiveness than controls, along with greater decreases in anxiety, anger, and grief. Control participants showed similar gains when given the intervention. The treatment effects of the earlier-treated group were maintained over the 12-week follow-up period. Participants who reported that self-forgiveness was an issue for them also showed improvements in this domain after treatment.

CONCLUSION: These results suggest the potential efficacy of one-on-one forgiveness interventions for men troubled by a partner's decision to have an abortion. After intervention, participants showed increased forgiveness toward the person they blamed most for the abortion, and those who had difficulty forgiving themselves also reported improvements in this area. Participants also showed decreases in anger, anxiety, and grief.

COMMENTARY: As with other treatment studies using similar methodologies (e.g., Freedman & Enright, 1996), this study found that an intervention designed to promote forgiveness did have some important therapeutic benefits in excess of what could be expected through the passage of time and repeated testing alone (i.e., compared with the no-treatment control condition). The relative efficacy of such forgiveness treatments, however, should still be compared with more standard approaches to recovery. Also, active ingredients responsible for the therapeutic effects of such interventions remain to be identified. Nonetheless, this study exemplifies another creative effort by Enright and his colleagues of how groups of people experiencing painful life circumstances might be succored by participating in interventions designed to help them forgive.

CORRESPONDENCE: Catherine T. Coyle, Department of Educational Psychology, University of Wisconsin–Madison, Madison, Wisconsin.

Darby, B.W., & Schlenker, B.R. (1982)

CHILDREN'S REACTIONS TO APOLOGIES

Journal of Personality and Social Psychology, 43, 742–753

OBJECTIVE: To examine the effects of different types of apologies on children under conditions in which the offender's motives and intentions vary.

DESIGN: Two randomized experiments.

SETTING: Two elementary schools and one middle school in Gainesville, Florida.

PARTICIPANTS: Study 1: 36 kindergarten/first graders (17 males, 19 females; mean age = 6.1 years); 34 fourth graders (16 males, 18 females; mean age = 9.3 years); and 40 seventh graders (20 males, 20 females; mean age = 12.3 years). Study 2: 37 kindergarten/first graders (17 males, 20 females; mean age = 6.3 years), 39 fourth graders (20 males, 19 females; mean age = 9.0 years); and 25 seventh graders (13 males, 12 females; mean age = 12.1 years).

MANIPULATED VARIABLES: Study 1: Participants listened to a vignette describing a transgression and an apology. Participants were randomly assigned to one of four groups (2 x 2) based on the level of responsibility of the actor (low versus high) and the consequences of the action (low versus high). As a within-subjects manipulation, each participant was presented with four types of responses by the actor (no apology, perfunctory apology, standard apology, and compensation apology) and was asked to rate his or her hypothetical response to each one. The grade of the participant was also used as a predictor variable.

Study 2: Participants again listened to a transgression/apology vignette. They were randomly assigned to one of four groups (2 x 2) based on the intention of the actor (intentional versus unintentional) and the motive (good versus bad). The within-subjects apology manipulation from Study 1 was used, and the grade of the participant was again used as a factor.

ASSESSMENT OF OUTCOME VARIABLES: Study 1: Participants were asked to indicate, on a 10-point scale, the extent to which the actor: (a) should be blamed, (b) should be forgiven, (c) should be punished, (d) felt sorry, (e) is a good versus bad person, and (f) would be liked by the participant.

Study 2: In addition to completing the ratings used in Study 1, participants were asked to assess how strong versus weak the actor was as a person.

MAIN RESULTS: Study 1: Participants advocated greater punishment for actors who were responsible for high-consequence transgressions. More elaborate apologies led to greater forgiveness, and apologies appeared especially effective in reducing punishment in the high-responsibility condition. Older children appeared to be more responsive than younger children to the types of apologies offered: For example, fourth and seventh graders thought that the story's offender was increasingly sorry as more elaborate apologies were used, a result not found with younger children.

Study 2: Actors with bad motives were judged more harshly than those with good motives. More elaborate apologies resulted in less blame, greater forgiveness, less desire for punishment, greater liking, greater attributions of strength, greater belief that the actor was sorry, and more positive evaluations. Older children were more responsive than younger ones to the type of apology; and the oldest children were especially harsh toward actors who offered no apology. Whereas elaborate apologies were effective in mitigating the effects of an accidental transgression, they were less effective with intentional transgressions. Having a good motive led to more favorable evaluations, but only when an apology was also used.

CONCLUSION: School-age children are capable of taking factors such as apologies, motives, and intentions into account when determining how harshly to judge a transgressor. Apologies—particularly elaborate ones—generally mitigated the effects of transgression. However, older children appeared to be more responsive to subtle differences in apologies than younger children.

COMMENTARY: The findings from this study provide experimental evidence that forgiveness is, at least in part, a social-psychological phenomenon that is influenced by the offender's actions following the offense and the way in which those actions are interpreted by the offended person. The fact of the offender's apology might not be as important as the specific qualities of that apology—such as the perceived motive and intentions of the offender—and the way in which the offended person perceives those elements of the apology. In addition, these results show that as children age, they become more sensitive to subtle differences in the apologies that offenders might offer for their actions.

CORRESPONDENCE: Barry R. Schlenker, Department of Psychology, University of Florida, Gainesville, Florida.

DiBlasio, F.A. (1993)

THE ROLE OF SOCIAL WORKERS' RELIGIOUS BELIEFS IN HELPING FAMILY MEMBERS FORGIVE

Families in Society, 74, 163–170

OBJECTIVE: To assess social workers' attitudes about forgiveness and their use of forgiveness techniques in clinical settings, with special emphasis on comparing highly religious practitioners with those less religious.

DESIGN: Cross-sectional survey.

SETTING: Maryland.

PARTICIPANTS: Written or oral invitations were extended to 243 clinical members of the American Association of Marital and Family Therapists, as well as other clinicians in the community (exact number not specified). A total of 167 persons responded. Of these, the 70 persons (50 women and 20 men) who identified themselves as social workers were included in this study. The mean age was 43 years. Participants held degrees at either the master's level (90%) or the doctoral level (10%). Religious affiliations included Christian (40%), Jewish (36%), Far Eastern (1%), and "other" (14%); 8% indicated no religious preference. Half the participants reported that their personal religious beliefs were very important, and many reported that their religious beliefs had either a significant impact (41%) or some impact (27%) on their interventions. More than half the participants (55%) reported agreement with a statement that religious ideologies should be separate from interventions.

ASSESSMENT OF PREDICTOR VARIABLES: A median split was performed on the therapist religiosity variable, dividing the sample into high religiosity and low religiosity groups (n = 35 in each group). These two groups did not differ significantly in gender, education, or age.

ASSESSMENT OF OUTCOME VARIABLES: Five composite variables were developed, each of which was composed of a series of 5-point Likert items: (a) forgiveness attitude, which assessed beliefs about the importance and usefulness of forgiveness in clinical practice (Cronbach's alpha = .71); (b) forgiveness techniques, which assessed strategies used in assisting clients with forgiveness issues (alpha = .81); (c) forgiveness and depression, which assessed the perception of the role of forgiveness in resolving depression (alpha = .77); (d) forgiveness and anger, which assessed the perception of the role of forgiveness in reducing anger (alpha = .74); and (e) religious openness, which assessed sensitivity toward clients' religious issues as part of the therapeutic process (alpha = .82).

MAIN RESULTS: The mean scores were just above the midpoint on the five dependent variables; that is, participants on average held slightly favorable attitudes toward forgiveness, its use in therapy, and the inclusion of religious issues in therapy. The highly religious therapists differed significantly ($p < .05$) from the less religious therapists on only one of the five dependent variables: the forgiveness attitude measure. Relative to less religious practitioners, highly religious practitioners reported more favorable attitudes toward forgiveness.

CONCLUSION: Relative to less religious practitioners, highly religious practitioners may have more favorable attitudes toward forgiveness in general. However, their more positive attitudes toward the concept of forgiveness do not necessarily translate to a greater emphasis on forgiveness in clinical practice.

COMMENTARY: Unlike DiBlasio and Proctor's (1993) analysis of the larger data set from which these data were derived, this study found that social workers' religious involvement was associated with more positive attitudes regarding the use of forgiveness in the clinical setting. Given the fact that at the time of this survey most clinical writing on forgiveness had appeared in professional journals targeted at religious clinicians, these results make sense. If future surveys of clinicians were to fail to find a relationship between therapists' religious involvement and their openness to forgiveness in the clinical setting, we might interpret that nonrelationship as evidence that forgiveness has been adopted as a mental health value by religious and nonreligious therapists alike.

CORRESPONDENCE: Frederick A. DiBlasio, Ph.D., School of Social Work, University of Maryland at Baltimore, Baltimore, Maryland.

DiBlasio, F.A., & Proctor, J.H. (1993)

THERAPISTS AND THE CLINICAL USE OF FORGIVENESS

American Journal of Family Therapy, 21, 175–184

OBJECTIVE: To examine the clinical use of forgiveness techniques within a sample of marital and family therapists.

DESIGN: Cross-sectional survey.

SETTING: Maryland.

PARTICIPANTS: Two hundred forty-three clinical members of the American Association of Marital and Family Therapists were invited by mail to participate, of which 128 responded. The mean age was 47 years, and 55% were female. Respondents had either a master's (61%) or a doctoral (39%) degree in fields such as social work (41%), psychology (18%), theology (12%), marital and family therapy (10%), and psychiatry (4%). Religious affiliations included Jewish (20%), Catholic (13%), Baptist or Methodist (11%), Episcopalian (10%), nondenominational Christian (7%), Lutheran (5%), Presbyterian (5%), Far Eastern (2%), and "other"

(18%); 10% indicated no religious preference. Fifty-five percent of participants reported that their personal religious beliefs were very important, and most reported that their religious beliefs had either a significant impact (43%) or some impact (52%) on their interventions. However, many (57%) reported a belief that their religious ideologies should be completely separate from their interventions.

ASSESSMENT OF PREDICTOR VARIABLES: An index of therapists' openness to their clients' religiousness (Cronbach's alpha = .79) was composed based on 5-point Likert items: inquiry about clients' religious affiliation, inquiry about clients' belief system, assessment of clients' level of religiosity, use of clients' religiosity in therapy, and validity of clients' religiosity for therapy. Therapists also rated the personal importance of their religious beliefs on a 5-point Likert scale (1 = not important; 5 = very important). Therapist age, gender, and highest educational level were also used as independent variables.

ASSESSMENT OF OUTCOME VARIABLES: An index of forgiveness techniques (Cronbach's alpha = .87) assessed the extent to which the therapist had developed specific techniques to help clients: (a) seek forgiveness, (b) grant forgiveness, and (c) forgive themselves. The three forgiveness items were rated on 5-point Likert scales (1 = techniques not developed at all, 5 = very well-developed techniques).

MAIN RESULTS: The mean score on the index of forgiveness techniques was 10.2, with scores ranging from 3 to 15. The mean religious openness score was 19.0, with scores ranging from 6 to 25. The index of forgiveness techniques correlated positively with religious openness (r = .46) and therapist age (r = .22), but did not correlate significantly with therapist gender, education, or personal religiosity. Multiple regression indicated that religious openness and therapist age, taken together, accounted for approximately 26% of the variance in the index of forgiveness techniques. Both variables made a significant independent contribution to the variance.

CONCLUSION: Therapists were more likely to have developed forgiveness techniques to the extent that they: (a) were older and (b) reported openness to assessing and using clients' religious-belief systems in therapy. Therapists' own levels of personal religiosity were not related to the development of forgiveness techniques.

COMMENTARY: In the clinical setting at least, forgiveness appears to be treated as a religious value. Therapists appear to be explore forgiveness in therapy as a function of their openness to exploring clients' religious commitments in therapy. Given the long history of forgiveness as a religious concept, this connection is perhaps unsurprising. The relationship between therapists' ages and their openness to forgiveness in the clinical setting might suggest (among other things) that as therapists gain experience (as clinicians and as human beings), they become more aware of the relevance of forgiveness in addressing human problems.

CORRESPONDENCE: Frederick A. DiBlasio, Ph.D., School of Social Work, University of Maryland at Baltimore, Baltimore, Maryland. Judith Harris Proctor, M.S.W., L.G.S.W., Virginia Theological Seminary, Alexandria, Virginia.

Enright, R.D., Santos, M.J., & Al-Mabuk, R. (1989)

THE ADOLESCENT AS FORGIVER

Journal of Adolescence, 12, 99–110

OBJECTIVE: To describe and empirically test a social cognitive developmental model of forgiveness.

DESIGN: Two cross-sectional surveys.

SETTING: Midwestern U.S.

PARTICIPANTS: Study 1: An age-stratified group of 59 persons was obtained, including a predominantly Catholic adult sample as well as members of parochial schools (grades 4, 7, and 10) and a parochial college. Most groups contained 6 males and 6 females.

Study 2: A similar age-stratified group of 60 persons was drawn, using 6 males and 6 females per group.

ASSESSMENT OF PREDICTOR VARIABLES: Participants' age groups were used as the predictor.

ASSESSMENT OF OUTCOME VARIABLES: For Studies 1 and 2, participants completed the following measures: (a) as a measure of reasoning about justice, the short form of Rest's (1974) Defining Issues Test (DIT), a measure of Kohlberg's moral development construct that requires participants to read and answer questions about moral dilemmas; (b) as a measure of reasoning about forgiveness, two revised dilemmas from the DIT followed by questions designed to tap each hypothesized stage of reasoning about forgiveness (1 through 6, with 6 being the most sophisticated stage of reasoning); and (c) a 10-item modification of the Religious Belief Scale (Allport, Gillespie, & Young, 1953) measuring religious conviction and participation. Fourth graders were not administered the justice or religious belief measures, both of which were designed for older persons.

MAIN RESULTS: Study 1 revealed a significant effect of age on forgiveness, with 4th, 7th, and 10th graders showing lower scores than college students and adults. The concepts of forgiveness and justice were found to be distinct but related, with forgiveness reasoning correlating positively with justice reasoning and religiosity. No gender differences were found on any of the measures. These results were essentially replicated in Study 2.

CONCLUSION: Two studies provided strong support for the notion that as people grow older they make more morally sophisticated judgments about forgiveness; in other words, people may pass through various "stages" in how they conceptualize forgiveness. Developmental advances in thinking about forgiveness appear to parallel those involved in justice-related thinking.

COMMENTARY: This study was the first, published empirical study dealing directly with the psychology of forgiveness. It provides good evidence that reasoning about forgiveness, changes in a similar fashion as does reasoning about justice. By using a Kohlbergian, moral development perspective, Enright and his colleagues linked research about forgiveness to a well-established psychological theory and research methodology. Nonetheless, moral development research would be greatly enriched by more intense examinations of how people's understandings of forgiveness change across the life span. Interestingly, the finding that religiousness was correlated with reasoning about forgiveness, suggests, as does Poloma and Gallup's (1991) study, that the relationship between religion and forgiveness might be an important area of future investigation.

CORRESPONDENCE: Robert D. Enright, Department of Educational Psychology, University of Wisconsin–Madison, Madison, Wisconsin.

Fagenson, E.A., & Cooper, J. (1987)

WHEN PUSH COMES TO POWER: A TEST OF POWER RESTORATION THEORY'S EXPLANATION FOR AGGRESSIVE CONFLICT ESCALATION

Basic and Applied Social Psychology, 8, 273–293

OBJECTIVE: To examine whether conflict escalation stems, in part, from a desire to restore one's personal power.

DESIGN: Laboratory experiment.

SETTING: College campus.

PARTICIPANTS: Forty-eight male undergraduates were paid for their participation.

MANIPULATED VARIABLES: Each participant was led to believe that he was one of three persons participating in a study of cognitive abilities. They were assigned to write a brief memo and were told that it would be evaluated by another participant ("Subject C") who had been assigned the role of "the appraiser"; the evaluation was actually standardized feedback. Participants were either antagonized (given an insulting review) or not antagonized (given an acceptable review). At this point, participants were led to believe that a second, unrelated role-play study would begin and that they would be randomly assigned to play various roles. (In actuality, all participants were placed into roles in which they would evaluate Subject C.) Participants were assigned to conditions of either relevant-power-enhancement (participant is president of the organization and, Subject C, his employee); zero-power-enhancement (no status hierarchy); or irrelevant-power-enhancement (participant is president of the organization and another participant, Subject B, his employee). Participants were then assigned the task of selecting a word game to give to the employee to perform. In the meantime, Subject C was said to be performing a different "creative association" task.

ASSESSMENT OF OUTCOME VARIABLES: Each participant evaluated the creative association assignment ostensibly done by Subject C in terms of creativity. He also rated Subject C on several semantic, differential personality scales (e.g., intelligent/dumb, interesting/dull).

MAIN RESULTS: Participants who had been antagonized were more derogatory toward Subject C than those who were not antagonized. On both dependent measures, the lowest level of derogation was shown by participants: (a) who were not antagonized or (b) who were antagonized but were subsequently given legitimate power over their antagonist. Participants who were antagonized but subsequently given power over a different person (not the antagonist) showed intermediate levels of derogation. The power-enhancement variable did not have an effect in the nonantagonized conditions.

CONCLUSION: Provoked students in this study appear less likely to retaliate if their personal power can be somehow restored. Although it appears most helpful to have one's power restored in reference to the antagonist, other forms of power restoration may also deter retaliation.

COMMENTARY: Like other studies included in this annotated bibliography (e.g., Brown, 1968), this study identifies an important motive that might govern people's decisions to retaliate against others who have harmed them: the motive to regain power that one perceives oneself to have lost through the offense. The restoration of victims' perceived power through elevating their status relative to their perpetrators appears to attenuate the tendency to retaliate. Without such elevations in power relative to one's perpetrator, victims appear to be more likely to retaliate. Thus, it appears that the motivation to retain power is an important one that must be understood to gain a more complete understanding of forgiveness and how it operates.

CORRESPONDENCE: Ellen A. Fagenson, Department of Management, School of Business Administration, George Mason University, Fairfax, Virginia.

Freedman, S.R., & Enright, R.D. (1996)

FORGIVENESS AS AN INTERVENTION GOAL
WITH INCEST SURVIVORS

Journal of Consulting and Clinical Psychology, 64, 983–992

OBJECTIVE: To assess the effectiveness of a forgiveness intervention program for improving mental health and well-being among female incest survivors.

DESIGN: Yoked, randomized, controlled experiment.

SETTING: A midwestern community.

PARTICIPANTS: Twelve adult women (average age 36 years; education 15 years) were recruited from the community through an advertisement. Participants were screened as follows: All reported a history of sexual abuse that involved physical contact by a male relative. All incidents of abuse had to occur more than 2 years before the screening, and participants had to report negative psychological effects. Persons reporting severe psychopathology (e.g., psychosis) or substance abuse were excluded.

ASSESSMENT OF PREDICTOR VARIABLES: Participants were randomly assigned into the experimental group or a wait-list control. Participants were matched as closely as possible on demographic and abuse history variables. The intervention consisted of one-on-one meetings with a graduate student therapist. A criterion-referenced format was used for planning treatment: Each participant's intervention ended after she had worked through all forgiveness topics. The average length of treatment was 14.3 months.

ASSESSMENT OF OUTCOME VARIABLES: At pretest and two posttests, participants completed: (a) the Psychological Profile of Forgiveness (Hebl & Enright, 1993), a 30-item measure of the degree to which one person has forgiven another; (b) the Hope Scale, a 30-item measure developed by Al-Mabuk, Enright, and Cardis (1995), to assess optimism about the future of one's relationship with another person; (c) the Spielberger State-Trait Anxiety Inventory (Spielberger et al., 1983); (d) the Beck Depression Inventory (Beck, Ward, Mendelson, Mock, and Erbaugh, 1961); (e) the Coopersmith Self-Esteem Inventory (Coopersmith, 1981); and (f) a Pseudo-Forgiveness Measure, consisting of five questions to assess whether the participant had truly forgiven.

MAIN RESULTS: Relative to the wait-list control, the experimental group reported significantly higher levels of forgiveness and hope, and lower levels of anxiety and depression. Members of the control group showed similar improvements once they were placed in the treatment group. Treatment gains persisted one year after the intervention.

CONCLUSION: Results of this study suggest that one-on-one, forgiveness-oriented interventions may constitute an effective treatment for incest survivors. Participants improved not only in forgiveness, but also in sub-jective well-being relative to a wait-list control group.

COMMENTARY: While other studies have evaluated the effects of group interventions for encouraging forgiveness, Freedman and Enright's study was the first intervention study evaluating the efficacy of an individual therapy intervention designed to encourage forgiveness. Also, Freed-man and Enright's study was the first study to evaluate whether thera-pies designed to encourage forgiveness, could be appropriate for address-ing one of the most severe and distressing interpersonal offenses that people encounter. These data provide important initial evidence that forgiveness does not lead to greater dysfunction among the victims of severe interpersonal hurts such as incest; in fact, it might actually facil-itate recovery from the psychological fallout associated with severe inter-personal trauma. Future studies might do well to compare the efficacy of Freedman and Enright's intervention to more traditional psy-chotherapeutic approaches, designed to help people recover from inter-personal victimization. Such comparisons between a forgiveness proto-col and more traditional protocols would help us to understand whether forgiveness is responsible for the therapeutic gains, or whether Freed-man and Enright's findings are the result of the common factors pre-sent in all effective psychotherapies.

CORRESPONDENCE: Suzanne R. Freedman, Department of Educational Psychology, University of Northern Iowa, Cedar Falls, Iowa.

Gonzales, M.H., Haugen, J.A., & Manning, D.J. (1994)

VICTIMS AS "NARRATIVE CRITICS":
FACTORS INFLUENCING REJOINDERS AND
EVALUATIVE RESPONSES TO OFFENDERS' ACCOUNTS

Personality and Social Psychology Bulletin, 20, 691–704

OBJECTIVE: To examine the effects of offender blameworthiness and accounts on the content and evaluative tone of victims' responses.

DESIGN: Scenario-based experiment.

SETTING: University of Minnesota.

PARTICIPANTS: A total of 235 undergraduate students (117 males, 118 females) were given extra course credit in introductory psychology for their participation.

MANIPULATED VARIABLES: Participants read questionnaires containing two hypothetical scenarios of a transgression by a friend: One focused on gossip overheard by a boss, while the other focused on the destruction of a computer disk. Participants were asked to imagine themselves in the role of the victim and to imagine the perpetrator as being of their same gender. As the first between-subjects variable, the scenarios included circumstances designed to reflect three levels of blameworthiness (accidental, negligent, and intentional). The second between-subjects variable was the type of account offered. After reading each scenario, participants were asked to imagine the offending friend offering an account from one of four categories: concessions, which imply acceptance of responsibility and often include apologies or requests for forgiveness; excuses, which deny full responsibility due to mitigating factors; justifications, which redefine the act to appear less blameworthy; and refusals, which includes denial of the offense or the perpetrator's role in it. Concessions and excuses are generally considered mitigating accounts; that is, they emphasize the face needs of the victim. Justifications and refusals are considered aggravating accounts; that is, they emphasize the face needs of the offender over those of the victim.

ASSESSMENT OF OUTCOME VARIABLES: After reading each scenario, participants were asked to write a response (or rejoinder) to the offender. Their responses were coded into five content categories based on Schonbach's (1990) taxonomy: (a) comments on the failure event, (b) comments on the account, (c) expressions of emotion, (d) comments on the offender's character, and (e) comments on the relationship between the victim and the offender. Coders also rated the affective tone of the responses on a 9-point Likert scale (1 = total acceptance/uniformly positive evaluation; 9 = total rejection/uniformly negative evaluation).

Participants also completed six rating scales, each on a 9-point Likert scale, to evaluate the interpersonal consequences of the offenders' transgressions and accounts. Items measured the degree of damage to the relationship and to the friend's image, the amount of anger toward the friend, the likelihood of forgiving the friend, and an overall evaluation of the explanation.

MAIN RESULTS: Across all three types of response measures, participants judged aggravating accounts (i.e., justifications and refusals) more harshly than mitigating accounts (i.e., concessions and excuses). However, analysis of the affective tone of responses revealed that participants evaluated intentional transgressions negatively, regardless of the type of account offered. Compared with intentional and negligent offenses, accidents yielded fewer negative comments on the perpetrators' conduct and on the consequences of the failure event. Sarcasm and negative evaluations were especially likely responses in the case of intentional offenses.

The data also suggested gender differences in responses to transgression. First, relative to men, women reported more negative effects of transgression (e.g., greater levels of anger, relationship damage, difficulty of forgiveness). Second, a significant interaction suggested the following: Men's rejoinders to accidents were more negative when they received aggravating as opposed to mitigating accounts. Women showed no such distinction between account type in the case of accidents. However, following negligent offenses, women's responses were more negative after refusals and more positive after concessions. Under conditions of negligence, men showed no distinction between account type. When transgressions were intentional, neither men's nor women's rejoinders were influenced by offender accounts; their responses were uniformly negative.

CONCLUSION: Victims' responses to perpetrators appear to depend on both the blameworthiness of the perpetrator and on the type of account offered. Increased blameworthiness of perpetrators is associated with more negative responses by victims. Similarly, aggravating accounts—in particular, outright refusals of one's responsibility—yield more negative responses than mitigating accounts. These data also raise the possibility of gender differences in responses to transgression.

COMMENTARY: This study elucidates some of the conditions under which various accounts for a perpetrator's behavior can influence the victim's response to the transgression. In general, mitigating accounts have important positive effects on victims' responses to unintentional (accidental and negligent) transgressions. In the case of intentional transgressions, however, these data suggest that the types of accounts used make little difference in how the victim responds to the perpetrator. In addition, these data suggest that women have more extreme responses to offenses of all kinds, regardless of whether the offense was accidental, negligent, or unintentional. These findings, when considered along with the findings of Hodgins, Liebeskind, and Enright (1996), suggest that men are less sensitive to interpersonal transgressions, both when they are victims and perpetrators: When they are victims, they seem to have less extreme negative responses than women, and when they are perpetrators, they respond with fewer mitigating accounts and less effort to repair the relationship. The differential sensitivity of men and women to interpersonal hurts might portend some important but heretofore unexplored gender differences in how forgiveness is construed and valued.

CORRESPONDENCE: Marti Hope Gonzales, Department of Psychology, Elliott Hall, University of Minnesota, Minneapolis, Minnesota.

Gonzales, M.H., Manning, D.J., & Haugen, J.A. (1992)

EXPLAINING OUR SINS: FACTORS INFLUENCING OFFENDER
ACCOUNTS AND ANTICIPATED VICTIM RESPONSES

Journal of Personality and Social Psychology, 62, 958–971

OBJECTIVE: To examine the effects of offender blameworthiness, consequence severity, and offender gender on accounts provided after a hypothetical predicament.

DESIGN: Two experiments using scenarios.

SETTING: University of Minnesota.

PARTICIPANTS: Participants were all undergraduates who were given extra course credit in introductory psychology. In Study 1, 90 students (45 males, 45 females) participated. In Study 2, 180 students (90 males, 90 females) participated.

MANIPULATED VARIABLES: Study 1: Participants read four hypothetical scenarios of transgression within a friendship and were asked to imagine themselves in the role of the offender. Two scenarios involved acts of omission, in which an offender failed to perform some positive action (while babysitting, failing to notice while a friend's child drinks cleaning fluid; failing to stop at a stop sign and getting into an accident). Two scenarios involved acts of commission, in which an offender performed a negative action (having sex with a friend's romantic partner; plagiarizing a friend's paper). Acts of commission were considered more blameworthy than acts of omission. Outcome severity (mild, moderate, or severe) was manipulated in a between-subjects fashion. Participant gender was also used as a predictor variable.

Study 2: Participants read three hypothetical scenarios of friendship transgression in which intent was varied (accidental, negligent, or intentional) as a within-subjects variable. Situations included failing to turn in a paper for a friend, destroying a friend's computer disk, and engaging in gossip about a friend, which is overheard by the friend's boss. Participant gender was again used as a predictor variable.

ASSESSMENT OF OUTCOME VARIABLES: Studies 1 and 2: After each scenario, the participant, imagining the self as the offender, was asked to give an account: "Your friend asks you to explain what happened. What do you say to him or her in this situation?" Raters coded these accounts for length and complexity and placed them into the categories of concessions, excuses, justifications, and refusals (cf. Schonbach, 1980). Participants also answered six questions on 9-point Likert scales regarding: (a) the degree of suffering likely to be caused in the relationship, (b) the extent to which one's image would suffer in the friend's eyes, (c) the extent to which the friend would hold the participant responsible, (d) the friend's level of anger, (e) the likelihood of forgiveness by the friend, and (f) the friend's overall evaluation of the explanation.

MAIN RESULTS: Study 1: Offenders expended more effort (i.e., gave longer and more complex accounts) after sins of commission than after sins of omission. Concessions were more frequent than excuses, which in turn were more frequent than justifications, which were more frequent than refusals. Women gave more complex accounts than did men, especially after blameworthy transgressions, which appeared to result from their use of more complex concessions. Participants expected more negative outcomes after sins of commission (versus omission) and after severe consequences (versus mild). Relative to men, women anticipated more negative outcomes from their transgressions.

Study 2: Concession was the most frequent strategy, as in Study 1. Women offered more concessions than did men, and their concessions were more complex. More concessions followed negligent acts than either accidental or intentional acts, suggesting a curvilinear relationship between blameworthiness and use of concessions. Accounts were more complex following accidental rather than negligent and intentional offenses; however, this effect seems due to the greater use of justifications and refusals in the accidental condition. Those committing intentional offenses told more lies than the other groups. Men also lied more than women. Participants expected the least negative outcomes following accidents, more negative outcomes following negligent acts, and the most negative outcomes following intentional acts.

CONCLUSION: People make greater use of concessions following sins of commission than sins of omission; however, there appears to be a curvilinear relationship between blameworthiness and accounts offered. People offer more concessions for negligent offenses than for accidental or intentional ones. In the case of intentional sins, offenders may be highly motivated to save face (as indicated by their higher rates of lying), whereas those who commit accidents may feel little need to explain themselves. Those who are negligent, however, appear particularly motivated to offer explanations and concessions. Women also tend to use more concessions and give more complex accounts than men, and they expect more negative outcomes from their transgressions.

COMMENTARY: This study distinguishes between sins of omission and sins of commission—and finds important differences in how people account for the two. People are more willing to "own up" to their sins of commission than to their sins of omission. Similar differences in how people account for accidental, negligent, and intentional sins were found as well. Based on these findings, we can expect that people would be more willing to seek forgiveness for sins of commission and for transgressions caused by negligence than those caused accidentally or intentionally. Also, the differences in the use of concessions by men and women might lead us to predict that women would be more likely to seek forgiveness after hurting other people, a tendency that might be related in part to womens' greater estimations of the harm caused by their transgressions.

CORRESPONDENCE: Marti Hope Gonzales, Department of Psychology, Elliott Hall, University of Minnesota, Minneapolis, Minnesota.

Gorsuch, R.L., & Hao, J.Y. (1993)

FORGIVENESS: AN EXPLORATORY FACTOR ANALYSIS AND ITS RELATIONSHIPS TO RELIGIOUS VARIABLES

Review of Religious Research, 34, 333–347

OBJECTIVES: (a) To examine whether forgiveness is best conceptualized as a unidimensional or multidimensional construct; (b) to examine the relationship between self-reported forgiveness and religious variables.

DESIGN: Cross-sectional survey.

SETTING: Part of 1988 Gallup poll on religious issues.

PARTICIPANTS: A nationwide random sample of 1,030 Gallup poll participants (513 males and 517 females) consisted of 80.5% white, 10.9% black, 6.6% Hispanic, and 2% other ethnic origin participants . Religious affiliations were 59.6% Protestant, 26.8% Roman Catholic, 2.6% Jewish, and 11% other.

ASSESSMENT OF PREDICTOR VARIABLES: Fifteen religious items were of interest for this study: self-identification items consisting of religious preference (Protestant, Catholic, Jewish, and no/other) and description of self as a "born again" or "evangelical Christian." Single-item measures assessed items such as the importance of religion in one's life, membership and attendance at church/synagogue, and intrinsic/extrinsic religious motivations. Factor analysis of the single-item measures suggested two factors: personal religiousness and religious conformity.

ASSESSMENT OF OUTCOME VARIABLES: Four forgiveness-related questions assessed: (a) participants' usual responses to deliberate offenses, (b) their reasons for their responses, (c) their reasons for not forgiving, and (d) their responses in situations in which they committed the offense. For each question, participants were given multiple-response options and could check as many as applied. Exploratory factor analysis was performed on the 25 response options.

MAIN RESULTS: In addition to a higher-order forgiveness factor, four correlated forgiveness factors emerged: forgiving motive (measuring an underlying motive facilitating forgiveness); religious response (measuring religious coping behaviors such as prayer); forgiving pro-action (measuring movement toward the other person); and hostility (measuring responses such as resentment, revenge, and self-justification). Considered as a set, these four factors contributed significantly to prediction of the religious variables even after the effects of the higher-order forgiveness factor were taken into account. Protestants were found to endorse significantly more religious responses than Catholics. Catholics, in turn, endorsed significantly more religious responses than Jews and participants with no/other religion. Protestants endorsed more proactive forgiving than those of no/other religious preference, while evangelical Christians endorsed significantly higher levels of each forgiveness factor compared with other groups. Personal religiousness was negatively correlated with hostility and positively correlated with the remaining three forgiveness factors.

CONCLUSION: Although there does appear to be a general factor representing forgiveness, the concept may be better explained using a multidimensional model. Religious variables appear to have some utility in predicting forgiveness-oriented responses, with evangelical Christians and those high in personal religiousness endorsing the highest levels of forgiving responses.

COMMENTARY: Gorsuch and Hao base their study on a representative sample of American adults, giving us unique insight into how the American population views the concept of forgiving. This study raises provocative questions about how religious groups—and religious involvement in general—instill values about forgiveness. These data suggest that Americans' attitudes about forgiving are strongly related to elements of their religious lives, and that religions might do much to impart values about forgiving. At best, however, Gorsuch and Hao's findings reveal only what people think and believe about forgiving; they do not reveal that religious involvement actually influences the extent to which people are willing to forgive others in ongoing relationships. The relationship between personal religiousness, spirituality, and forgiveness remains to be investigated more fully through more in-depth measurement of people's thoughts, feelings, and behaviors toward people who have actually hurt them in the past. Attention should be given as well to biases such as social desirability that might lead religious respondents to report that they are actually more "forgiving" than they actually appear to be when less obtrusive means of data collection are used.

Haley, W.E., & Strickland, B.R. (1986)

INTERPERSONAL BETRAYAL AND COOPERATION: EFFECTS ON SELF-EVALUATION IN DEPRESSION

Journal of Personality and Social Psychology, 50, 386–391

OBJECTIVE: To determine whether depressed persons respond differently to interpersonal betrayal than nondepressed persons.

DESIGN: Laboratory experiment.

SETTING: University of Massachusetts.

PARTICIPANTS: Fifty-four female undergraduates received course credit for participation. Approximately 2 weeks before the start of the experiment, a sample of 199 females had completed a modified version of the Zung Self-Rating Depression Scale (Zung, 1965). Participants for this study were taken from the top and bottom quartiles of the distribution on the Zung Scale.

ASSESSMENT OF PREDICTOR VARIABLES: Depressed participants (those scoring in the top quartile) were compared with those who were not depressed (those scoring in the bottom quartile). In addition, each participant was paired with a confederate and was randomly assigned to either a betrayal condition (the confederate promised to cooperate in the Prisoner's Dilemma Task but instead played competitively) or a positive interaction condition (the confederate provided a useful hint in a puzzle-solving task).

ASSESSMENT OF OUTCOME VARIABLES: After the experimental manipulation, participants completed the Multiple Affect Adjective Check List (MAACL; Zuckerman & Lubin, 1965) as a measure of mood. Participants were then asked to work on an individual problem-solving task (block design from the Wechsler Adult Intelligence Scale; Wechsler, 1955). They were subsequently given a pile of colored chips and asked to evaluate their own performance by adding or subtracting up to 10 chips from their pile. A second MAACL was then administered, as was a personality checklist based on the Gough Adjective Checklist (Gough, 1952).

MAIN RESULTS: Data from the MAACL suggested that participants in the betrayal condition were subsequently in worse moods than those in the positive interaction condition; however, this effect had faded by the time of the second MAACL. No significant interactions with depression were noted. However, within the betrayal condition, depressed participants were more likely to be maximally competitive than those who were not depressed. Although the depressed participants were more self-critical than nondepressed participants on the personality checklist, the effects of betrayal were apparent on the behavioral self-criticism measure (chip allocation): According to this measure, depressed participants who had been betrayed were more self-critical than those in the other three groups (that is, they were more likely to remove chips from their allocated pile of chips).

CONCLUSION: At least among women, depression is related to responses to interpersonal betrayal. Relative to those who are not depressed, depressed women appear more likely to retaliate against those who have betrayed them. In addition, according to behavioral measures of self-criticism, the greater self-criticism of depressed women may emerge primarily under negative interpersonal conditions such as betrayal.

COMMENTARY: This study is one of very few studies examining how interpersonal offenses (in this case, betrayals) influence both the victims' behavior toward perpetrators and victims' appraisals of themselves. Depressed women appear more likely to retaliate against their perpetrators than those who are not depressed. Also, women who are depressed appear unable to avoid deflations in their appraisals of their own actions after they have been betrayed by perpetrators. These results have important implications for understanding forgiveness, and converge nicely with psychometric investigations (e.g., Mauger et al., 1992; Subkoviak et al., 1995) showing that people who are depressed actually score lower on standardized measures of forgiveness (both forgiveness of self and forgiveness of other people).

CORRESPONDENCE: William E. Haley, Department of Psychology, University of Alabama at Birmingham, Birmingham, Alabama.

....

Hargrave, T.D., & Sells, J.N. (1997)

THE DEVELOPMENT OF A FORGIVENESS SCALE

Journal of Marital and Family Therapy, 23, 41–62.

....

OBJECTIVE: To test the validity and reliability of the Interpersonal Relationship Resolution Scale (IRRS), a self-report measure of forgiveness.

DESIGN: Three cross-sectional administrations of the IRRS instrument, as part of a five-stage scale development procedure. Study 1: Factor analysis and internal consistency analysis. Study 2: Concurrent validity. Study 3: Predictive validity.

SETTING: College campus.

PARTICIPANTS: Study 1: 164 persons (118 females, 46 males) recruited from graduate and undergraduate psychology, and counseling classes and various occupational sites. Age range: 19 to 77 years, average = 31.9

years. Ethnicity: 81.7% white, 7.9% Hispanic, 6.7% Asian, 3.7% black. Marital status: 42.8% married, 41.5% never married, 12.3% divorced, 3% remarried, 0.4% widowed.

Study 2: 35 volunteers participated. Age range: 19 to 55 years, average = 25 years. Ethnicity: 46.7% white, 20% Hispanic, 17.15% Asian, 17.15% black. Marital status: 37.15% married, 34.29% never married, 11.43% divorced, 14.28% remarried, 2.85% widowed.

Study 3: 98 volunteers participated, of which 35 represented a clinical group recruited from therapy situations. Age range: 19 to 61 years, average = 28 years. Ethnicity: 68.7% white, 15.2% Hispanic, 13.1% Asian, 3.0% black. Marital status: 47.4% married, 30.9% never married, 7.2% divorced, 14.4% remarried, 1.1% widowed.

ASSESSMENT OF PREDICTOR VARIABLES: In Study 1, factor analysis and internal consistency analysis were performed on the 162-item preliminary IRRS to determine which items would be retained. In Studies 2 and 3, the 44-item IRRS was administered. Cronbach's alpha for Forgiveness Scale: .92. Pain Scale: .95.

ASSESSMENT OF OUTCOME VARIABLES: In Study 2, participants completed: (a) the Personal Authority in the Family System Questionnaire (Bray, Williamson, & Malone, 1984a, 1984b), a 132-item measure of eight family systems constructs; (b) the Relational Ethics Scale (Hargrave, Jennings, & Anderson, 1991), a 24-item measure of trust, justice, loyalty, and entitlement within relationships; (c) the Fundamental Interpersonal Relations Orientation-Behavior Scale (Shutz, 1958), a 54-item measure of expressed and wanted inclusion, control, and affection; and (d) the Burns Depression Checklist (Burns, 1994), a 15-item measure of depressive symptoms.

MAIN RESULTS: In Study 1, 44 of the 162 true/false items were selected for inclusion in the final scale. From the two main scales, Forgiveness and Pain, eight subscales were created (for Forgiveness—Insight, Understanding, Giving the Opportunity for Compensation, and Overt Act of Forgiving; for Pain—Shame, Rage, Control, and Chaos). The Forgiveness and Pain Scales were not significantly correlated.

Study 2 showed acceptable concurrent validity of the IRRS, as demonstrated by its relations with various measures of family/relationship functioning and depressive symptoms.

In Study 3, a clinical sample was shown to have lower scores than a nonclinical sample on Forgiveness, and higher scores on Pain. In general, people reporting greater forgiveness for specific offenders, reported good boundary-setting within the family as well as a lack of intergenerational intimidation and violation. People reporting greater pain regarding a specific relational injury, reported more intergenerational intimidation, greater triangulation between parents, and low levels of justice and trust in family relationships.

CONCLUSION: The IRRS was demonstrated to have acceptable levels of internal consistency, concurrent validity, and predictive validity. It appears to serve as a good measure of Hargrave's theoretical model (1994a).

COMMENTARY: This measure of forgiveness, based on the family therapy theorizing of Boszormenyi-Nagy and Hargrave, was designed to operationalize a variety of constructs that have been traditionally considered to be conceptually related to forgiveness, although not necessarily part of forgiveness *per se*. Hargrave and Sells' focus on constructs, such as giving opportunities for compensation and the overt act of forgiving, make the measure potentially quite useful for understanding how forgiveness might unfold; and lead to relational repair in the context of family relationships, and other close relationships, that have been damaged by interpersonal transgressions. The Pain Scales (Shame, Rage, Control, and Chaos) might also prove useful for examining whether, and the extent to which, interpersonal injuries continue to exert negative effects within individuals and their families.

CORRESPONDENCE: Terry D. Hargrave, Ph.D., Associate Professor of Behavioral Studies, Amarillo College, Amarillo, Texas. James N. Sells, Ph.D., Assistant Professor of Counseling, West Texas A & M University, Canyon, Texas.

Hebl, J.H., & Enright, R.D. (1993)

FORGIVENESS AS A PSYCHOTHERAPEUTIC GOAL
WITH ELDERLY FEMALES

Psychotherapy, 30, 658–667

OBJECTIVE: To examine the efficacy of a group-based forgiveness intervention with elderly females.

DESIGN: Controlled, randomized experiment.

SETTING: Christian church community in middle-class area of midsize midwestern city.

PARTICIPANTS: Twenty-four females with a mean age of 74.5 years; all were over age 65. Letters of invitation were sent to 204 persons in the community. Respondents were selected for the study if they reported a specific, painful forgiveness issue and were not currently grieving over a major loss.

ASSESSMENT OF PREDICTOR VARIABLES: Participants were randomly assigned to the experimental group (the group forgiveness intervention) or to a control group (a discussion group focusing on topics generated by its members). Both groups were held for 1 hour per week for 8 weeks.

ASSESSMENT OF OUTCOME VARIABLES: At pretest, participants completed: (a) the Spielberger State-Trait Anxiety Inventory (Spielberger et al., 1983), (b) the Beck Depression Inventory (Beck et al., 1961), and (c) the Coopersmith Self-Esteem Inventory (Coopersmith, 1981). At posttest, each of these measures was administered again, with the addition of the following measures: (a) the Psychological Profile of Forgiveness, a 30-item scale that measures the degree to which one person has forgiven an offender, and (b) the Willingness-to-Forgive Scale, a 16-item measure of willingness to choose forgiveness as a problem-solving strategy.

MAIN RESULTS: The Psychological Profile of Forgiveness Scale demonstrated good internal consistency and validity. Results from the Psychological Profile of Forgiveness and Willingness-to-Forgive Scales favored the experimental group. However, no significant differences in anxiety and depression emerged between the groups; instead, both groups had decreased anxiety and depression. Across the entire sample, the Psychological Profile of Forgiveness was positively correlated with self-esteem, and negatively correlated with anxiety and depression at posttest.

CONCLUSION: Both the experimental and control groups appear to have been therapeutic for participants. However, the experimental group appears to have met its goal of increasing forgiveness in its participants. Forgiveness, in turn, was associated with greater mental health within the entire sample.

COMMENTARY: This study was the first published study designed to investigate the efficacy of a protocol designed to encourage a specific sample of people to forgive someone who had hurt them in the past. It should be recognized that the publication of this piece in a mainstream journal such as *Psychotherapy*, was a major achievement in introducing the health and social sciences to the concept of forgiving. Also, these data suggested that a protocol designed to help people forgive might also be beneficial in reducing psychological symptoms. Because the alternative-treatment condition also facilitated reductions in anxiety and depression, it would be premature to conclude that "forgiving makes people less depressed and anxious"; nonetheless, these data do suggest that such interventions might lead to important psychological benefits that are quite distinct from their effects in helping people to forgive those who have injured them.

Hodgins, H.S., Liebeskind, E., & Schwartz, W. (1996)

GETTING OUT OF HOT WATER: FACEWORK IN SOCIAL PREDICAMENTS

Journal of Personality and Social Psychology, 71, 300–314

OBJECTIVE: To examine perpetrator accounts of face-threatening predicaments and whether such accounts vary according to: (a) the perpetrator's motivational orientation, (b) the status of the victim, (c) relationship closeness, and (d) the blameworthiness of the perpetrator.

DESIGN: Experiment using written scenarios.

SETTING: Skidmore College in New York State.

PARTICIPANTS: Ninety-six undergraduates (48 women, 48 men) enrolled in various psychology classes.

MANIPULATED VARIABLES: All participants received a questionnaire including four scenarios of transgression. Participants were instructed to take the role of the perpetrator. The following variables were experimentally manipulated: As a between-subjects variable, the level of blameworthiness of the perpetrator was varied (low, moderate, or high); as a within-subjects variable, victim status (low versus high) and relationship closeness (low versus high) were varied.

ASSESSMENT OF ADDITIONAL PREDICTOR VARIABLES: Gender was used as a predictor variable. Participants also completed a 17-vignette version of the General Causality Orientation Scale (GCOS) (Deci & Ryan, 1985), which assesses motivational orientation. (Motivational orientation refers to a person's tendency to either initiate action or to perceive events as initiating from someplace outside the self.) The GCOS assesses three types of motivational orientation: autonomous (initiating behavior from choices based on awareness of one's own needs, feelings, and goals); control-oriented (seeking out external controls; experiencing events as pressures that determine behavior and feelings); and impersonal (experiencing desired outcomes as unattainable; displaying little sense of intentionality). Relative to control orientation, autonomous orientation is usually associated with lower levels of interpersonal defensiveness. Participants were categorized into one of the three orientations based on their scores.

Assessment of Outcome Variables: After reading each scenario, participants were asked to provide an account by answering the question: "What do you say to the other person in this situation?" Responses were rated by two judges according to the number of mitigating elements (concessions and excuses), which primarily help the victim save face, and aggravating elements (justifications and refusals), which primarily help the perpetrator save face. Accounts were also coded by length, complexity, and the number of lies used. Lengthy, complex accounts using few lies are generally considered less defensive (or more mitigating) than short, simple accounts or those using lies.

Participants answered two questions about the role of obtaining forgiveness on their situational self-esteem: "How will you feel about yourself if the person forgives/does *not* forgive you?" They also answered five questions about their future relationship with the victim (how much the relationship would suffer, how much the perpetrator's image would suffer, how responsible the victim would consider the perpetrator, how angry the victim would be, and how likely the victim would be to forgive). Participants answers were rated on 9-point scales.

Main Results: Overall, participants gave more mitigating than aggravating accounts; mitigating accounts were given more frequently: (a) by autonomous participants (relative to those with control-oriented or impersonal styles); (b) to a higher-status person; (c) to friends—except under conditions of high blame; and (d) by women. Relative to low- and moderate-blame participants, high-blame participants: (a) gave shorter, less complex accounts; (b) used more lies; and (c) used a greater proportion of aggravating strategies. These results occurred even though the high-blame participants appeared aware that their offense would harm the relationship. In general, perpetrators expected to feel better about themselves if they were forgiven than if they were not; however, being unforgiven appeared to be especially deflating for women in conflicts with friends.

CONCLUSION: The likelihood of receiving a mitigating account from a perpetrator appears to depend on: (a) who the perpetrator is (females and those with autonomous orientations are more likely); (b) the relative status of the victim (high-status victims are more likely); (c) the relationship between the parties (friends are more likely than acquaintances); and (d) the blameworthiness of the perpetrator (those with low or moderate blameworthiness are more likely than those with high levels of blameworthiness). When perpetrators feel highly blameworthy, they may put more energy into defensive, face-saving actions and less energy into actions that would preserve the relationship. Finally, although people appear to feel better about themselves if forgiven, these results may be especially pronounced for women in close relationships.

COMMENTARY: This study differs from most studies reviewed in this bibliography in that it takes the perspective of the perpetrator and attempts to elucidate the variables that lead to concessions and excuses (accounts that promote relational repair). Interestingly, it appears that relationship closeness, gender, and power—three relatively understudied variables in the forgiveness literature—might be important variables to appraise in future studies. In addition, these results suggest that at high levels of offense severity perpetrators are less likely to offer concessions or excuses, probably because admissions of guilt for such serious offenses are, from a social-psychological perspective, extremely costly and involve an enormous loss of face. Finally, the results suggest that actually receiving forgiveness is important for restoring perpetrators' self-esteem following concessions and excuses. As concessions and excuses come at a great loss of face, actually receiving forgiveness from victims appears to be an important variable leading to the restoration of face for perpetrators who offer frank, mitigating accounts for their negative actions.

CORRESPONDENCE: Holley S. Hodgins, Department of Psychology, Skidmore College, Saratoga Springs, New York.

Holbrook, M.I., White, M.H., & Hutt, M.J. (1995)

THE VENGEANCE SCALE: COMPARISON OF GROUPS
AND AN ASSESSMENT OF EXTERNAL VALIDITY

Psychological Reports, 77, 224–226

OBJECTIVE: To examine the validity of the Vengeance Scale (Stuckless & Goranson, 1992).

DESIGN: Cross-sectional survey.

SETTING: Three sites in Maine: The University of Southern Maine, the Windham Correctional Center, and the Brunswick Police Department.

PARTICIPANTS: Group 1 consisted of 68 undergraduates (20 males, 48 females) who received extra credit in an introductory psychology course for participating. Group 2 consisted of 45 inmates (37 males, 5 females, 3 unreported) who participated voluntarily. Group 3 consisted of 13 police officers (10 males, 3 females) who participated voluntarily.

ASSESSMENT OF PREDICTOR VARIABLES: The three groups of participants (students, inmates, and police officers) were compared.

ASSESSMENT OF OUTCOME VARIABLES: Participants completed the Vengeance Scale (Stuckless & Goranson, 1992), a 20-item measure of attitudes toward revenge.

MAIN RESULTS: Main effects of both gender and participant groups were found. Inmates scored higher on the Vengeance Scale than police officers or students, suggesting that the inmates held more favorable attitudes toward revenge. However, the higher scores of inmates appear attributable to the elevated scores of men in the inmate group; investigation of means suggests that female inmates were no more likely than female students or police officers to have high vengeance scores. Across all groups, males scored higher than females, a result that was also found in the original study (Stuckless & Goranson, 1992).

CONCLUSION: In addition to providing support for the external validity of the Vengeance Scale, this study suggests a positive link between attitudes toward revenge and criminal behavior, at least among males. Results also replicated Stuckless and Goranson's original (1992) finding of more positive attitudes toward revenge in males.

COMMENTARY: Stuckless and Goranson (1992) found that people who had favorable attitudes toward revenge reported more aggressive and vengeful behavior than people with less favorable attitudes toward revenge. The Holbrook, White, and Hutt (1995) study used the known-groups method of construct validation to marshal additional evidence about the validity of the Vengeance Scale. Their results suggest that criminality might be related, at least in males, to the attitudes one holds about revenge. This insight might have some important applications for examinations of criminality in the future, and the positive roles that forgiveness might play in reducing violent, vengeful responses to perceived transgressions.

CORRESPONDENCE: M.I. Holbrook, Department of Psychology, Auburn University at Montgomery, Montgomery, Alabama.

Komorita, S.S., Hilty, J.A., & Parks, C.D. (1991)

RECIPROCITY AND COOPERATION IN SOCIAL DILEMMAS

Journal of Conflict Resolution, 35, 494–518

OBJECTIVE: To examine the effects of delayed reciprocity in the Prisoner's Dilemma Game (PDG)—a tool used to simulate conflict situations in the laboratory.

DESIGN: Two laboratory experiments.

SETTING: College campus.

PARTICIPANTS: Participants for both studies were males from under-graduate psychology courses, all of whom received course credit for participation. Study 1 had a sample size of 96, and Study 2 had a sample size of 64.

MANIPULATED VARIABLES: Study 1: In the PDG, two participants are repeatedly faced with the decision to choose a cooperative or a competitive strategy. Participants win a moderate number of points if they both cooperate. If one defects while the other cooperates, the defector wins a large sum while the cooperator receives nothing. If both defect, both win a small sum. In both studies, participants were led to believe that they would be competing against another person in the PDG; in actuality they were playing against a preprogrammed strategy. They were told that the aim was to maximize one's own points and that prizes would be awarded based on points earned.

The program was designed to start the game with a cooperative move and to immediately reciprocate any repeated choice by the participant. Two variables were manipulated, each dealing with the program's response to changes in participants' choices: (a) the immediacy with which the program would retaliate by reciprocating the participant's change from a cooperative to a defective choice (immediate versus delayed by 1 trial); and (b) the immediacy of forgiving by reciprocating the participant's change from a defective to a cooperative choice (immediate versus delayed by 1 trial). Thirty-six trials were performed and were broken into three blocks of 12 trials.

Study 2: The same immediacy manipulations as in Study 1 were used within the context of a highly similar paradigm, a "public goods paradigm" in which participants choose to invest goods in either a personal account (competitive) or a joint account (cooperative). The payoffs and strategies are essentially the same as for the PDG.

ASSESSMENT OF OUTCOME VARIABLES: Study 1: Choices (cooperative versus competitive) made in the PDG were analyzed. In addition, before their own choice on each trial, participants were asked to predict the choice of the other player on a 5-point scale (where 1 = very likely to defect and 5 = very likely to cooperate).

Study 2: Choices made by participants were analyzed using an equivalent procedure to that used in the PDG.

MAIN RESULTS: Study 1: Relative to delayed reciprocity, immediate reciprocity of a switch from competition to cooperation led to more cooperation by participants. Participants were most accurate in predicting the behavior of the "toughest" opponent, the condition representing the player that was slow to forgive and quick to retaliate.

Study 2: Again, relative to delayed reciprocity, immediate reciprocity of a competitive-to-cooperative switch promoted greater cooperation by participants. This tendency became stronger over trials: Those who had to wait for cooperation showed less cooperation over time, while those who received immediate cooperation showed more cooperation over time.

CONCLUSION: These findings highlight the importance of immediate cooperation for inducing forgiveness in others. People are more likely to respond in forgiving ways if their attempts at cooperation are immediately reciprocated. In terms of facilitating cooperation, having a clear understanding of another person's strategy may not be as important as receiving immediate cooperation from the other person.

COMMENTARY: Many of the studies in this annotated bibliography point to the severe limits on people's abilities to process information and make valid inferences about their offenders after interpersonal transgressions occur. Similarly, these two studies also show that people have a difficult time detecting transgressors' desires to return to cooperative relationships, unless victims' returns to cooperative behavior are immediately reciprocated by cooperative behavior by the transgressor. The major implication of this finding is that in close relationships (e.g., marriages, family relationships, friendships) where mutual hurts have occurred, it is in both relational partners' best interests to return to cooperative behavior and to forgive the transgressions of one's partner as quickly as possible. Moreover, as soon as one's partner returns to cooperative behavior, one should reciprocate that cooperative behavior.

CORRESPONDENCE: S.S. Komorita, Department of Psychology, University of Illinois at Urbana–Champaign, Champaign, Illinois.

Kremer, J.F., & Stephens, L. (1983)

ATTRIBUTIONS AND AROUSAL AS MEDIATORS OF MITIGATION'S EFFECT ON RETALIATION

Journal of Personality and Social Psychology, 45, 335–343

OBJECTIVE: To examine whether the timing of mitigating information affects subsequent retaliation by a victim.

DESIGN: Laboratory experiment.

SETTING: A university in the midwestern U.S.

PARTICIPANTS: Forty males were recruited from introductory classes and were given extra credit ($n = 32$) or money ($n = 8$) for participation.

MANIPULATED VARIABLES: All participants met with a "polite" male experimenter and submitted to a blood pressure recording before engaging in a bogus perception task using slides. They were asked to sit still for the recording. After a second reading was taken, a "rude" male experimenter entered the room, examined the data, and provoked the participant: "Can't you sit still for just a few minutes?" The polite experimenter then returned.

At this point, the procedure diverged depending on the experimental condition. Participants were randomly assigned to one of four conditions: (a) provocation only (PO) (the polite experimenter took another blood pressure reading, then left); (b) early mitigation (EM) (the polite experimenter told the participant that the rude experimenter was very worried about a midterm exam); (c) early mitigation with additional provocation (EMP) (same as condition [b] except that the rude exper-

imenter subsequently returned and verbally attacked the polite experimenter); and (d) late mitigation (LM) (the polite experimenter took
another blood pressure reading and left; he returned later, after a second
slide-rating task had been completed, and mentioned the rude experimenter's worry over the exam).

ASSESSMENT OF OUTCOME VARIABLES: After completing the procedure
described above, participants completed a questionnaire. First, they rated
the politeness of each experimenter to provide a manipulation check.
To measure retaliation, participants were asked if the laboratory should
continue to fund each experimenter next year (where 1 = give funds
to a new person, 7 = give funds to this person). Physiological measures
(heart rate and blood pressure) were also taken periodically, and attributions about the experimenter's behavior were assessed. (These questions were raised at the end of the study because of the high likelihood
of raising suspicion.)

MAIN RESULTS: Men who heard the early mitigation (EM) retaliated less
than those who did not receive any information (PO). However, those
who heard mitigating information later (LM) or who met with additional provocation (EMP) retaliated almost as much as those in the PO
condition. Multiple regression analyses demonstrated that these effects
could not be attributed to differences in physiological arousal. Finally,
the EM group was also more likely than the other groups to attribute
the rude experimenter's behavior to external causes.

CONCLUSION: To be effective in preventing retaliation, information about
mitigating circumstances: (a) should be communicated as early as possible and (b) should not be followed by another offense.

COMMENTARY: Strong norms of politeness govern people's role-based
interactions. This study shows that when such norms are broken, retaliation often does occur. Men who perceive themselves to have been
treated rudely in the course of a role-based interaction, are likely to curb
their tendency to retaliate when they receive information that helps
them to view their transgressors in a more generous and forgiving light.

However, equal amounts of information can have very different mitigating effects depending on the conditions under which the information is provided to victims. Mitigating information should be offered as early as possible in order to curb victims' tendencies to retaliate. These findings, along with the finding that additional provocation also exacerbates victims' tendencies to retaliate, suggest the presence of an upper bound on people's abilities to process mitigating information when they are in the aftermath of an interpersonal offense.

CORRESPONDENCE: John F. Kremer, Psychology Department, Indiana University-Purdue University at Indianapolis, Indianapolis, Indiana.

Mauger, P.A., Perry, J.E., Freeman, T., Grove, D.C., McBride, A.G., & McKinney, K.E. (1992)

THE MEASUREMENT OF FORGIVENESS: PRELIMINARY RESEARCH

Journal of Psychology and Christianity, 11, 170–180

OBJECTIVE: To develop and validate two self-report measures of dispositional forgiveness: Forgiveness of Others (FOO) and Forgiveness of Self (FOS). FOO ostensibly measures respondents' self-reported tendency or capacity to forgive people who hurt them, whereas FOS ostensibly measures respondents' tendency or capacity to forgive themselves.

DESIGN: Cross-sectional survey.

SETTING: Outpatient Christian counseling centers in Georgia.

PARTICIPANTS: Two hundred thirty-seven persons receiving outpatient Christian counseling services.

ASSESSMENT OF PREDICTOR VARIABLES: The FOO and FOS Scales were completed by participants. Each scale has 15 items. These measures were included as subscales of a larger personality inventory, the Behavioral Assessment System (BAS), which was completed by participants. Using a separate sample, both scales demonstrated adequate internal consistency (Cronbach's alpha = .79 for FOO; .82 for FOS) and test–retest reliability (.94 for FOO, .67 for FOS).

ASSESSMENT OF OUTCOME VARIABLES: Counselors rated a subset of 46 clients on a 132-item rating scale designed to measure a wide range of psychologically relevant behavior. The Minnesota Multiphasic Personality Inventory (MMPI) was also utilized.

MAIN RESULTS: The correlation between the FOO and FOS Scales was .37. FOO was shown to be related to the BAS Scale, Alienation from Others (e.g., negative attitudes toward others, cynicism, passive-aggressive behavior), while FOS was more closely related to Neurotic Immaturity (e.g., negative self-image, deficits in self-control and motivation). Counselor ratings of client behavior yielded findings mirroring these self-report data. Problems with both types of forgiveness were associated with psychopathology as measured by the MMPI; however, symptoms such as depression, anxiety, and low self-esteem were more closely linked with FOS scores than with FOO scores.

CONCLUSION: The FOO and FOS Scales, both of which have adequate psychometric properties, appear to measure two related but conceptually distinct constructs. Problems related to forgiving others appear to be "extrapunitive"; that is, they are focused on punishing others. In contrast, problems with forgiving the self are more "intropunitive"; that is, they deal with a tendency to turn punishment on the self.

COMMENTARY: This article is unique among approaches to the measurement of forgiveness in two ways. First, Mauger and his colleagues attempt to measure forgiveness at a dispositional level (i.e., as a trait or global interpersonal tendency) rather than as a response to an isolated interpersonal offense. Second, Mauger and his colleagues have also attempted to measure forgiveness for oneself. While the concept of self-forgiveness is discussed in some conceptual articles, only Mauger has tried to develop a sound psychometric instrument for assessing this construct. Forgiveness of Self and Forgiveness of Others, as measured with Mauger's Scales, appear to be related cross-sectionally to a variety of important mental health variables. Future research should establish whether these relationships hold up in longitudinal and clinical studies. Also, future studies would do well to differentiate these constructs from related constructs such as anger, hostility, guilt, and shame. To the extent that Mauger's Scales do measure unique constructs, they may be important tools for advancing our understanding of forgiveness as an aspect of the healthy personality.

CORRESPONDENCE: Paul A. Mauger, Ph.D., The Psychological Studies Institute, Atlanta, Georgia.

McCullough, M.E., & Worthington, E.L., Jr. (1995)

PROMOTING FORGIVENESS: A COMPARISON OF TWO BRIEF PSYCHOEDUCATIONAL GROUP INTERVENTIONS WITH A WAIT-LIST CONTROL

Counseling and Values, 40, 55–68

OBJECTIVE: To test the effectiveness of two brief, group-based, psychoeducational forgiveness interventions, one using a self-enhancement rationale and one using an interpersonal rationale.

DESIGN: Controlled field experiment.

SETTING: A university in the southeastern U.S.

PARTICIPANTS: Eighty-six students from psychology classes received course credit for participating. Gender: 76% female, 24% male. Ethnicity: 21% black, 72% white, 7% other. Average age: 22 years. Participants were eligible if they had incurred an interpersonal hurt that they had wanted, but were unable, to forgive. Those having suffered very severe offenses such as abuse and incest were not included in this study.

INTERVENTION: Participants were randomly assigned to one of three conditions: a wait-list control or one of two forgiveness intervention groups. Each forgiveness intervention consisted of an hour-long structured group ($n = 7$ to 14 per group). Groups were led by two male students from an American Psychological Association–approved doctoral program in counseling psychology. Both interventions included didactic material, individual exercises, and discussion, and both helped participants generate empathy, reframe their own victimization experiences, and distinguish between forgiveness and reconciliation. The only difference between the interventions was the rationale given for the importance of forgiveness: The Self-Enhancement group emphasized benefits for the self, whereas the Interpersonal group emphasized benefits for relationships.

ASSESSMENT OF OUTCOME VARIABLES: In addition to providing demographic information and answering basic questions about the offense, participants completed the Wade Forgiveness Scale (Wade, 1989), an 83-item scale measuring forgiveness of an offender. The scale contains nine subscales: Revenge, Freedom from Obsession, Affirmation, Victimization, Feelings, Avoidance, Toward God, Conciliation, and Holding a Grudge. This measure was completed three times: before intervention, after intervention, and at a 6-week follow-up.

MAIN RESULTS: Relative to the control group, persons who had participated in one of the interventions reported less desire for revenge, more positive feelings toward the offender, and more desire for reconciliation than the control group participants. However, some differences emerged between the two intervention groups: Relative to the Interpersonal group, the Self-Enhancement group reported reduced feelings of revenge, increased affirming thoughts about the offense, and more conciliatory thoughts and behaviors. Scores on five subscales (Freedom from Obsession, Victimization, Avoidance, Toward God, and Holding a

Grudge) did not appear to be affected by either intervention; however, this may have occurred in part because the entire sample improved on some of these variables over time (Victimization, Holding a Grudge, and Freedom from Obsession).

CONCLUSION: Brief psychoeducational forgiveness interventions can lead to increases in various aspects of forgiveness, and these improvements can be maintained over time. People may also be more responsive to interventions that initially focus on benefits for the self, rather than relationship benefits, as a rationale for forgiveness.

COMMENTARY: This study, which employed two very weak (i.e., one-hour) psychoeducational treatments, sought to examine whether minimal psychoeducational training could be helpful in encouraging forgiveness. Given how short these interventions were (in comparison to typical group psychoeducational interventions, which typically last from 8 to 50 sessions), it was indeed surprising that the forgiveness interventions had detectable effects on participants' self-reports of forgiveness. The efficacy of such interventions might be improved by focusing treatment on the issues specific to more homogeneous populations, as others (e.g., Freedman & Enright, 1996; Coyle & Enright, 1997) have done so cleverly. Finally, these results are instructive because they point out that people can be motivated to forgive for many reasons, and not all rationales are equally effective. It seems especially important to provide a convincing rationale for the benefits that forgiveness might have for personal well-being, in addition to other relational benefits that forgiveness might bring.

CORRESPONDENCE: Michael E. McCullough, National Institute for Healthcare Research, Rockville, Maryland.

McCullough, M.E., Worthington, E.L., Jr., & Rachal, K.C. (1997)

INTERPERSONAL FORGIVING IN CLOSE RELATIONSHIPS

Journal of Personality and Social Psychology, 73, 321–336

OBJECTIVE: To examine the determinants, structure, and consequences of forgiving from a social-psychological perspective. In particular, the causal role of empathy in promoting forgiveness was investigated.

DESIGN: One cross-sectional survey and one controlled field experiment.

SETTING: Two university campuses.

PARTICIPANTS: Study 1: 239 undergraduates (131 females, 108 males) received course credit for participation. Ethnicity: 83% white, 14% black, 3% other.

Study 2: Students ($n = 134$) volunteered from introductory psychology courses. The sample was 80% female with a mean age of 22 years. Ethnicity: 52% white, 35% black, 7% Asian-American, 4% Latinos. Participants were screened to ensure that they: (a) wanted to learn information and skills to help them forgive a specific offender; (b) were not taking psychotropic medications or receiving counseling; (c) did not show substance abuse problems, psychotic behavior, or personality disorders that might disrupt the group; and (d) agreed to be randomly assigned to either a seminar or a wait list. A total of 70 were available to participate on the weekend the intervention was offered.

ASSESSMENT OF PREDICTOR VARIABLES: Study 1: In addition to providing demographic information, participants completed the following measures: (a) two Likert items about the offense—a 5-point item indicating the degree to which the offense hurt them and a 6-point item indicating how wrong they believed the offense to be; (b) two 5-point Likert items measuring the degree to which their offenders apologized and attempted to explain their hurtful behavior; and (c) an eight-item empathy scale used in previous research (e.g., Fultz, Batson, Fortenbach, McCarthy, & Varney, 1986).

Study 2: Participants were blocked on gender and randomly assigned to one of three conditions: an empathy seminar ($n = 13$), a comparison seminar ($n = 17$), or a wait list ($n = 40$). The empathy seminar encouraged forgiving using affective and cognitive empathy; whereas the comparison seminar encouraged forgiveness without focusing explicitly on empathy. Each seminar leader received pre-training and used a treatment manual. Two weeks after assignment to groups, seminar participants met for a total of 8 hours over a 2-day period (Friday evening/Saturday). Trainees in an American Psychological Association-approved psychology program conducted each seminar. All group leaders were naive to study hypotheses and randomly assigned to experimental conditions.

ASSESSMENT OF OUTCOME VARIABLES: Study 1: Participants completed the following measures: (a) a 5-item measure of forgiving that emphasized the participant's disposition toward the offender (constructed from a subset of items on the Enright Forgiveness Inventory; Subkoviak et al., 1995); (b) 20 items from Wade's (1989) Forgiveness Scale; (c) 2 items measuring conciliatory behavior toward the offender; and (d) 3 items measuring avoidance behavior toward the offender, which were also adapted from Wade's (1989) Forgiveness Scale.

Study 2: Participants completed the following measures at pretest, at posttest (immediately after the seminars), and at follow-up (6 weeks after the seminars): (a) the 4-item version of Batson's empathy adjectives (Coke, Batson, & McDavis, 1978) to measure affective empathy; (b) the Self-Dyadic Perspective-Taking Scale (Long, 1990) to measure cognitive empathy toward the offender; and (c) the same 5-item measure of forgiving used in Study 1.

MAIN RESULTS: Study 1: The forgiving and empathy measures were first refined. Structural equation modeling techniques suggested that the well-established relationship between apology and forgiving is likely to be partially mediated by empathy. However, relative to empathy, forgiving appears to be a stronger predictor of interpersonal behavior toward the offender.

Study 2: Results suggested that, overall, more forgiveness and affective empathy occurred in the empathy seminar than in the comparison seminar or the wait-list control, with the comparison seminar and the wait-list control not differing significantly. However, at follow-up, the comparison group showed an increase in forgiveness that diminished the difference between the two seminar groups. The wait-list control showed no such increase in forgiveness.

CONCLUSION: Taken together, results from these studies suggest that empathy is likely to play a central role in promoting forgiveness. Study 2 also provides further support for the notion that forgiveness can be fostered through clinical intervention, even when the intervention is brief and uses nonclinical populations.

COMMENTARY: By viewing forgiveness as a particular form of prosocial behavior, the researchers were able to capitalize on a rich body of theorizing about the role of empathy as a motivator of prosocial behavior. Their data give some initial evidence to suggest that the experience of emotional empathy for one's offender might indeed be crucial for facilitating forgiveness. It is puzzling that the comparison group in Study 2 became so much more forgiving by the follow-up assessment, despite the lack of structured activities designed explicitly to encourage empathy for the offender. Future research might shed more light on how the empathy-forgiveness model might be used productively in clinical interventions.

CORRESPONDENCE: Michael E. McCullough, National Institute for Healthcare Research, Rockville, Maryland.

McGraw, K.M. (1987)

GUILT FOLLOWING TRANSGRESSION:
AN ATTRIBUTION OF RESPONSIBILITY APPROACH

Journal of Personality and Social Psychology, 53, 247–256

OBJECTIVE: To examine the attributional mediators of post-transgression guilt.

DESIGN: Two experiments: one scenario based and one based on recollection of an autobiographical event.

SETTING: Northwestern University in Chicago.

PARTICIPANTS: Undergraduates participated for course credit. Study 1 had 84 participants, and Study 2 had 119 participants. Approximately equal numbers of men and women participated.

MANIPULATED VARIABLES: Study 1: Each participant read four scenarios describing an incident involving two same-sex college students, one portrayed as a victim and the other as a harmdoer. Participants were asked to imagine themselves in the role of the harmdoer, the victim, or a detached observer. Scenarios varied in a within-subjects fashion by the level of responsibility attributable to the harmdoer (accidental/unforeseeable, accidental/foreseeable, intentional/unjustified, and intentional/justified), and the specific nature of the harm (suffering a broken arm, being ridiculed about a weight problem, having a blouse ruined, and losing $20).
    Study 2: Participants were asked to describe an interpersonal transgression incident from their own experience. Between-subjects factors included the participant's role in the conflict (victim, harmdoer, or observer) and level of responsibility (accidental/unforeseeable, accidental/foreseeable, intentional/unjustified, and intentional/justified).

ASSESSMENT OF OUTCOME VARIABLES: Study 1: Participants used 7-point scales to rate the level of responsibility attributable to the victim and the harmdoer, the level of guilt likely to be experienced by the harmdoer, and the level of upset likely to be experienced by the victim.

Study 2: Using 9-point scales, participants in the intentional conditions rated the justifiability of the harmdoer's behavior. Those in the accidental conditions rated the foreseeability of the harmdoer's behavior. All participants were asked to rate the level of responsibility attributable to the harmdoer and the victim, and the level of blame deserved by the harmdoer. They also rated the extent to which the harmdoer's behavior was due to personal versus situational characteristics. Finally, they were asked about the level of guilt likely to be experienced by the harmdoer and the level of upset likely to be experienced by the victim.

MAIN RESULTS: Study 1: Participants imputed most responsibility to those who committed intentional/unjustified transgressions, less responsibility in the case of intentional/justified and unintentional/foreseeable transgressions, and least responsibility in the case of unintentional/unforeseeable transgressions. However, participants believed that harmdoers would experience more guilt following accidental than intentional transgressions. Guilt about foreseeable transgressions was also believed to be higher than guilt about unforeseeable transgressions, and guilt about justified transgressions was believed to be higher if the harm was justified rather than unjustified. This pattern was the same across participant roles (victim, perpetrator, and observer). No gender effects were observed.

Study 2: As in the first study, accidental transgressions were associated with higher self-reports and estimates of guilt than intentional transgressions. In addition, guilt was negatively related to causality and the likelihood of future transgression, and positively related to attributions of blame to the harmdoer. Again, no gender effects were observed.

CONCLUSION: Harmdoers appear to experience greater guilt after committing transgressions that are accidental as opposed to intentional. This is true even though higher levels of responsibility are assigned to harmdoers whose transgressions are intentional.

COMMENTARY: These findings are quite interesting because they suggest two psychological factors that might make forgiving transgressors, who are perceived to have behaved intentionally, doubly difficult. First, intentional actions lead to more attributions of blame and responsibility, which has been shown to make empathy for the offender less likely (e.g., Weiner et al., 1991). Second, the perpetrators of intentional actions are perceived to feel less guilty, which might also make empathy for them less likely, and also make them less likely to seek forgiveness (see, e.g., O'Malley & Greenberg, 1983).

Correspondence: Kathleen M. McGraw, Department of Political Science, State University of New York at Stony Brook, Stony Brook, New York.

Meek, K.R., Albright, J.S., & McMinn, M.R. (1995)

RELIGIOUS ORIENTATION, GUILT, CONFESSION, AND FORGIVENESS

Journal of Psychology and Theology, 23, 190–197

Objective: To explore the relationship between religious orientation, experiences of guilt and forgiveness, and subjective well-being.

Design: Cross-sectional survey.

Setting: Loyola University of Chicago.

Participants: Fifty-five undergraduate psychology students and 53 members of InterVarsity Christian Fellowship (for a total of 64 females and 44 males).

Assessment of Predictor Variables: Participants completed the Religious Orientation Scale (Allport & Ross, 1967), a measure of intrinsic religiousness (religiousness that is motivated by the conviction that one's religious faith is the "master motive" for one's life) and extrinsic religiousness. A median split was performed on this measure to create intrinsic and extrinsic groups. In addition, three levels of information about a hypothetical guilt-inducing situation were presented to each participant (skipping work to go on a date, encountering and talking to a co-worker who worked extra hours to take the day off, and confessing to the boss). Participants were asked to imagine themselves as the offender in each of these situations. Finally, participants were randomly assigned to one of two versions of the third scenario: In the "grace" version, confession was met with understanding and forgiveness by the boss. In the "no-grace" version, confession was met with a harsh, unforgiving response.

Assessment of Outcome Variables: Short Likert-type scales were given after each scenario to assess the extent to which each participant (imagining the self as the offender) would experience guilt, grace, and forgiveness. Participants were also asked how likely they would be to commit and to repeat the transgression; 6 items were given after the first scenario, 4 after the second, and 10 after the third.

Main Results: Relative to extrinsics, intrinsics reported higher levels of guilt, lower likelihood of repeating the offense, less probable satisfaction with getting the day off, and a greater likelihood that they would confess. All participants showed an increase in guilt ratings after the second scenario (encountering and talking to the co-worker) and a decrease after the third scenario (confession). Following the last (confession) scenario, (a) those in the grace condition were more likely than those in the no-grace condition to state that they would feel better after having confessed, and (b) intrinsics reported a greater likelihood than extrinsics of forgiving themselves and feeling forgiven by God. Guilt appeared to mediate the relationship between intrinsic religiousness and feeling good about getting the day off; in other words, although intrinsics were less likely than extrinsics to report that they would feel good about getting the day off, this effect was largely explainable through the greater guilt reported by intrinsics.

Conclusion: Intrinsically religious persons may be somewhat more susceptible to guilt than extrinsically religious persons. However, these data suggest that intrinsics' greater guilt coexisted with some adaptive reactions: Relative to extrinsics, intrinsics reported greater intentions to confess their transgressions. They also reported a greater likelihood that they would feel better after confession, be able to forgive themselves, and feel forgiven by God after committing an interpersonal transgression.

COMMENTARY: Feeling forgiven constitutes one of the most important personal motivations for seeking forgiveness. Even without being forgiven, however, people appear to gain relief simply from confessing and coming clean *regardless of the response of the offended person*. Meek and her colleagues have also found data that intrinsic religiousness is a major motivation for one's willingness to confess following an interpersonal transgression. People with intrinsic motivations for being religious appear to be highly motivated toward prosocial responses—including prosocial levels of guilt—following interpersonal transgressions. These findings add important data regarding the variables that predict willingness to confess and seek forgiveness, and regarding the effects of confessing and seeking forgiveness on the well-being of the transgressor.

CORRESPONDENCE: Katheryn Rhoads Meek, Department of Psychology, Wheaton College, Wheaton, Illinois.

Mongeau, P.A., Hale, J.L., & Alles, M. (1994)

AN EXPERIMENTAL INVESTIGATION OF ACCOUNTS AND ATTRIBUTIONS FOLLOWING SEXUAL INFIDELITY

Communication Monographs, 61, 326–344

OBJECTIVE: To determine whether intentionality and revenge motives would influence: (a) attributions about infidelity and (b) accounts generated to explain it.

Design: Scenario-based experiment.

SETTING: Medium-sized university in the midwestern U.S.

PARTICIPANTS: A total of 239 undergraduates (142 females, 97 males) participated for course credit.

MANIPULATED VARIABLES: Participants read a scenario describing a heterosexual dating relationship in which one partner (the infidel) goes to a bar, meets a friend of the opposite sex, and ends up having sexual intercourse with the friend later that evening. Participants are asked to imagine themselves in the role of the infidel. The following variables were manipulated in a between-subjects fashion: intention of meeting friend at bar (low versus high), sex of infidel (male versus female), and revenge motive (yes versus no). In the revenge condition, the infidel just discovered that his/her romantic partner was having sex with someone else. In the no-revenge condition, the infidel was alone because his/her romantic partner was visiting parents. Participant gender was also used as a predictor variable.

ASSESSMENT OF OUTCOME VARIABLES: After reading the scenario, participants (who envisioned themselves as the infidel) gave attributional ratings of their intent, responsibility, blame, and guilt. They were then asked to provide a written account: "If you were [the infidel], what would you say to [partner's name] in an attempt to explain your behavior?" Two coders, who were blind to the experimental conditions, placed the accounts into as many of five account categories as appropriate (concessions, excuses, justifications, refusals, and silence; cf. McLaughlin, Cody, & O'Hair, 1983). They also rated the degree of aggravation or mitigation characterizing each account.

MAIN RESULTS: Intentionality and revenge motives were associated with decreased guilt. Revenge motives were associated with decreases in attributions of blame and responsibility to self. Although revenge accounts were more aggravating than non-revenge accounts, there was no effect of intent on mitigation/aggravation. Three-fourths of accounts in the no-revenge conditions were concessions and excuses, whereas three-fourths of accounts in the revenge conditions were justifications and refusals. Female infidels were perceived as being more responsible for their actions and feeling greater guilt; and male participants perceived the female's infidelity as more intentional than the male's infidelity. Males' accounts were generally more aggravating than females' accounts.

CONCLUSION: Having a revenge motive appears to influence both people's attributions about infidelity and the accounts given in response to it. People appear to experience less guilt and self-blame about infidelity under conditions of revenge, and they also give more aggravating accounts. The role of gender in infidelity was also highlighted in this study: In general, women are judged more harshly for infidelity and tend to give more mitigating accounts when in the role of the infidel.

COMMENTARY: This study, like others in this annotated bibliography (e.g., McGraw, 1987) suggests that people feel less guilt about intentionally hurting others (e.g., through actions motivated by revenge), than they feel when they hurt others unintentionally. Perhaps because of this lack of guilt, people who have acted out of revenge also appear to offer accounts for their behavior that make reconciliations more difficult following interpersonal transgressions. These findings suggest that when people become convinced of their right to seek revenge, the normal, prosocial effects of guilt cease to operate, making the processes of seeking forgiveness, granting forgiveness, and reconciliation more difficult.

CORRESPONDENCE: Paul A. Mongeau, Associate Professor of Speech Communication, Miami University, Oxford, Ohio.

Ohbuchi, K., Kameda, M., & Agarie, N. (1989)

APOLOGY AS AGGRESSION CONTROL: ITS ROLE IN MEDIATING APPRAISAL OF AND RESPONSE TO HARM

Journal of Personality and Social Psychology, 56, 219–227

OBJECTIVE: To examine the effects of apologies on subsequent aggression by a victim, and the psychological mechanisms underlying such effects.

DESIGN: Two experiments: one laboratory based and one scenario based.

SETTING: University campus in Japan.

PARTICIPANTS: Study 1: 58 female undergraduates received a small amount of money for participation. Study 2: 80 male undergraduates received course credit for participation.

MANIPULATED VARIABLES: Study 1: Participants were led to believe that their performance on a bogus intellectual task was harmed by an experimental assistant's mistake. They then received a poor evaluation of performance by the experimenter. Participants were randomly assigned to one of four conditions, based on a 2 x 2 manipulation of apology (the assistant did versus did not apologize to the participant) and harm removal (the experimenter either did or did not change his evaluation of the participant's performance).

Study 2: Participants read a scenario of an incident in which a man was physically injured by two other men dashing out from an alley. Manipulated variables included level of harm (severe or mild) and apology (presence versus absence).

ASSESSMENT OF OUTCOME VARIABLES: Study 1: After the experimental manipulation, participants filled out a questionnaire in which they rated: (a) three distinct, negative aspects of the assistant's personality (insincerity, irresponsibility, and carelessness); (b) their own level of unpleasant affect (on a 0–10 scale); and (c) the competence of the assistant. Participants were told that their ratings on the competence item would influence the assistant's grade; thus this last item served as a strong measure of aggression or retaliation.

Study 2: After reading the scenario, participants rated, on Likert–type scales, their assumptions about: (a) the perpetrator's negative personality traits (bad-naturedness, insincerity, unfriendliness, irresponsibility, and maliciousness); (b) the victim's affective state (unpleasantness and anger); (c) the victim's desire for seven different aspects of apology (saying "excuse me," a detailed explanation, accepting responsibility, showing consideration for the victim, expressing remorse, begging for forgiveness, and promising future good deeds); and (d) the victim's probable aggressive responses (physical and verbal aggression).

MAIN RESULTS: Study 1: Across all dependent variables, assistants who apologized received more favorable ratings than those who did not. In a multiple-regression analysis predicting aggressive responses, the effect of apology was not significant; instead, aggressive responses were more directly linked to: (a) the victim's impression of the perpetrator and (b) the victim's level of unpleasant affect.

Study 2: Apologies caused reductions in negative impressions of the perpetrator, negative affect, and verbal aggression by victims. A trend in the same direction was found for physical aggression. Trends also suggested that lower levels of physical aggression and fewer unfavorable impressions would occur when harm was mild rather than severe. The ability of an apology to reduce verbal aggression and negative affect was attenuated under conditions of severe harm.

On all but one of the apology scales (expressing remorse, which showed a trend), participants perceived the victim as having a stronger desire for an apology when harm was severe rather than mild. On four apology scales (saying "excuse me," accepting responsibility, showing consideration, and begging for forgiveness), participants viewed the victim as having a weaker desire for an apology when an apology was actually received than when not. On four of the scales (saying "excuse me," a detailed explanation, accepting responsibility, and showing consideration), an interaction between apology and harm level occurred: a spontaneous apology reduced the desire for an apology more under conditions of mild as opposed to severe harm. In a multiple-regression analysis, both the victim's affect and desire for an apology—but not whether the perpetrator actually apologized—predicted verbal aggression. Both apologies and impressions of the perpetrator predicted physical aggression.

CONCLUSION: Apologies appear to be helpful in reducing negative impressions of a perpetrator, negative affect for the victim, and the victim's aggression against the perpetrator. They may be most helpful under the condition of mild rather than severe harm. The effectiveness of apologies can be partially explained through their effects on the victim's affect, impressions of the perpetrator, and desire for an apology.

COMMENTARY: This study, conducted on a Japanese sample, provides another interesting look at the power of apologies in reducing victims' negative affect, thoughts about perpetrators, and likely verbal and physical aggression toward perpetrators. The effects of apologies on reduced retaliation appear to be mediated, in part, by their effects in reducing victims' negative affect and repairing victims' negative perceptions of their perpetrators. Thus, these data cross-validate—using a non-American sample—the power of apologies at creating cognitive and emotional change following interpersonal offenses (see also Darby & Schlenker, 1982; McCullough, Worthington, & Rachal, 1997; Weiner et al., 1991). Also, these data show that under conditions of moderate to mild degrees of harm, perfunctory apologies are perceived as sufficient to meet victims' desires for an apology.

CORRESPONDENCE: Ken-ichi Ohbuchi, Department of Psychology, Faculty of Arts and Letters, Tohoku University, Kawauchi, Japan.

O'Malley, M.N., & Greenberg, J. (1983)

SEX DIFFERENCES IN RESTORING JUSTICE:
THE DOWN PAYMENT EFFECT

Journal of Research in Personality, 17, 174–185

OBJECTIVE: To determine whether a perception that a harmdoer is experiencing guilt or remorse will partially vindicate the harmdoer.

DESIGN: Three scenario-based experiments.

SETTING: College campus.

PARTICIPANTS: Participants were all undergraduates. In Studies 1 and 2, participation was part of a classroom exercise. In Study 3, partial course credit was given for participation. Number of participants: Study 1, 120; Study 2, 64; Study 3, 144.

ASSESSMENT OF PREDICTOR VARIABLES: In all studies, participants were given questionnaires including scenarios of driving situations (crashes in all studies; the factor of recklessness was added in Study 2). Gender was also used as a predictor variable in all studies. In Study 1, manipulated variables included the amount of damage caused by the crash (major versus minor), and the admission of responsibility by the harmdoer (admission versus no admission). In Study 2, apology (apology offered versus no apology offered) was manipulated. In Study 3, negligence (negligent versus unlucky) and remorsefulness (none, moderate, or extreme) were manipulated.

ASSESSMENT OF OUTCOME VARIABLES: Study 1: Using a 9-point scale, participants rated: (a) the amount of reparations that the harmdoer should fairly pay the victim; (b) the degree to which the harmdoer appeared to be suffering psychologically; and (c) two aspects of the harmdoer's character (e.g., likability, competence, morality).

Study 2: On 10-point scales, participants rated: (a) the harmdoer's

feelings following the accident; (b) the feelings of the driver of the damaged car; (c) likeableness of the harmdoer; (d) negligence of the harmdoer; (e) whether a fine should be used as punishment; and (f) whether
a fine should be used as a deterrent. Based on results of a factor analysis,
items a, b, and c were combined into an index of social aspects of the
incident. Items e and f were combined to form an index of the use of
fines.

Study 3: On 10-point scales, participants rated: (a) how much the harmdoer suffered psychologically; (b) the extent to which the harmdoer
deserved reproach for negligence; and (c) the appropriate fine (in $5
increments ranging from $0 to $45).

MAIN RESULTS: Study 1: Participants rated harmdoers who accepted
responsibility as suffering more psychologically than those who did not.
They also assigned them much higher ratings on the character scales
than those who did not accept responsibility. Greater reparations were
recommended in the major damage condition than the minor damage
condition, and males recommended greater reparations than females.
Closer inspection of means suggested that women, in rating a harmdoer
who accepted responsibility, assigned a less severe penalty than men or
women in the non-admission condition.

Study 2: When determining whether a fine should be used, females,
to a greater extent than males, considered the likeableness and negligence of the driver as well as the feelings of the harmdoer and victim.
Regardless of participant gender, desire to exact a fine was stronger for
nonapologetic than apologetic drivers.

Study 3: Unremorseful drivers were rated as suffering less psychologically than moderately remorseful drivers, who in turn were perceived
as suffering less than extremely remorseful drivers. Greater blame was
assigned to negligent drivers than to unlucky ones. In general, females
tended to recommend more lenient fines to the extent that the harmdoer was remorseful, whereas males' ratings were not affected by the
remorsefulness manipulation.

CONCLUSION: This study suggests the presence of a "down-payment
effect" for females in which harmdoers who experience guilt or remorse

are partially vindicated: their psychological suffering serves as a down payment in terms of just reparations. Males, in contrast, are less likely to take the perceived remorsefulness of the harmdoer into account when assigning reparations. However, both males and females appear to moderate their retributive actions when transgressors offer apologies.

COMMENTARY: This study, like others, shows the power of remorsefulness and apologies for reducing people's tendencies to infer negative character traits of the perpetrator, blame the perpetrator, and enact retributive courses of action following the perpetrators' transgressions (in this case, car crashes). Also, this study suggests that women might be more open than men to tempering their tendencies toward retribution when social-psychological factors such as admissions of responsibility, remorsefulness, and apologies are present. Finally, these findings suggest that when perpetrators express remorse and responsibility, victims often infer that the perpetrator is suffering psychologically—a factor that might weigh heavily in people's decisions to forgive their perpetrators.

CORRESPONDENCE: Michael O'Malley, Department of Psychology, University of Colorado, Colorado Springs, Colorado.

Park, Y.O., & Enright, R.D

THE DEVELOPMENT OF FORGIVENESS IN THE CONTEXT OF ADOLESCENT FRIENDSHIP CONFLICT IN KOREA

Journal of Adolescence, 20, 393–402.

OBJECTIVE: Using a nonwestern sample to investigate the role of developmental factors in people's understanding of forgiveness and actual forgiveness for an offending close friend.

DESIGN: Cross-sectional, self-report data (interview and questionnaires).

SETTING: Junior high school and college settings in Seoul, Korea.

PARTICIPANTS: Thirty, seventh and eighth graders (mean age = 13.31 years) and 30 juniors and seniors in college (mean age = 21.34 years), with an equal number of males and females in each group. All participants resided in Seoul, Korea and identified themselves as Christians. A total of 1,800 students were screened. Inclusion criteria included the presence of a serious, unfair conflict caused by a same-gender friend during the last 5 to 6 months.

ASSESSMENT OF PREDICTOR VARIABLES: Age, gender, and education level were reported.

ASSESSMENT OF OUTCOME VARIABLES: Participants completed (a) the Understanding Forgiveness Interview, which contained questions pertaining to the strategies, manifestations, and conditions specific to each of three types of forgiveness (revengeful, external, and internal); (b) the Restoring Friendship Strategy Scale, a 10-item measure of the extent to which the participant used proactive reconciliation strategies with the offending friend; and (c) the Degree of Forgiveness Scale, a 10-item scale measuring the extent to which a participant reported that he or she had forgiven the friend.

MAIN RESULTS: Age was positively correlated with the understanding of forgiveness. Understanding of forgiveness and actual forgiveness were positively correlated with the use of proactive strategies for friendship restoration. However, the correlation between the understanding of forgiveness and actual forgiveness suggested only a weak relationship ($p < .08$). (When the mode rather than the mean was used, the relationship was significant.) The average junior high student appeared to be in a transitional period between Revengeful and External Forgiveness, whereas the average college student was in transition between External and Internal Forgiveness. No gender differences were found.

CONCLUSION: Older participants appeared to have a deeper understanding of the forgiveness concept than younger participants. Although understanding of forgiveness was related to the self-reported manner in which friendship conflicts were resolved, it was not strongly predictive of actual forgiveness. In other words, understanding what forgiveness is only weakly implied an ability to forgive in a specific situation.

COMMENTARY: As in previous research by Enright and his colleagues, this study finds evidence that people have a moral sense regarding forgiveness that develops as they age, just as their reasoning about moral concepts such as justice and care appear to develop over time. In the same way that Kohlberg found support for his theorizing about the universality of moral development from cross-cultural replications, Enright's theory about the universality of the development of reasoning about forgiveness receives support from this cross-cultural replication of his earlier findings. However, the very small correlations between people's level of reasoning about forgiveness and their actual self-reported forgiveness for an offending relationship partner, reveal the disjunction between reason and action. Alternatively, the lack of correspondence between reasoning and self-reported forgiveness for a specific relationship partner might reveal that forgiveness, in such instances, remains under the control of particular aspects of the relationship or the offense itself.

CORRESPONDENCE: Younghee Oh Park, Department of Psychology, Duksung Women's University, Seoul, Korea.

Poloma, M.M., & Gallup, G.H. (1991)

UNLESS YOU FORGIVE OTHERS: PRAYER AND FORGIVENESS

In Varieties of prayer *(pp. 85–106). Philadelphia: Trinity Press*

OBJECTIVE: To assess forgiveness-related beliefs and behaviors, examine the relationship between forgiveness and well-being, and explore the association of religious variables and prayer with forgiveness.

DESIGN: Cross-sectional survey, as part of larger Gallup poll.

SETTING: 1988 Gallup poll.

PARTICIPANTS: Nationwide random sample of 1,030 adult men and women.

ASSESSMENT OF PREDICTOR VARIABLES: Various religious factors were assessed, including religious salience, participation, beliefs, and prayer experience.

ASSESSMENT OF OUTCOME VARIABLES: The forgiveness question asked, "Which of these do you usually do when you feel that someone has done something wrong to you?" Respondents selected as many of the eight choices as applied to them: Two were coded as negative (getting even, resentment); one neutral (overlook offense or push it out of mind); and five positive (try to forgive, pray for the person, pray for comfort and guidance, discuss with the person, do something nice for the person). Life satisfaction was also assessed with a single-item measure.

MAIN RESULTS: Although the vast majority (94%) of respondents said that it was fairly, or very important, for religious people to forgive, only 48% said that they usually tried to forgive others. Positive attitudes toward forgiveness were significantly (although not strongly; $r = .16$) associated with life satisfaction. To control for interaction among forgiveness-related responses, all eight responses were entered into a multiple-regression analysis to predict life satisfaction. Results suggested that life satisfaction was negatively related to resentment and positively related to praying for the offender.

Other relationships between religion and forgiveness emerged. For example, a clear majority of participants (83%) reported that God's help was needed to be able to truly forgive someone, whereas only 15% reported that they could forgive using their own power and resources. Positive correlations emerged between acts of forgiveness and prayer experience, religious salience, feeling close to God, being a born-again Christian, and meditative prayer. Prayer experience—particularly meditative prayer—appeared to be an especially important predictor of forgiveness.

CONCLUSION: Forgiveness appears to have a small, positive relationship with life satisfaction. Yet although most people appear to view forgiveness as important, only about half of individuals report that they usually try to forgive others. There appears to be a positive association between many religious variables and forgiveness, with prayer experiences emerging as a major predictor.

COMMENTARY: In contrast with other studies (e.g., Subkoviak et al., 1995), this study provides some evidence that religious involvement does indeed play a factor in understanding the propensity to forgive others (see also Enright, Santos, & Al-Mabuk, 1989). People involved in their religious traditions, particularly traditions that give forgiveness a central theological emphasis, tend to report a greater willingness to forgive others than those who are less involved in religious faiths that place such emphasis on forgiveness. How religious involvement might dispose people to forgive other people remains, however, a topic for future investigation. Additionally, there exists a small tendency for more forgiving people to report greater life satisfaction. Thus, these study data provide some initial evidence to drive future investigations on how forgiveness might promote health and well-being.

CORRESPONDENCE: No information listed.

Roloff, M.E., & Janiszewski, C.A. (1989)

OVERCOMING OBSTACLES TO INTERPERSONAL
COMPLIANCE: A PRINCIPLE OF MESSAGE CONSTRUCTION

Human Communication Research, 16, 33–61

OBJECTIVE: To examine the effects of relationship closeness and request type on: (a) wording of requests and (b) responses to refusal of a request. Only the material relevant to refusal of a request will be presented here.

DESIGN: Cross-sectional survey with both scenario and autobiographical components.

SETTING: Medium-sized midwestern university.

PARTICIPANTS: A total of 120 undergraduates (39 males, 80 females, 1 that did not indicate gender) participated for course credit. Most (60%) of the participants were sophomores and juniors.

MANIPULATED VARIABLES: Participants were randomly assigned questionnaires in which they were asked to think about one specific "target" person in their class: a friend, an acquaintance, or a stranger. Participants were asked to imagine themselves making a request from the target. Participants were also randomly assigned to read about one of four help-seeking situations, two of which were requests to borrow a resource (class notes shortly before an exam or $25), and two of which were requests for favors (a time-consuming ride downtown or typing an eight-page paper). Participants were asked to imagine themselves approaching the target and making the request.

All requests were chosen to appear costly. However, when a request focuses on borrowing something that is readily available and can be returned in the same condition (such as money or class notes), it entails lower risk for the helper than a request that will consume considerable energy and may not be easily compensated (such as driving someone downtown or typing a paper). Thus the borrowing condition in this study represented less of an imposition than the favor condition.

ASSESSMENT OF ADDITIONAL PREDICTOR VARIABLES: As a measure of intimacy, participants completed an 11-item, 7-point Likert scale developed by Roloff, Janiszewski, McGrath, Burns, and Manrai (1988). The scale, which has an internal consistency reliability (alpha) of .97, assesses the level of intimacy of typical interactions between the participant and the target.

ASSESSMENT OF OUTCOME VARIABLES: After indicating how they would phrase their request, participants were asked to write down exactly what, if anything, they would say to the target if their request were denied.

Responses were coded as forgiving if the requester acknowledged the target's right to refuse compliance; expressed no resentment; or indicated appreciation for the target's consideration. Responses were coded as counterpersuasion attempts if they repeated the request; made a revised or reduced request; elaborated on the need for assistance; or stressed the ease with which compliance might occur.

MAIN RESULTS: When a request to borrow a resource was refused, forgiving responses were less likely to the extent that the relationship was intimate (using both the intimacy manipulation and the self-report measure). When a request for a favor was refused, the opposite pattern was found: forgiving responses were more likely to the extent that the relationship was intimate. Use of counterpersuasion was negatively related to use of forgiveness in participant responses. In the borrowing condition, counterpersuasion attempts were positively associated with self-reported intimacy. In the favor condition, counterpersuasion was negatively associated with self-reported intimacy.

CONCLUSION: Due to obligations posed by relational bonds, people generally expect greater compliance from people with whom they are close than from strangers. Yet their responses to a refused request depend not only on relationship closeness but also on the type of request. When a potential helper refuses a comparatively small request (borrowing something that can be readily returned), requesters are more likely to respond in an unforgiving manner to the extent that the relationship is close. This presumably occurs because people expect more from intimates and are more comfortable asserting themselves with them. However, if a larger imposition (a time-consuming favor) is refused, requesters are more likely to give a forgiving response to the extent that the relationship is close. Realizing that a large favor constitutes substantial risk for the potential helper, requesters within close relationships may choose to reduce pressure to avoid putting further strain on the close other and, possibly, the relationship.

COMMENTARY: Relational closeness has been thought by some to be an important variable governing people's willingness to forgive others whom they perceive to have offended them. This study finds an interesting phenomenon: people are more willing to forgive intimates when they refuse to honor an "expensive" request, but are actually less willing to forgive when intimates fail to honor a small request. Nonetheless, the interaction of intimacy and level of refusal is interesting, and might lead to important insights into the combination of factors that shape people's decisions to forgive.

CORRESPONDENCE: No mailing address listed. The first author was at Northwestern University at the time of this writing.

Rusbult, C.E., Verette, J., Whitney, G.A., Slovik, L.F., & Lipkus, I. (1991)

ACCOMMODATION PROCESSES IN CLOSE RELATIONSHIPS: THEORY AND PRELIMINARY EMPIRICAL EVIDENCE

Journal of Personality and Social Psychology, 60, 53–78

OBJECTIVE: To pinpoint factors associated with the use of accommodation in close relationships. Accommodation refers to the willingness, when one relationship partner has engaged in a potentially destructive act, to react constructively while inhibiting destructive impulses.

DESIGN: Six studies: two scenario-based experiments (Studies 1 and 2), three cross-sectional surveys (Studies 3, 4, and 5), and one laboratory experiment (Study 6).

SETTING: University of North Carolina at Chapel Hill.

PARTICIPANTS: Participants for Studies 1 through 5 were all undergraduates participating for course credit. In Study 6, participants were 41 couples involved in ongoing heterosexual dating relationships; one member of each couple participated for course credit, while the other was a volunteer.

ASSESSMENT OF PREDICTOR VARIABLES: Studies 1 and 2: Participants read essays detailing interpersonal transgression incidents and were asked to imagine themselves as the victim. In Study 1, the primary between-subjects variable was the level of social concern evoked. In the normal concern condition, participants were told only that the perpetrator was a casual acquaintance. The reduced concern condition added the caveat that the perpetrator's response: (a) would not be affected by the participant's response and (b) would be viewed as largely irrelevant. Study 2 varied the level of interdependence between the parties (acquaintances, casual dates, regular dates, or seriously involved).

Studies 3 through 5: These studies used cross-sectional, self-report surveys to assess various predictors of accommodation. Relationship factors, which were assessed on 9-point scales, included commitment, satisfaction, quality of alternatives, investment in relationship, comparison level, normative support, and centrality of relationship. Study 3 also included 21 items to measure one's relative involvement in the relationship (compared with one's partner). Study 4 included a self-esteem measure, the Multifaceted Evaluation-of-Self Inventory (Hoyle, 1987), as well as Bem's (1974) Sex-Role Inventory. Study 5 included Davis's (1983) Interpersonal Reactivity Index as a measure of empathic concern and perspective taking. Study 5 also included measures of cognitive rigidity (Wesley, 1953) and Machiavellianism (Christie & Geis, 1970).

Study 6: To measure relationship distress/nondistress, participants (both members of a couple) filled out measures of commitment and satisfaction.

ASSESSMENT OF OUTCOME VARIABLES: Studies 1 and 2: After each essay, participants indicated how likely they would be to respond in each of 12 hypothetical ways, each of which signified either exit, voice, loyalty, or neglect (cf. Rusbult & Zembrodt, 1983). In all analyses, exit and neglect were considered destructive responses, whereas voice and loyalty were considered constructive.

Studies 3 through 5: A 24-item scale was used as a structured measure of self-reported tendencies toward constructive (voice, loyalty) and destructive (exit, neglect) responses. In Studies 3 and 4, participants also answered several open-ended questions about how they would respond to specific relationship transgressions. Responses were coded for degree of exit, voice, loyalty, and neglect.

Study 6: A self-report questionnaire similar to those in Studies 3 through 5 was used. The other three elements consisted of behavioral measures: (a) an interaction between the partners, which was audio-taped and coded for the number and proportion of constructive and destructive acts; (b) responses in a matrix games task; and (c) behavioral accommodation to a response discrepant from their own (actually a bogus response, but ostensibly made by their partner and stubbornly adhered to) on a moral dilemmas task.

MAIN RESULTS: Studies 1 and 2 suggested that people are less likely to accommodate if normal social concerns are lifted (Study 1) and if the relationship is not highly interdependent (Study 2).

Studies 3 through 5 suggested that greater accommodation was associated with greater relationship satisfaction, stronger commitment, poorer quality alternatives, greater investment size, greater centrality of the relationship, higher levels of psychological femininity, greater perspective taking, and greater normative support. Self-esteem, cognitive rigidity, empathic concern, and Machiavellianism were not related to accommodation. Commitment emerged as a partial mediator of the associations between relationship factors and accommodation.

Study 6 suggested that relationship distress was greater when both partners engaged in high levels of destructive reactions. Self-reported tendencies toward accommodation were also found to predict actual accommodation behavior.

CONCLUSION: Willingness to accommodate—that is, to inhibit destructive impulses while reacting constructively—is associated with greater relationship satisfaction. However, because accommodation implies a certain degree of self-sacrifice, people are not equally willing to accommodate in all interpersonal contexts. Accommodation appears more likely in relationships characterized by high commitment, poorer quality alternatives, greater investment, higher psychological femininity, mutual perspective-taking, and greater normative support.

COMMENTARY: This is a study of major importance that identifies some of the variables associated with willingness to accommodate in the face of destructive actions from one's relationship partner. Accommodation seems to be a crucial process for minimizing relational damage following the occurrence of an interpersonal transgression. While the study does not address forgiving directly, it would seem that accommodation and forgiveness would be two sides of the same coin, and that Rusbult and colleagues' understanding of accommodation would be an important theoretical starting point for understanding how forgiveness occurs in close relationships.

CORRESPONDENCE: Caryl E. Rusbult, Department of Psychology, University of North Carolina, Chapel Hill, North Carolina.

Stillwell, A.M., & Baumeister, R.F. (1997)

THE CONSTRUCTION OF VICTIM AND PERPETRATOR MEMORIES: ACCURACY AND DISTORTION IN ROLE-BASED ACCOUNTS

Personality and Social Psychology Bulletin, 23, 1157–1172

OBJECTIVE: To study how roles shape the construction of narrative accounts by victims and perpetrators; to test for the presence of self-serving distortions in victim and perpetrator accounts.

DESIGN: Three scenario-based experiments.

SETTING: A private research university in Ohio and a small public university in New York State.

PARTICIPANTS: In all studies, participants were undergraduates participating for course credit. Studies 1 and 2 were conducted at a private research university, while Study 3 was conducted at a small public univer-

sity. Study 1: 50 participants; 21 males, 29 females. Study 2: 30 participants; 17 males, 13 females. Study 3: 87 participants; 29 males, 58 females.

MANIPULATED VARIABLES: In each study, participants were asked to read
about a fictional transgression incident and to picture themselves in a
certain role. The story involved a promise by one student to help another
student study, an externally caused change in the terms of the commitment, a refusal to honor the commitment, and a bad outcome.

In Study 1, between-subjects manipulations included two role variations: perpetrator versus victim perspective, and first-person versus
third-person retelling of story. (The data from the third-person perspective were not emphasized in this article.) A control condition was also
included in which participants were simply asked to read the story and
to answer questions about it, without taking a role. After reading the
story, participants were given a 5-minute filler task to prevent them
from thinking about the story. They were then asked to write the story
as they remembered it.

Study 2: The same basic procedure was used as in Study 1. Before
reading the story, participants were asked to take either a victim or perpetrator perspective (for the control group, no suggestions on perspective-
taking were given). They then rewrote the story from the appropriate
perspective (Time 1). After a 3- to 5-day interval (Time 2), participants
returned and were again asked to write the story from memory.

Study 3: A similar procedure was used: manipulated roles included
victim, perpetrator, and control. To ensure that the results of Studies 1
and 2 were not due to demand characteristics, an additional condition was
added: when asked to write the story, participants were either given the
same directions as in Studies 1 and 2 (simple replication condition) or
were asked to furnish as accurate a story as possible (accuracy condition).

ASSESSMENT OF OUTCOME VARIABLES: All studies: after being typed, stories
were coded for the presence of various distortions including omission
of facts, insertion of new material, and alteration of information.

MAIN RESULTS: Study 1: Primary analyses focused on the first-person stories. Persons assigned to victim and perpetrator roles made more distor-

tions than control participants. Victims distorted by omitting details about mitigating circumstances and adding or emphasizing details about exacerbating circumstances, while perpetrators showed the opposite pattern.

Study 2: The general pattern of results from Study 1 was replicated: those assigned to victim and perpetrator roles showed self-serving distortions in their accounts. Furthermore, these distortions remained at Time 2.

Study 3: Again, the patterns of self-serving distortions were replicated. The results showed no clear evidence of demand characteristics: participants told to emphasize accuracy did not respond in less biased ways than those not specifically given such instructions.

CONCLUSION: Both victims and perpetrators distort information in self-serving ways, both by omitting information that might weaken their positions and by adding or changing information to strengthen their positions. These biases remain in effect at a 3- to 5-day interval and do not appear attributable to demand characteristics.

COMMENTARY: Some of the difficulties associated with forgiving, as this study shows, emerge from the fact that victims appear to fail to encode much of the information that would facilitate forgiving (e.g., mitigating circumstances), and add details to stories that would make forgiveness more difficult. Conversely, perpetrators appear to fail to encode many of the details that would make them more contrite and willing to seek forgiveness. These cognitive errors, associated with the victim and perpetrator roles, probably contribute to the great challenge of helping victims and perpetrators to be reconciled through the processes of seeking and granting forgiveness. Also, these tendencies toward distortion should be taken seriously in studies of forgiveness in close relationships, or in attempts to facilitate forgiveness through interventions involving both victim and perpetrator.

CORRESPONDENCE: Arlene M. Stillwell, Department of Psychology, State University of New York College at Potsdam, Potsdam, New York.

Stuckless, N., & Goranson, R. (1992)

THE VENGEANCE SCALE: DEVELOPMENT OF A MEASURE OF ATTITUDES TOWARD REVENGE

Journal of Social Behavior and Personality, 7, 25–42

OBJECTIVE: To develop and validate a measure of attitudes toward revenge. Study 1 focused on item generation, refinement, and selection. Study 2 emphasized validation; whereas Study 3 assessed test-retest reliability.

DESIGN: Three studies using survey methods: two cross-sectional and one longitudinal.

SETTING: York University, Ontario, Canada.

PARTICIPANTS: Study 1: 402 undergraduates in both day and evening classes (267 females, 121 males, 14 who did not identify gender). Age range = 18–59 years, mean age = 23 years; 88% were single.

Study 2: 151 day and evening undergraduates. Age range = 18–56 years mean age = 27 years; 65% percent were single.

Study 3: 85 undergraduates (no demographic information provided for this sample).

SCALE ITEMS ADMINISTERED: Study 1: After a pool of 85 potential items was refined through feedback from graduate students and faculty, 57 revenge-related items were administered in a questionnaire.

Studies 2 and 3: The Vengeance Scale developed in Study 1 was administered.

OTHER MEASURED VARIABLES: Study 1: The following scales were administered: (a) the 13-item short form of the Marlowe-Crowne Scale (Reynolds, 1982); (b) the 16-item Jackson Social Desirability Scale (Jackson, 1970); (c) the Trait Anger Scale (Spielberger, Jacobs, Russell, & Crane, 1983); and (d) an Empathy Scale composed of the perspective-taking and empathic-concern subscales of the Interpersonal Reactivity Index (Davis, 1980). Demographic questions were also asked.

Study 2: In addition to the anger, empathy, and social desirability measures used in Study 1, participants completed a 12-item questionnaire on vengeance behavior to provide concurrent validation for the Vengeance Scale. Domains sampled by this scale included (a) the likelihood of one's own vengeful or helpful responses in hypothetical situations and (b) one's own vengeful behavior and desires in the present and recent past.

Study 3: The Vengeance Scale was administered a second time, after a 5-week period, to assess test-retest reliability.

MAIN RESULTS: Study 1: The scale was refined to 20 items using standard measurement methods. It was found to have good internal consistency and minimal contamination by social desirability. A factor analysis suggested that the Vengeance Scale was best viewed as a unidimensional measure. Males showed higher scores than females. The scale correlated positively with trait anger and negatively with dispositional empathy.

Study 2: Study 2 largely replicated the results of Study 1 in terms of internal consistency ratings, unidimensionality of the construct, low correlations with social desirability scales, a negative correlation with empathy, and a positive correlation with trait anger. Males again scored higher on average than females. Concurrent validity was demonstrated through correlations with the 12-item, vengeance behavior questionnaire. Vengeance was shown to be distinguishable from general reciprocity.

Study 3: Test-retest reliability was established with a correlation of $r = .90$ ($p < .01$).

CONCLUSION: The Vengeance Scale was demonstrated to be a reliable and valid measure of attitudes toward vengeance. It correlates positively with trait anger and negatively with empathy. In addition, scale scores appear to be relatively independent of social desirability.

COMMENTARY: As Stuckless and Goranson point out in an earlier paper, the concept of revenge—like the concept of forgiveness—has received virtually no systematic attention from social scientists. Given the pervasiveness of behaviors that many people perceive to be motivated by the desire for revenge on the highways, in the office, and in family feuds—it is odd that social scientists have been so silent on the topic. The Vengeance Scale is an important first step in making a measurement tool available to researchers interested in taking an initial look at what vengeance is, what kinds of people are likely to be vengeful, and how people with positive attitudes toward revenge are likely to behave in social situations in which they are provoked or offended. In a sense, vengeance is the obverse side of forgiveness, making it an important variable to consider in future research on forgiveness.

CORRESPONDENCE: Richard Goranson, Psychology Department, York University, North York, Ontario, Canada.

Subkoviak, M.J., Enright, R.D., Wu, C., Gassin, E.A., Freedman, S., Olson L.M., & Sarinopoulos, I. (1995)

MEASURING INTERPERSONAL FORGIVENESS IN LATE ADOLESCENCE AND MIDDLE ADULTHOOD

Journal of Adolescence, 18, 641–655

OBJECTIVE: To validate a measure of interpersonal forgiveness and to examine its relation to anxiety, depression, religiosity, and social desirability.

DESIGN: Cross-sectional survey.

SETTING: Public university in the midwestern U.S.

PARTICIPANTS: A total of 394 participants (204 females, 190 males). College students (mean age = 22.1 years) formed half the sample, while the other half consisted of their same-gender parents (mean age = 49.6 years).

Data were eliminated for those pairs in which at least one member scored high on pseudo-forgiveness as measured by the Enright Forgiveness Inventory.

ASSESSMENT OF PREDICTOR VARIABLES: Participants were instructed to recall the most recent experience of being hurt deeply and unfairly by someone. They then completed the Enright Forgiveness Inventory (EFI), a 60-item scale that assesses positive and negative aspects of behavior, cognition, and affect toward an offending person. Five pseudo-forgiveness items, which measured denial and condonation, were also included, as were three consistency-check items.

ASSESSMENT OF OUTCOME VARIABLES: Participants completed (a) the Spielberger State-Trait Anxiety Scale (Spielberger et al., 1983); (b) the Beck Depression Inventory (Beck & Steer, 1987); (c) a seven-item scale assessing religious practice; (d) the Crowne-Marlowe Social Desirability Scale (Crowne & Marlowe, 1960); (e) one item assessing the extent of forgiveness (included as a validity-check); and (f) background questions (age, gender, educational level, religious affiliation).

MAIN RESULTS: The subscales and full scale of the EFI were shown to have good internal consistency, validity, and test-retest reliability. Forgiveness was associated with lower anxiety scores, a relationship that was especially strong for students experiencing deep hurt. No significant correlations with depression were found. Within developmentally normative relationships (male-female relationships in the students; spouse/child relationships for the parents), the student group appeared to find forgiveness more difficult than the parent group. Under conditions of deep hurt, however, parents and *their own* children (note: not parents and children *in general*) forgave to similar degrees. Although there was no relationship between forgiveness and the seven-item religiosity measure, persons who were affiliated with a religion showed slightly higher levels of forgiveness than those who were not affiliated.

CONCLUSION: The EFI appears to have adequate psychometric properties. Scores on the EFI were found to be negatively correlated with anxiety.

Results demonstrated the importance of examining factors such as the depth of hurt caused by an offense and whether an offense is developmentally normative. When offenses are developmentally normative, children may find it more difficult to forgive than do their parents. In the case of deep hurt, parents and their children show similar levels of forgiveness.

COMMENTARY: The development of a body of research on forgiveness has been traditionally hindered by the lack of instrumentation for measuring forgiveness. Enright's 60-item scale is likely to be a highly useful instrument. The balance of positive and negative items and small correlations with social desirability are extremely useful properties. Enright's ongoing work to refine and validate this measure in many cultures shall only improve its utility for many research applications.

CORRESPONDENCE: Robert D. Enright, Department of Educational Psychology, University of Wisconsin–Madison, Madison, Wisconsin.

Tangney, J.P., Wagner, P.E., Hill-Barlow, D., Marschall, D.E., & Gramzow, R. (1996)

RELATION OF SHAME AND GUILT TO CONSTRUCTIVE VERSUS DESTRUCTIVE RESPONSES TO ANGER ACROSS THE LIFESPAN

Journal of Personality and Social Psychology, 70, 797–809

OBJECTIVE: To examine how proneness to shame and guilt relate to constructive versus destructive responses to anger among children, adolescents, college students, and adults.

DESIGN: Cross-sectional survey.

SETTING: East coast of the U.S.

PARTICIPANTS: Participants were 302 children (grades 4 through 6) and 427 adolescents (grades 7 through 11) recruited from public schools, 176 college students attending a large state university, and 194 adult travelers passing through a large urban airport. Samples contained both males and females, were composed largely of whites and blacks, and primarily represented Catholic and Protestant religious affiliations.

ASSESSMENT OF PREDICTOR VARIABLES: Each participant completed a version of the Test of Self-Conscious Affect (TOSCA) appropriate either for children (TOSCA-C; Tangney, Wagner, Burggraf, Gramzow, & Fletcher, 1990), adolescents (TOSCA-A; Tangney, Wagner, Gavlas, & Gramzow, 1991b), or adults (TOSCA; Tangney, Wagner, & Gramzow, 1989). The TOSCA was designed to assess shame-proneness, guilt-proneness, externalization, detachment-unconcern, alpha pride (pride in self), and beta pride (pride in behavior). It consists of 10 negative and 5 positive scenarios that respondents would be likely to encounter in everyday life. Participants read each scenario and used a 5-point scale to rate their likelihood of reacting in various ways (including those related to shame and guilt). In this study, internal consistencies (alphas) ranged from .74 to .78 for the Shame scales and .61 to .83 for the Guilt scales.

ASSESSMENT OF OUTCOME VARIABLES: As an assessment of characteristic responses to anger, each participant completed a version of the Anger Response Inventory (ARI) appropriate either for children (ARI-C; Tangney, Wagner, Hansbarger, & Gramzow, 1991), adolescents (ARI-A; Tangney, Wagner, Gavlas, & Gramzow, 1991a), or adults (ARI; Tangney, Wagner, Marschall, & Gramzow, 1991). The ARI includes a series of scenarios of common, developmentally appropriate situations that are likely to elicit anger. Participants were asked to imagine themselves in each situation. After reading each scenario, participants rated on a 5-point scale: (a) how angry they would be in such a situation (anger arousal); (b) their behavioral intentions (constructive, malicious, or fractious); (c) their likely behavioral and cognitive responses (e.g., aggressive and nonaggressive behaviors, escapist-diffusing tactics, and cognitive reappraisals); and (d) the likely long-term consequences (for self, other, and relationship). Internal consistencies (alphas) were .76 for children, .80 for adolescents, .78 for college students, and .80 for adults.

MAIN RESULTS: Due to the substantial overlap between shame and guilt (rs ranging from .40 to .48), the primary analyses of interest are partial correlations using the residuals of shame and guilt—that is, those parts that represent the "unique" portion of each construct (shame-free guilt and guilt-free shame). All analyses reported below use these residuals. Across all age groups, shame-proneness was positively related to anger arousal and to both malevolent intentions (e.g., felt like getting back at the target of anger) and fractious intentions (e.g., felt like "letting off steam"), but was not related to constructive intentions (e.g., felt like fixing the situation). Shame-proneness was also associated with destructive responses to anger, including higher levels of: (a) direct physical, verbal, and symbolic aggression toward the target; (b) indirect aggression (e.g., harming something important to the person); (c) malediction (talking maliciously behind the target's back); (d) displaced aggression (aggression displaced onto another person such as one's spouse); (e) anger held in (ruminative anger); and (f) self-aggression (tendency to become disproportionately angry with the self for the anger-eliciting situation; e.g., "I was furious with myself for trusting him in the first place"). Shame-proneness was largely unrelated to constructive responses, positively related to reappraisal of one's own role, and negatively related to optimism about the outcome of the anger episode.

Guilt-proneness, in contrast, was positively related to constructive intentions, negatively related to malevolent intentions, and not related to fractious intentions. It also correlated negatively with aggression indices (direct, indirect, malediction, and displaced) across all age groups. There was, however, a positive relationship between guilt-proneness and self-aggression. Guilt-proneness was positively associated with: (a) constructive responses (e.g., taking corrective action; discussing situation with the target); (b) reappraisal (e.g., "I wonder if I made a mistake?"; "Maybe she couldn't help it"); (c) optimism about long-term consequences; and (d) in childhood and adolescence only, with the use of escapist-diffusing tendencies.

CONCLUSION: These findings strongly suggest that shame-prone persons are likely to respond to anger-inducing situations in nonconstructive ways. Shame-proneness was associated with higher levels of anger and aggression across a wide variety of indices. Guilt-proneness, in contrast, was negatively related to aggression and positively related to a variety of constructive responses.

COMMENTARY: Shame and guilt are related, but distinct, psychological phenomena. These results suggest that the tendency to experience shame might play a major role in facilitating people's tendencies toward destructive forms of retaliation following anger-eliciting situations. Thus, we might hypothesize that shame-proneness is a major deterrent of the capacity to forgive others. Conversely, proneness to guilt appears to facilitate more constructive responses following anger-eliciting situations, suggesting that people with high guilt-proneness might be more prone to forgive than are other people. Thus, like other studies (e.g., Baumeister, Stillwell, & Heatherton, 1995) reviewed in this annotated bibliography, this study suggests that guilt might serve some important—although unappreciated—functions in helping people overcome the negative, personal, and relational effects of interpersonal transgressions.

CORRESPONDENCE: June Price Tangney, Department of Psychology, George Mason University, Fairfax, Virginia.

Weinberg, N. (1994)

SELF-BLAME, OTHER BLAME, AND DESIRE FOR REVENGE: FACTORS IN RECOVERY FROM BEREAVEMENT

Death Studies, 18, 583–593

OBJECTIVE: To examine the relationship between cause of death, attributional processes, and self-reported recovery from bereavement.

DESIGN: Quasi-experiment using cross-sectional survey.

SETTING: Major midwestern university.

PARTICIPANTS: Questionnaires were sent to a total of 5,000 nonacademic employees (i.e., secretaries, maintenance workers, and food service personnel) and 2,500 graduate students, all from the same university. The response rate was 18%. A total of 200 participants were selected for the study, all of whom: (a) identified the death of a loved one as the most distressing event that they had ever experienced and (b) indicated the cause of their loved one's death. Identity of deceased person: 48% parent, 12% child, 10% sibling, 8% spouse, 4% grandparent, 10% other relatives, 6% unrelated persons such as friends and mentors. Causes of death included cancer (79), accidents (30), unspecified disease (38), stroke or heart disease (21), chronic health conditions (13), miscarriages or neonatal death (9), suicide (6), and murder (4). The mean time since the death was 8 years.

The sample was composed of 45 males and 155 females with a mean age of 40 years. Marital status: 29% single, 38% married for the first time, 12% separated or divorced, 15% married for the second time, 7% widowed. Respondents had 1.4 children on average with a mean age of 11 years. Highest education level attained: 28% high school, 23% junior college or trade school, 21% college undergraduate, 22% graduate school. The majority (90% of the 77% who answered a race item) were white.

ASSESSMENT OF PREDICTOR VARIABLES: After describing the distressing experience, participants completed the Inventory of Responses to Distressing Events (IRDE), which is based on the Revised Ways of Coping Checklist (Folkman, Lazarus, Dunkel-Schetter, DeLongis, & Gruen, 1986). The IRDE lists 66 emotional, cognitive, and behavioral responses that people might make when distressing experiences occur. Participants were asked to rate (on 4-point Likert scales) the extent to which they engaged in each response at the time the death occurred. Self-blame was measured by the statement "I blamed myself," other blame by "I blamed others," and desire for revenge by "I thought about or sought revenge." Using a separate sample of social work students who had completed the IRDE, test–retest reliabilities were found to be: .86 for self-blame, .61 for other blame, and .69 for desire for revenge.

ASSESSMENT OF OUTCOME VARIABLES: Participants rated the extent to which they believed they had recovered from the other person's death on a 10-point scale. Test–retest reliability: .75.

MAIN RESULTS: Relative to deaths from natural causes (i.e., illness, miscarriage), unnatural deaths (accidents, murders, and suicides) were associated with greater blame. In the case of unnatural deaths, 84% of mourners blamed a person, with 40% blaming both themselves and others ("dual blame"), 26% blaming others alone, and 18% blaming themselves alone. In contrast, only 38% of mourners reporting naturally caused death reported blame (14% self- and other blame, 12% self-blame, 13% other blame). Self-reported recovery was greater: (a) for natural deaths than for unnatural ones and (b) for mourners who did not blame themselves than for those who did. Overall, other blame was not related to recovery. However, in the case of unnatural death, those who blamed others but did not desire revenge reported greater recovery than those who blamed others and did desire revenge.

CONCLUSION: People are more likely to assign blame—particularly dual blame—in the case of unnatural versus natural deaths. Self-blame is associated with poorer recovery from bereavement. The relationship between other-blame and recovery appears more complex: Among people who have lost others through unnatural causes, poorer recovery is predicted by other blame—but only if it is accompanied by a desire for revenge.

COMMENTARY: Despite the unusual methods of data analyses, this fascinating study is the only study of which we are aware, that has actually examined whether blaming others and desiring revenge influence how people adjust to the unnatural death of loved ones. Interestingly, these data suggest that it is not blame of other people that prevents people from adjusting (in fact, the lack of blame predicts poorer adjustment), but rather, the combination of blame and the quest for revenge. Thus, it appears that the processes of blaming and desiring revenge operate somewhat independently, and it is only in combination that they interfere with adjustment to bereavement.

CORRESPONDENCE: Nancy Weinberg, School of Social Work, University of Illinois, Urbana, Illinois.

Weiner, B., Graham, S., Peter, O., & Zmuidinas, M. (1991)

PUBLIC CONFESSION AND FORGIVENESS

Journal of Personality, 59, 281–312

OBJECTIVE: To examine the effects of confessing one's transgressions on forgiveness and other related judgments toward an offender.

DESIGN: Five experiments, four of which used vignettes and a fifth using a laboratory-based manipulation.

SETTING: The University of California, Los Angeles.

PARTICIPANTS: Participants for all five studies were college undergraduates enrolled in introductory psychology courses. Both males and females participated. Numbers of participants ranged from 61 (Study 2) to 125 (Study 1).

MANIPULATED VARIABLES: All participants were randomly assigned to groups. In Studies 1 through 4, participants were presented with a vignette in which an actor committed a moral transgression. Variables manipulated included the status of the transgressor (Study 1), the attribution for the transgression (Study 2), and the spontaneity of the confession, with (Study 3) or without (Study 4) an accusation. Study 5 employed a mixed-motive game in which a confederate confessed either spontaneously or following an accusation.

ASSESSMENT OF OUTCOME VARIABLES: Dependent variables, each of which was used in one or more of the studies, included the perceived personal character of the transgressor, attributions of responsibility for the transgression, sympathetic and angry responses, future expectations, inferred reasons for the confession, forgiveness, and behavioral judgments. The effectiveness of confession was also compared with several other accounts offered by the actor for his transgressions, including denial of responsibility (Studies 1 and 2), denial of the act itself (Studies 3 and 4), or no information (a control condition in Studies 1 through 5). In Study 5, the effects of confessions on subsequent cooperation and competition were assessed, as were perceptions of the offender.

MAIN RESULTS: Across the studies, results consistently demonstrated that when an accused transgressor was definitely guilty, confession yielded more favorable reactions than denial of the offense. Confession was shown to be especially adaptive under conditions of: (a) attributional uncertainty—that is, when the exact cause of the transgression remains unclear (Study 2) and (b) spontaneity—that is, before accusation (Studies 4 and 5). However, Study 5 suggested that even a spontaneous confession may prompt more negative inferences than situations that do not raise any suspicion about guilt (which was, in this case, the control condition).

CONCLUSION: In this series of experiments, confession was shown to have beneficial effects on how the transgressors were evaluated by others. Confession appears to be most helpful in facilitating forgiveness when: (a) it is offered before an accusation occurs—but only if an accusation does seem to be forthcoming, (b) the actor is perceived as having truly committed a transgression, and (c) the attribution for the act is ambiguous.

COMMENTARY: Like the studies by Darby and Schlenker, these data from Weiner and his colleagues illuminate the basic social-psychological elements of interpersonal forgiving, particularly how confession might influence an offended person's willingness and/or ability to forgive. Such experimental data are helpful for pointing out how basic variables, such as the style with which one confesses and the timing of the confession, influence forgiveness. The data from Study 5 also show that the basic findings about confession are important in real-life interactions, not simply in people's hypothetical responses to vignettes. Taken together, these five studies provide convincing evidence that forgiveness is strongly shaped by social events that occur *after the offense itself is already completed.*

CORRESPONDENCE: Bernard Weiner, Department of Psychology, University of California, Los Angeles, California.

Wu, J., & Axelrod, R. (1995)

HOW TO COPE WITH NOISE IN THE ITERATED PRISONER'S DILEMMA

Journal of Conflict Resolution, 39, 183–189

OBJECTIVE: To compare three approaches to coping with noise in the Prisoner's Dilemma Game (PDG), a tool used to simulate conflict situations in the laboratory. A noisy environment is one in which people sometimes draw incorrect inferences because they lack perfect information about the actions of others.

DESIGN: Revised version of earlier round-robin tournament (Axelrod, 1980b) in which various computer-simulated strategies were pitted against each other. Ecological simulation techniques, which involve repeated use and weighing of strategies over multiple "generations," were also used.

SETTING: No information given.

PARTICIPANTS: Four strategy programs were compared, each of which was pitted against 63 strategies from an earlier tournament (Axelrod, 1980b).

ASSESSMENT OF PREDICTOR VARIABLES: In the PDG, two participants are repeatedly faced with the decision to choose a cooperative or a competitive strategy. The object is to win as many points as possible. If both cooperate, they each win 3 points. If one defects while the other cooperates, the defector wins 5 points while the cooperator receives 0 points. If both defect, both win 1 point.

In this version, the average number of moves per game was 151. Noise (ranging from 0.1% to 10%) was programmed into each run (cf. Bendor, Kramer, & Stout, 1991), and an ecological simulation was performed: That is, the games were run repeatedly (in this case, 2,000 times), with the fraction of the population represented by a given rule, based on the rule's tournament score in the previous run. In this way, the resulting environment tends to emphasize rules that have done relatively well in the noisy setting.

The strategies compared included generous TIT FOR TAT (which is based on reciprocity norms but cooperates 10% of the time that it would otherwise defect), contrite TIT FOR TAT (which is based on reciprocity norms but can recover from its own unintentional defections—caused by noise—by cooperating on the next move), and two other strategies not based on reciprocity.

ASSESSMENT OF OUTCOME VARIABLES: The scores of the four strategies were compared in two ways: first, each score was repeatedly paired with the 63 rules of the prior tournament at various levels of noise. Second, all rules (the new 4 and the other 63) were placed into the ecological simulation and run through 2,000 iterations (or "generations"). This second method demonstrated which strategies worked best in an environment that had adapted to noise.

MAIN RESULTS: When the prior tournament was again run, both generous TIT FOR TAT and contrite TIT FOR TAT fared better than the non-reciprocity-based strategies at all levels of noise. However, contrite TIT FOR TAT (reciprocity with contrition) was by far the most effective strategy after 1,000 trials of the ecological simulation (with its lead increasing as of 2,000 trials), suggesting that it is well adapted to survive in an environment that has "learned" how to deal with the presence of noise.

CONCLUSION: When noise (i.e., communication breakdown and occasional mistaken inference) is present, reciprocity still works, assuming that it is qualified by either generosity or contrition. Both generosity and contrition, by enabling some recovery from transgressions, can reduce the risk of ongoing conflict. However, in an environment in which others have also adapted to dealing with breakdowns in communication, a strategy of contrite reciprocity appears superior.

COMMENTARY: The results from this study point out a principle that is critical for future studies of forgiveness with samples of human subjects: Even though we sometimes hurt other people—either intentionally or unintentionally—in relationships, returning to productive, cooperative modes of interaction is nearly always facilitated by reciprocity. Also, this study suggests that inadvertent transgressions can be overcome through overlooking some of the offenses of one's partner (which might have been prompted by one's own hurtful behavior), and also, by refraining from allowing one's own inadvertently hurtful behavior from starting a precedent for mutual hurt in the relationship. Thus, willingness to forgive the inadvertent transgressions of one's relationship partner, but especially contrition for one's own hurtful behavior, might be critical ingredients for long-term success in interpersonal relations.

CORRESPONDENCE: No mailing address listed. The first author was at the University of Michigan at the time of this writing.

Zillmann, D., Bryant, J., Cantor, J.R., & Day, K.D. (1975)

IRRELEVANCE OF MITIGATING CIRCUMSTANCES IN RETALIATORY BEHAVIOR AT HIGH LEVELS OF EXCITATION

Journal of Research in Personality, 9, 282–293

OBJECTIVE: To explore the effects of mitigating circumstances on retaliation at moderate versus high levels of arousal.

DESIGN: Laboratory experiment.

SETTING: Indiana University.

PARTICIPANTS: Sixty male undergraduates participated for course credit.

MANIPULATED VARIABLES: Two participants were run at a time. They met a "polite experimenter" and completed an easy, bogus perceptual task. A second "rude experimenter" later entered and made insulting comments to the participants while administering a frustrating task (a listening task for which the tape was full of static and extraneous noise). Based on a coin toss, participants were assigned to perform either a high-excitation task (riding a bike exerciser) or a moderate-excitation task (disc threading). Participants then observed the rude experimenter provoking the polite experimenter. They were either told by the polite experimenter, "He's really uptight about his prelims" (mitigation condition), or given no information (no mitigation condition).

ASSESSMENT OF OUTCOME VARIABLES: Participants rated their satisfaction with the experiment and listed any complaints. They were also asked to rate each experimenter in terms of competence and courtesy, and to recommend whether the experimenter should be reappointed as a research assistant. The last question was considered to be the most direct measure of retaliation because it carried implications for the future of the rude experimenter.

MAIN RESULTS: More complaints about the experiment and the rude experimenter were offered in the high excitation condition than the moderate excitation condition. No main effects of mitigation were found on these variables. Ratings of the experimenter's competence and courtesy were influenced both by mitigation and excitation conditions, with less favorable ratings given under conditions of high excitation and no mitigation. Recommendations to reappoint the experimenter showed the same pattern. Finally, in the case of courtesy ratings and recommendations for reappointment, a significant interaction appeared between mitigation and excitation condition: whereas mitigating circumstances reduced negative and retaliatory ratings under conditions of moderate excitation, they had no effect under conditions of high excitation.

CONCLUSION: Mitigating information may lose its ability to reduce hostility and retaliation when the victim is in a state of high (physiological) excitation.

COMMENTARY: This study reveals that people are not able to use mitigating information to reduce their tendency to retaliate following interpersonal offenses when they are physiologically aroused in the same way as when they are not physiologically aroused. As in other studies reviewed in this bibliography (Kremer & Stevens, 1983; Zillmann & Cantor, 1976), these findings suggest that the value of mitigating information in reducing retaliation can be easily corrupted by subtle timing effects and increased cognitive load on the victim. As even casual interpersonal offenses themselves are stressful (see Zillmann & Cantor, 1976) significant interpersonal transgressions might be so difficult to forgive, in part, because the increased physiological arousal associated with such hurts increases people's cognitive load, limiting their ability to do cognitive work that would make forgiveness possible. The interplay between social, cognitive, and physiological variables remains an interesting area for future research into the structure of forgiveness.

CORRESPONDENCE: Dr. Dolf Zillmann, Institute for Communication Research, Radio-TV Center, Indiana University, Bloomington, Indiana.

Zillmann, D., & Cantor, J.R. (1976)

EFFECT OF TIMING OF INFORMATION ABOUT MITIGATING CIRCUMSTANCES ON EMOTIONAL RESPONSES TO PROVOCATION AND RETALIATORY BEHAVIOR

Journal of Experimental Social Psychology, 12, 38–55

OBJECTIVE: To determine whether physiological arousal and retaliation are influenced by both the presence and the timing of mitigating circumstances.

DESIGN: Laboratory experiment.

SETTING: Indiana University.

PARTICIPANTS: Forty-five male undergraduates were recruited through a campus advertisement and were paid for their participation.

MANIPULATED VARIABLES: After participants were told by a "polite experimenter" that their physiological reactions to television segments would be monitored, their blood pressure, heart rate, and skin temperature were assessed. All participants, after performing the first, bogus video-rating task, were provoked by a "rude experimenter" about a supposed failure to sit still. The rude experimenter also insulted the polite experimenter. Participants then performed a second video-rating task. In the prior mitigation condition, the polite experimenter gave participants mitigating information ("He's really uptight about a midterm he has tomorrow") before being provoked. In the subsequent mitigation condition, the mitigating information was given after the participant was provoked (after the second video-rating task). In the no mitigation condition, this explanation was not provided at any time.

ASSESSMENT OF OUTCOME VARIABLES: To measure changes in arousal, a total of six measurements of heart rate, blood pressure, and skin temperature were taken to assess the effects of the experimental manipulations. Retaliation was measured via a questionnaire given at the end of the session: Participants rated their satisfaction with the experiment and listed any complaints. They were also asked to rate each experimenter and offer an opinion as to whether the experimenter should be reappointed as a research assistant. The last question was considered to be the most direct measure of retaliation because it carried implications for the future of the rude experimenter.

MAIN RESULTS: All participants showed increased systolic blood pressure after provocation. However, those in the prior mitigation condition showed significantly less intense physiological responses. The blood pressure readings of the prior mitigation group dropped to baseline levels after the second video-rating task, while those of the other two groups remained elevated. When the subsequent mitigation group received the mitigating information, systolic pressure dropped significantly and eventually returned to baseline levels. Similar results were found for heart rate and skin temperature, although the skin temperature results were weaker.

Regardless of its timing, mitigation reduced dissatisfaction and complaining about the experiment. However, timing of mitigating information was a predictor of direct retaliation against the rude experimenter. In ratings of the rude experimenter's performance and courtesy and recommendations about reappointment, participants in the prior mitigation condition gave more favorable ratings than those in the other two conditions (which did not differ significantly). Whereas only one of the 15 participants in the prior mitigation group gave the rude experimenter a negative reappointment rating, 12 of the participants in the subsequent mitigation group gave him negative ratings. In addition, coding of written comments revealed that those in the prior mitigation condition wrote comments that were significantly less hostile than those in the other two conditions (which did not differ significantly).

CONCLUSION: The physiological arousal data strongly suggest that information about mitigating circumstances leads to reduced arousal, regardless of its timing. However, the timing of mitigation appears very important in terms of retaliation: compared with mitigating information received after provocation, prior mitigation appears to be a substantial deterrent to hostility and retaliation. Thus, while late mitigation may be better than none at all (at least in terms of reducing arousal), its ability to dampen hostile responses appears limited.

COMMENTARY: These results provide a link between social processes, cognitive processes, and physiological processes that could be extremely important for future theorizing about how forgiveness might influence physical health. To the extent that people receive mitigating information (in the form of apologies, for example) after social transgressions *with appropriate timing* (see also Kremer & Stevens, 1983), they appear to be able to reduce their elevated physiological arousal following interpersonal transgressions in short order. Without such mitigating information, however, physiological arousal remains high. These mitigation-mediated reductions in physiological arousal following interpersonal offenses might also be influenced by the increased ability of victims to forgive perpetrators, about whose offensive behavior they have received some appropriately timed mitigating information. Whether the extended elevations in physiological arousal—associated with inappropriately timed mitigating information—are clinically significant remains to be investigated in future studies.

CORRESPONDENCE: Dr. Dolf Zillmann, Institute for Communication Research, Radio-TV Center, Indiana University, Bloomington, Indiana.

LIST OF ARTICLES BY SUBJECT

Accounts

Gonzales, Manning, & Haugen, 1992

Gonzales, Haugen, & Manning, 1994

Hodgins, Liebeskind, & Schwartz, 1996

Mongeau, Hale, & Alles, 1994

Anger

Stuckless & Goranson, 1992

Tangney, Wagner, Hill-Barlow, Marschall, & Gramzow, 1996

Apology

Baumeister, Stillwell, & Wotman, 1990

Baumeister, Stillwell, & Heatherton, 1995

Darby & Schlenker, 1982

Gonzales, Haugen, & Manning, 1994

McCullough, Worthington, & Rachal, 1997

Ohbuchi, Kameda, & Agarie, 1989

O'Malley & Greenberg, 1983

Attributions

Boon & Sulsky, 1997

Darby & Schlenker, 1982

Gonzales, Manning, & Haugen, 1992

Gonzales, Haugen, & Manning, 1994

Hodgins, Liebeskind, & Schwartz, 1996

Kremer & Stephens, 1983

McGraw, 1987

Mongeau, Hale, & Alles, 1994

O'Malley & Greenberg, 1983

Weinberg, 1994

Weiner, Graham, Peter, & Zmuidinas, 1991

Blame (self)

Weinberg, 1994

Blame (others)

Baumeister, Stillwell, & Heatherton, 1995

Boon & Sulsky, 1997

McGraw, 1987

Interventions
    Al-Mabuk, Enright, & Cardis, 1995
    Coyle & Enright, 1997
    Freedman & Enright, 1996
    Hebl & Enright, 1993
    McCullough, Worthington, & Rachal, 1997
    McCullough & Worthington, 1995

Marriage/Family/Romantic Relationships
    Al-Mabuk, Enright, & Cardis, 1995
    Baumeister, Stillwell, & Heatherton, 1995
    Boon & Sulsky, 1997
    Coyle & Enright, 1997
    Hargrave & Sells, 1997
    Mongeau, Hale, & Alles, 1994
    Roloff & Janiszewski, 1989
    Rusbult, Verette, Whitney, Slovik, & Lipkus, 1991

Mental Health
    Al-Mabuk, Enright, & Cardis, 1995
    Coyle & Enright (in press)
    DiBlasio, 1993
    DiBlasio & Proctor, 1993
    Freedman & Enright, 1996
    Haley & Strickland, 1986
    Hargrave & Sells, 1997
    Hebl & Enright, 1993
    Mauger et al., 1992

Physiological Measures
    Kremer & Stephens, 1983
    Zillmann & Cantor, 1976

Prisoner's Dilemma Game
    Axelrod, 1980a
    Axelrod, 1980b
    Bendor, Kramer, & Stout, 1991
    Haley & Strickland, 1986
    Komorita, Hilty, & Parks, 1991
    Wu & Axelrod, 1995

Religious Variables
  DiBlasio, 1993
  DiBlasio & Proctor, 1993
  Enright, Santos, & Al-Mabuk, 1989
  Gorsuch & Hao, 1993
  Meek, Albright, & McMinn, 1995
  Poloma & Gallup, 1991
  Subkoviak et al., 1995
Retaliation/Revenge
  Brown, 1968
  Fagenson & Cooper, 1987
  Haley & Strickland, 1986
  Holbrook, White, & Hutt, 1995
  Kremer & Stephens, 1983
  Mongeau, Hale, & Alles, 1994
  Ohbuchi, Kameda, & Agarie, 1989
  Stuckless & Goranson, 1992
  Tangney, Wagner, Hill-Barlow, Marschall, & Gramzow, 1996
  Zillmann, Bryant, Cantor, & Day, 1975
  Zillmann & Cantor, 1976
Self-Forgiveness
  Mauger et al., 1992
Victim/Perpetrator Differences
  Baumeister, Stillwell, & Wotman, 1990
  Baumeister, Stillwell, & Heatherton, 1995
  Stillwell & Baumeister, 1997

REFERENCES

*Al-Mabuk, R.H., Enright, R.D., & Cardis, P.A. (1995). Forgiveness education with parentally love-deprived late adolescents. *Journal of Moral Education, 24*, 427–444.

Allport, G.W., Gillespie, J.M., & Young, J. (1953). The religion of the postwar college student. In J.M. Seidman (Ed.), *The adolescent* (pp. 266–285). New York: Dryden.

Allport, G.W., & Ross, J.M. (1967). Personal religious orientation and prejudice. *Journal of Personality and Social Psychology, 5*, 432–443.

*Axelrod, R. (1980a). Effective choice in the Prisoner's Dilemma. *Journal of Conflict Resolution, 24*, 3–25.

*Axelrod, R. (1980b). More effective choice in the Prisoner's Dilemma. *Journal of Conflict Resolution, 24*, 379–403.

Baumeister, R.F., Stillwell, A.M., & Heatherton, T.F. (1994). Guilt: An interpersonal approach. *Psychological Bulletin, 115*, 243–267.

*Baumeister, R.F., Stillwell, A.M., & Heatherton, T.F. (1995). Personal narratives about guilt: Role in action control and interpersonal relationships. *Basic and Applied Social Psychology, 17*, 173–198.

*Baumeister, R.F., Stillwell, A.M., & Wotman, S.R. (1990). Victim and perpetrator accounts of interpersonal conflict: Autobiographical narratives about anger. *Journal of Personality and Social Psychology, 59*, 994–1005.

Beck, A.T., & Steer, R.A. (1987). *Beck depression inventory.* San Antonio: Psychological Corporation.

Beck, A.T., Ward, C.H., Mendelson, M., Mock, J., & Erbaugh, J. (1961). An inventory for measuring depression. *Archives of General Psychiatry, 4*, 561–571.

Bem, S.L. (1974). The measurement of psychological androgyny. *Journal of Consulting and Clinical Psychology, 47*, 155–162.

*Bendor, J., Kramer, R.M., & Stout, S. (1991). When in doubt...Cooperation in a noisy prisoner's dilemma. *Journal of Conflict Resolution, 35*, 691–719.

Biglan, A., Rothlind, J., Hops, H., & Sherman, L. (1989). Impact of distressed and aggressive behavior. *Journal of Abnormal Psychology, 98*, 218–228.

*Boon, S.D., & Sulsky, L.M. (1997). Attributions of blame and forgiveness in romantic relationships: A policy-capturing study. *Journal of Social Behavior and Personality, 12*, 19–44.

*Articles reviewed in this bibliography

Bray, J.H., Williamson, D.S., & Malone, P.E. (1984a). Personal authority in the family system: Development of a questionnaire to measure personal authority in intergenerational family processes. *Journal of Marital and Family Therapy, 10*, 167–178.

Bray, J.H., Williamson, D.S., & Malone, P.E. (1984b). *Manual for the personal authority in the family system questionnaire.* Houston, TX: Houston Family Institute.

*Brown, B.R. (1968). The effects of need to maintain face on interpersonal bargaining. *Journal of Experimental Social Psychology, 4*, 107–122.

Burns, D. (1994). *The therapist's toolkit: Comprehensive treatment and assessment tools for mental health professionals.* Los Altos, CA.

Christie, R., & Geis, F.L. (1970). *Studies in Machiavellianism.* San Diego, CA: Academic Press.

Coke, J.S., Batson, C.D., & McDavis, K. (1978). Empathic mediation of helping: A two-stage model. *Journal of Personality and Social Psychology, 36*, 752–766.

Coopersmith, S. (1981). *Self-esteem inventories.* Palo Alto, CA: Consulting Psychologists, Inc.

*Coyle, C.T., & Enright, R.D. (1997). Forgiveness intervention with post-abortion men. *Journal of Consulting and Clinical Psychology, 65*, 1042–1045.

Crowne, D.P., & Marlowe, D. (1960). A new scale of social desirability independent of psychopathology. *Journal of Consulting Psychology, 24*, 349–354.

*Darby, B.W., & Schlenker, B.R. (1982). Children's reactions to apologies. *Journal of Personality and Social Psychology, 43*, 742–753.

Davis, M.H. (1980). A multidimensional approach to individual differences in empathy. *JSAS Catalog of Selected Documents in Psychology, 10*, 85.

Davis, M.H. (1983). Measuring individual differences in empathy: Evidence for a multi-dimensional approach. *Journal of Personality and Social Psychology, 44*, 113–126.

Deci, E.L., & Ryan, R.M. (1985). The General Causality Orientations Scale: Self-determination in personality. *Journal of Research in Personality, 19*, 109–134.

Deutsch, M., & Krauss, R. (1960). The effects of threat on interpersonal bargaining. *Journal of Abnormal and Social Psychology, 61*, 223–230.

*DiBlasio, F.A. (1993). The role of social workers' religious beliefs in helping family members forgive. *Families in Society, 74*, 163–170.

*DiBlasio, F.A., & Proctor, J.H. (1993). Therapists and the clinical use of forgiveness. *American Journal of Family Therapy, 21*, 175–184.

*Enright, R.D., Santos, M.J., & Al-Mabuk, R. (1989). The adolescent as forgiver. *Journal of Adolescence, 12*, 99–110.

*Fagenson, E.A., & Cooper, J. (1987). When push comes to power: A test of power restoration theory's explanation for aggressive conflict escalation. *Basic and Applied Social Psychology, 8,* 273–293.

Folkman, S., Lazarus, R., Dunkel-Schetter, C., DeLongis, A., & Gruen, R.J. (1986). Dynamics of a stressful encounter: Cognitive appraisal, coping and encounter outcomes. *Journal of Personality and Social Psychology, 50,* 992–1003.

*Freedman, S.R., & Enright, R.D. (1996). Forgiveness as an intervention goal with incest survivors. *Journal of Consulting and Clinical Psychology, 64,* 983–992.

Fultz, J., Batson, C.D., Fortenbach, V.A., McCarthy, P.M., & Varney, L.L. (1986). Social evaluation and the empathy-altruism hypothesis. *Journal of Personality and Social Psychology, 50,* 761–769.

*Gonzales, M.H., Haugen, J.A., & Manning, D.J. (1994). Victims as "narrative critics": Factors influencing rejoinders and evaluative responses to offenders' accounts. *Personality and Social Psychology Bulletin, 20,* 691–704.

*Gonzales, M.H., Manning, D.J., & Haugen, J.A. (1992). Explaining our sins: Factors influencing offender accounts and anticipated victim responses. *Journal of Personality and Social Psychology, 62,* 958–971.

*Gorsuch, R.L., & Hao, J.Y. (1993). Forgiveness: An exploratory factor analysis and its relationships to religious variables. *Review of Religious Research, 34,* 333–347.

Gough, H. (1952). *The adjective checklist.* Palo Alto, CA: Consulting Psychologists Press.

*Haley, W.E., & Strickland, B.R. (1986). Interpersonal betrayal and cooperation: Effects on self-evaluation in depression. *Journal of Personality and Social Psychology, 50,* 386–391.

Hargrave, T.D. (1994). *Families and forgiveness: Healing intergenerational wounds.* New York: Brunner/Mazel.

Hargrave, T.D., Jennings, G., & Anderson, W. (1991). The development of a relational ethics scale. *Journal of Marital and Family Therapy, 17,* 145–158.

*Hargrave, T.D., & Sells, J.N. (1997). The development of a forgiveness scale. *Journal of Marital and Family Therapy, 23,* 41–62.

*Hebl, J.H., & Enright, R.D. (1993). Forgiveness as a psychotherapeutic goal with elderly females. *Psychotherapy, 30,* 658–667.

*Hodgins, H.S., Liebeskind, E., & Schwartz, W. (1996). Getting out of hot water: Facework in social predicaments. *Journal of Personality and Social Psychology, 71,* 300–314.

*Holbrook, M.I., White, M.H., & Hutt, M.J. (1995). The Vengeance Scale: Comparison of groups and an assessment of external validity. *Psychological Reports, 77,* 224–226.

Hoyle, R.H. (1987, November). *Factorial validity of the Multifaceted-Evaluation-of-Self Inventory (MESI)*. Paper presented at the twenty-seventh annual meeting of the New England Psychological Association, Amherst, MA.

Hudson, W.W. (1976). Child's attitudes toward father. In C.A. Giuli & W.W. Hudson (Eds.), *Assessing parent-child relationship disorders in clinical practice: The child's point of view*. Honolulu, HI: University of Hawaii Department of Educational Psychology and School of Social Work.

Jackson, D. (1970). A sequential system for personality scale development. In C. D. Spielberger (Ed.), *Current topics in clinical and community psychology* (pp. 61–96). New York: Academic Press.

* Komorita, S.S., Hilty, J.A., & Parks, C.D. (1991). Reciprocity and cooperation in social dilemmas. *Journal of Conflict Resolution, 35*, 494–518.

* Kremer, J.F., & Stephens, L. (1983). Attributions and arousal as mediators of mitigation's effect on retaliation. *Journal of Personality and Social Psychology, 45*, 335–343.

Long, E.C.J. (1990). Measuring dyadic perspective-taking: Two scales for assessing perspective-taking in marriage and similar dyads. *Educational and Psychological Measurement, 50*, 91–103.

* Mauger, P.A., Perry, J.E., Freeman, T., Grove, D.C., McBride, A.G., & McKinney, K.E. (1992). The measurement of forgiveness: Preliminary research. *Journal of Psychology and Christianity, 11*, 170–180.

* McCullough, M.E., & Worthington, E.L., Jr. (1995). Promoting forgiveness: A comparison of two brief psychoeducational group interventions with a wait-list control. *Counseling and Values, 40*, 55–68.

* McCullough, M.E., Worthington, E.L., Jr., & Rachal, K.C. (1997). Interpersonal forgiving in close relationships. *Journal of Personality and Social Psychology 73*, 321–336.

* McGraw, K.M. (1987). Guilt following transgression: An attribution of responsibility approach. *Journal of Personality and Social Psychology, 53*, 247–256.

McLaughlin, M.L., Cody, M.J., & O'Hair, H.D. (1983). The management of failure events: Some contextual determinants of accounting behavior. *Human Communication Research, 9*, 208–224.

* Meek, K.R., Albright, J.S., & McMinn, M.R. (1995). Religious orientation, guilt, confession, and forgiveness. *Journal of Psychology and Theology, 23*, 190–197.

* Mongeau, P.A., Hale, J.L., & Alles, M. (1994). An experimental investigation of accounts and attributions following sexual infidelity. *Communication Monographs, 61*, 326–344.

* Ohbuchi, K., Kameda, M., & Agarie, N. (1989). Apology as aggression control:

Its role in mediating appraisal of and response to harm. *Journal of Personality and Social Psychology, 56,* 219–227.

*O'Malley, M.N., & Greenberg, J. (1983). Sex differences in restoring justice: The down payment effect. *Journal of Research in Personality, 17,* 174–185.

*Park, Y.O., & Enright, R.D. (1997). The development of forgiveness in the context of adolescent friendship conflict in Korea. *Journal of Adolescence, 20,* 393–402.

*Poloma, M.M., & Gallup, G.H. (1991). *Varieties of prayer.* Philadelphia: Trinity Press.

Potvin, L., Lasker, J., & Toedter, L. (1989). Measuring grief: A short version of the perinatal grief scale. *Journal of Psychopathology and Behavioral Assessment, 11,* 29–45.

Rest, J. (1974). *Manual for the Defining Issues Test.* Unpublished manuscript, University of Minnesota.

Reynolds, W.M. (1982). Development of reliable and valid short forms of the Marlowe-Crowne Social Desirability Scale. *Journal of Clinical Psychology, 38,* 119–125.

*Roloff, M.E., & Janiszewski, C.A. (1989). Overcoming obstacles to interpersonal compliance: A principle of message construction. *Human Communication Research, 16,* 33–61.

Roloff, M.E., Janiszewski, C.A., McGrath, M.A., Burns, C.S., & Manrai, L.A. (1988). Acquiring resources from intimates: When obligation substitutes for persuasion. *Human Communication Research, 14,* 364–396.

*Rusbult, C.E., Verette, J., Whitney, G.A., Slovik, L.F., & Lipkus, I. (1991). Accommodation processes in close relationships: Theory and preliminary empirical evidence. *Journal of Personality and Social Psychology, 60,* 53–78.

Rusbult, C.E., & Zembrodt, I.M. (1983). Responses to dissatisfaction in romantic involvements: A multidimensional scaling analysis. *Journal of Experimental Social Psychology, 19,* 274–293.

Schonbach, P. (1980). A category system for account phases. *European Journal of Social Psychology, 10,* 195–200.

Schonbach, P. (1990). *Account episodes: The management and escalation of conflict.* Cambridge: Cambridge University Press.

Schutz, W.C. (1958). *FIRO: A three-dimensional theory of interpersonal behavior.* New York: Reinhart.

Spanier, G. (1976). Measuring dyadic adjustment: New scales for assessing the quality of marriage and similar dyads. *Journal of Marriage and the Family, 38,* 15–28.

Spielberger, C.D., Gorsuch, R.L., Lushene, R.,Vagg, P.R., & Jacobs, G.A. (1983). *State-trait anxiety inventory, Form V: Self-evaluation questionnaire.* Palo Alto, CA: Consulting Psychologists Press.

Spielberger, C.D., Jacobs, G.A., Russell, S., & Crane, R.S. (1983). Assessment of anger: The State-Trait Anger Scale. In J.N. Butcher & C.D. Spielberger (Eds.), *Advances in personality assessment* (vol. 2, pp. 161–189). Hillsdale, NJ: Lawrence Erlbaum.

* Stillwell, A.M., & Baumeister, R.F. (1997). The construction of victim and perpetrator memories: Accuracy and distortion in role-based accounts. *Personality and Social Psychology Bulletin, 23,* 1157–1172.

* Stuckless, N., & Goranson, R. (1992). The Vengeance Scale: Development of a measure of attitudes toward revenge. *Journal of Social Behavior and Personality, 7,* 25–42.

* Subkoviak, M.J., Enright, R.D., Wu, C., Gassin, E.A., Freedman, S., Olson, L.M., & Sarinopoulos, I. (1995). Measuring interpersonal forgiveness in late adolescence and middle adulthood. *Journal of Adolescence, 18,* 641–655.

Tangney, J.P., Wagner, P.E., Burggraf, S.A., Gramzow, R., & Fletcher, C. (1990). *The Test of Self-Conscious Affect for Children (TOSCA-C).* Fairfax,VA: George Mason University.

Tangney, J.P., Wagner, P.E., Gavlas, J., & Gramzow, R. (1991a). *The Anger Response Inventory for Adolescents (ARI-A).* Fairfax,VA: George Mason University.

Tangney, J.P., Wagner, P.E., Gavlas, J., & Gramzow, R. (1991b). *The Test of Self-Conscious Affect for Adolescents (TOSCA-A).* Fairfax,VA: George Mason University.

Tangney, J.P., Wagner, P., & Gramzow, R. (1989). *The Test of Self-Conscious Affect (TOSCA).* Fairfax,VA: George Mason University.

Tangney, J.P., Wagner, P.E., Hansbarger, A., & Gramzow, R. (1991). *The Anger Response Inventory for Children (ARI-C).* Fairfax,VA: George Mason University.

* Tangney, J.P., Wagner, P.E., Hill-Barlow, D., Marschall, D.E., & Gramzow, R. (1996). Relation of shame and guilt to constructive versus destructive responses to anger across the lifespan. *Journal of Personality and Social Psychology, 70,* 797–809.

Tangney, J.P., Wagner, P.E., Marschall, D., & Gramzow, R. (1991). *The Anger Response Inventory (ARI).* Fairfax,VA: George Mason University.

Templeton, J.M. (1997). *Worldwide laws of life.* Philadelphia, PA: Templeton Foundation Press (0-8264-1018-9, hbd; 1-890151-15-7, pbk).

Wade, S.H. (1989). *The development of a scale to measure forgiveness.* Unpublished doctoral dissertation, Fuller Graduate School of Psychology, Pasadena, CA.

Wechsler, D. (1955). *Manual for the Wechsler Adult Intelligence Scale*. New York: Psychological Corporation.

* Weinberg, N. (1994). Self-blame, other blame, and desire for revenge: Factors in recovery from bereavement. *Death Studies, 18*, 583–593.

* Weiner, B., Graham, S., Peter, O., & Zmuidinas, M. (1991). Public confession and forgiveness. *Journal of Personality, 59*, 281–312.

Wesley, E. (1953). Perseverative behavior, manifest anxiety and rigidity. *Journal of Abnormal and Social Psychology, 48*, 129–134.

* Wu, J., & Axelrod, R. (1995). How to cope with noise in the iterated Prisoner's Dilemma. *Journal of Conflict Resolution, 39*, 183–189.

* Zillmann, D., Bryant, J., Cantor, J.R., & Day, K.D. (1975). Irrelevance of mitigating circumstances in retaliatory behavior at high levels of excitation. *Journal of Research in Personality, 9*, 282–293.

* Zillmann, D., & Cantor, J.R. (1976). Effect of timing of information about mitigating circumstances on emotional responses to provocation and retaliatory behavior. *Journal of Experimental Social Psychology, 12*, 38–55.

Zuckerman, M., & Lubin, B. (1965). *Manual for the Multiple Affect Adjectives Checklist*. San Diego, CA: Educational and Industrial Testing Service.

Zung, W.W.K. (1965). A self-reporting depression scale. *Archives of General Psychiatry, 12*, 63–70.

Part V

✦

Forgiveness in Future Research

CHAPTER 9

Empirical Research in Forgiveness: Looking Backward, Looking Forward

Everett L. Worthington, Jr.

FIVE PILLARS OF FORGIVENESS RESEARCH

BY NOW, YOU HAVE ABSORBED chapters by a broad array of experts—theologians, basic researchers, and applied researchers—who have described their conceptual constructs and research directions. As you read, you no doubt filtered their ideas through your perceptual scheme, and you probably have numerous ideas about how to further your own research. If you have not scientifically investigated forgiveness previously, you likely have more new ideas than you will ever be able to pursue.

A solid, if limited, platform of empirical research on forgiveness has been established (witness the annotated bibliography by McCullough, Exline, & Baumeister, Chapter 8, expanded from http://www.templeton. org, Grant Opportunities, Forgiveness RFP [1997]). Numerous talented researchers are now building pillars from that base. If the building is to progress efficiently and effectively, five weight-bearing columns must be constructed; that is, five central issues must be addressed by the scientist-builders. If, within 10 years, fundamental issues are addressed, I believe the scientific study of forgiveness will have both a foundation and a frame. Subsequent scientist-builders will add to the existing structure and build new wings and stories we cannot now imagine.

What are the five pillars?

1. *Conceptual clarity* (this is now often lacking).

2. *Theoretical advances* (more are needed).

3. *Methods and measurements of granting forgiveness and related concepts* (these must be developed; for example: confession, repentance, reconciliation, seeking forgiveness, accepting forgiveness, apology, and letting go of anger and hurt; developing a diversity of measurement modalities is especially important).

4. *Applications to populations for which forgiveness is highly relevant* (such applications need to be identified and their effectiveness evaluated).

5. *Publication and dissemination of information* (this must be broad, yet focused on respected outlets).

The following discussion suggests an ambitious research agenda to advance the scientific study of unforgiveness and forgiveness. Rather than review completed research (cf. Chapter 8), I have identified research that, I think, is yet to be done. I hope the agenda will guide those who are just entering the field and provide a context for established researchers to evaluate their future contributions. Furthermore, I hope this research agenda will serve as a benchmark to evaluate the progress of the field 10 years from now.

Conceptual Clarity

Definition. One important yet unresolved conceptual issue is the definition of forgiveness. Several authors (e.g., Enright, Eastin, Golden, Sarinopoulos, & Freedman, 1992; Enright & the Human Development Study Group, 1994; Enright & Zell, 1989; McCullough, Worthington, & Rachal, 1997) have defined forgiveness precisely (see various chapters in the present volume). Enright and his colleagues (1992) have done the most to identify the philosophical and theological underpinnings of forgiveness and thus provide a basis for understanding its various contexts. However, despite overlaps in the definitions, no consensus definition of forgiveness has yet been developed.

In the Hope College conference on forgiveness in October, 1997, where this book originated, debate occurred about whether development of a consensus definition of forgiveness would stimulate or curtail advancement in the scientific study of forgiveness. Those who argued in favor of a consensus definition hoped to save effort, reduce duplication, and increase efficiency. Those who argued against attempts to formulate a consensus suggested that a multiplicity of definitions would result in healthy competition that would guide research into complementary, theoretically informed paths. The general hope was that, eventually, a consensus definition would evolve and focus research efforts more sharply than in the present situation.

Conceptual Issues. Forgiveness of others is a complex topic and might be investigated at several levels. Researchers may study discrete acts of offense or harm and their causes and sequelae. They may also study broad determinants of unforgiveness and forgiveness, such as historical cultural influences and personality characteristics. Researchers may also focus on seeking, granting, and accepting forgiveness for specific acts of offense or harm (Enright & the Human Development Study Group, 1996). However, much unforgiveness results from the aggregation of numerous hurts or offenses. While forgiveness is granted by individuals, forgiveness might involve interpersonal relations (see especially Dorff, Chapter 2; Baumeister, Exline, & Sommer, Chapter 4). Forgiveness usually occurs in an interpersonal context, although some forgiveness might be granted for events that occurred in terminated relationships. Just as important, relationships in which hurtful acts have become so numerous or painful that the partners conceptualize the relationship as being unforgiving might also require forgiveness. Forgiveness could be studied as a personality trait or characteristic; that is, the propensity to forgive might generalize across situations and over time such that some people seem to have forgiving personalities. Investigations of the development of such a characteristic, which might be called "forgivingness," might be fruitful.

Forgiveness of self for doing a reprehensible act (see Enright & the Human Development Study Group, 1996) provides a special case of forgiveness: One is both subject and object, forgiver and offender. Another special case is forgiveness by God—divine forgiveness—which has long been seen as the bailiwick of theologians, especially from the Christian perspective (see Marty, Chapter 1). However, experiences or perceptions of forgiveness by God incorporate psychological, physical, and spiritual correlates and could be examined from a variety of perspectives (see Jones, 1995). Forgiveness *of* God (see Moon, in press), while theologically troublesome, is often an experience with which people struggle. In one study of a clinical population, forgiveness of God for one's hardships was one of the most frequently addressed theological issues in psychotherapy (Worthington, Dupont, Berry, & Duncan, 1988). It, too, could be investigated psychologically.

In addition, conceptual clarity must distinguish forgiveness from related processes (e.g., reconciliation, exoneration, condoning, pardoning, confessing). For instance, one woman told me that she could never forgive a man who abused her because she was afraid he would do so again. She was confusing forgiveness (an intrapersonal act) with reconciliation (an interpersonal transaction). Clear conceptual differentiation of topics is needed as a scientist begins to investigate forgiveness or forgiveness-related concepts.

While forgiveness has received a modest amount of research attention, *unforgiveness* has been virtually ignored. Unforgiveness is a state brought about by hurt, injury, offense, or injustice. Conceivably, the unforgiveness arising from an unintentionally inflicted hurt might differ both qualitatively and quantitatively from the unforgiveness arising from an intentional insult.

Forgiveness is a state that reflects a process. Interventions to promote forgiveness lead people through a series of activities that more or less control their thoughts; forgiveness processes in naturally occurring situations might be dissimilar to those instigated by intervention researchers (see Part III in this volume).

Variables Associated with Forgiveness. The precursors of unforgiveness and forgiveness are not well understood. Because the field of forgiveness is not well developed, additional baseline research must demonstrate how the propensity to forgive might vary by religious orientation, race, class, gender, and the like. Of particular, but not exclusive, interest is how religion and spirituality might be related to unforgiveness or forgiveness. Because forgiveness figures prominently within several religions, the effect of religion on forgiveness deserves investigation (see Pargament & Rye, Chapter 3).

Besides investigating the precursors of unforgiveness and forgiveness, researchers need to examine their covariates. Emotional experience, and sometimes emotional expression, occurs simultaneously with experiences of both unforgiveness and forgiveness: but which emotions in what mixture under what conditions? Similarly, unforgiveness and forgiveness are related to stress reactions. Researchers need to investigate the relationships between unforgiveness and stress. Does stress cause unforgiveness? Does unforgiveness cause stress? Does stress potentiate unforgiveness or make it likely to recur? Or do stress and unforgiveness simply co-vary, perhaps because they are related to a mediating variable such as perceived loss of control? Or, as is likely, does each of the above occur under different circumstances?

Unforgiveness as a pattern of life, which might be called "unforgivingness," is possibly related to negative health consequences or sequelae such as cardiovascular dysfunction (perhaps due to chronic anger), immune-system deficiencies, or stress-related disorders. "Forgivingness" might ameliorate the course of the disorders or even prevent disorders from occurring. Dispositional or trait forgivingness might even promote health and well-being—directly by affecting chronic bodily states or indirectly through mechanisms such as increasing social support and prolonging marriage (both of which are associated with positive health outcomes).

Forgiveness might not always be appropriate. Not only must attention be given to factors that make forgiveness (and unforgiveness) likely, and perhaps desirable, but it also must be given to the possible negative effects of forgiving (on the forgiver, on the perpetrator, and perhaps on interested and involved parties, such as family members). Identifying contraindications for forgiveness remains vital to advancing the practice and scientific study of forgiveness. Longitudinal research is necessary to determine these relationships and clarify precursors, covariates, and effects of discrete acts of forgiveness, as well as a general lifestyle of forgivingness.

Theoretical Advances

Generally, little theory has been advanced about unforgiveness and forgiveness. Enright has applied a cognitive-developmental-structural model to the development of thinking about forgiveness (see Enright, Gassin, & Wu, 1992; Enright & the Human Development Study Group, 1991), and he has empirically investigated his contentions about the cognitive-structural model (see Enright, Santos, & Al-Mabuk, 1989; Subkoviak et al., 1995). He has also developed an integrated process model to describe the promotion of forgiveness, and he has investigated that model in four published studies (see Al-Mabuk, Enright, & Cardis, 1995; Coyle & Enright, 1997; Freedman & Enright, 1996; Hebl & Enright, 1993).

McCullough and his colleagues have elaborated on the role of empathy in forgiving (and empirically investigated their contentions; see McCullough & Worthington, 1995; McCullough et al., 1997; McCullough et al., 1998). DiBlasio has stressed willful decision making as the basis of forgiveness (DiBlasio, 1998). Hargrave (1994a, 1994b) has described interpersonal forgiveness within the family. Other than those theoretical approaches, no theoretical models have addressed mechanisms involved directly in forgiveness.

Theoretically informed approaches, such as application of attributional differences in people acting in different roles (e.g., victim versus perpetrator; see Baumeister et al., Chapter 4); interpersonal trust (see VanLange et al., 1997); accommodation (see Rusbult, Verette, Whitney, Slovik, & Lipkus, 1991); reconciliation (see Courtright, Millar, Rogers, & Bagarozzi, 1990; Patterson & O'Hair, 1992; Worthington & Drinkard, 1998); relationship development, relationship dynamics, giving an account of an interpersonal offense (see Mongeau, Hale, & Alles, 1994; Sitkim & Bies, 1993); and saving face (see Hodgins, Liebeskind, & Schwartz, 1996) have been, or offer the potential to be, applied to forgiveness. Neuroscience, psychoneuroimmunology, primatology, and behavior genetics could yield theoretical constructs that might fruitfully be applied to investigations of forgiveness, but as yet have not been.

In general, model and theory development is particularly needed in four areas:

1. the motives and processes of unforgiveness (how and why it happens and the physiological and psychological mechanisms involved);

2. how forgiveness develops in naturally occurring situations;

3. how forgiveness can be promoted through intentional interventions at the individual, dyadic, naturally occurring group, national, or international level, followed by theoretical research on why forgiveness might occur; and

4. component analyses to determine which parts of interventions are actively causing the effects and relations among forgiveness-related concepts (such as reconciliation, apology, confession, justice, retaliation, revenge, blame, etc.).

Subfield-specific models of forgiveness are also needed. For example, What would be involved in a cognitive-neuroscience model of forgiveness? What is the social psychology of forgiveness? What personality processes are active in forgivingness and unforgivingness? What would be involved in a behavior-genetics model of forgiveness? How are religion and forgiveness related (or not) and in whom? In addition, theory-relevant models of the measurement of forgiveness are needed.

Models and theories that connect disparate fields—for example, those that connect theories of unforgiveness and naturally occurring forgiveness, unforgiveness and interventions to promote forgiveness, and two or more subfields—are not currently extant. At present, some theories (such as evolutionary theory within the life sciences and social-cognitive-behavioral, biopsychosocial, and other theories within psychology) can provide a broad framework for understanding forgiveness; however, much attention must be given to theory and model development.

Theoretical explanations are needed for describing how unforgiveness, naturally occurring forgiveness, and intervention-promoted forgiveness occur. As the research now stands, theoretical advances would be especially valuable. Other works should identify and empirically test factors that might facilitate and inhibit unforgiveness and forgiveness, mediate unforgiveness and forgiveness, and be affected consequentially when forgiveness does or does not occur in particular situations or with particular populations. That is, antecedents, mediators and moderators, and consequences of forgiveness need to be carefully explicated.

Methods and Measurements

Methodological Diversity. The scientific study of forgiveness is a developing field. It is reasonable to expect that methods used to investigate phenomena will not necessarily always involve quantitative methods. For instance, applications of interventions to forgiveness on a grand scale might not yield to precise quantitative measurement. One example of large-scale efforts to promote forgiveness is South Africa's Truth and Reconciliation Commission, which represents a national initiative established by President Nelson Mandela to promote honest disclosure of political crimes in South Africa, as well as to promote amnesty for perpetrators and healing for victims. Or, learning forgiveness within a religious community by observation of exemplars of forgiveness (see Jones, 1995) might not yield to quantitative study. Observational studies in human interactions involving unforgiveness and forgiveness might yield hypotheses. In addition, studies of reconciliation in primates (de Waal, 1989, 1993) might advance research on forgiveness and reconciliation. Qualitative methods are thus necessary and appropriate for reasonable approaches to some scientific questions, as long as they are supplemented by quantitative methods.

Measurement Issues. Generally, few good self-report instruments are accepted in the field. The Enright Forgiveness Inventory has substantial psychometric support (see Subkoviak et al., 1995) and is available from Enright on request (see Chapter 6 and Contributors list). Hargrave and Sells (1997) have published an instrument in the *Journal of Marital and Family Therapy* that seems particularly appropriate for assessing forgiveness in a family context (see also Pollard, Anderson, Anderson, & Jennings, 1998). The Wade Forgiveness Scale (Wade, 1989), a long scale made up of nine subscales, is weakly connected to any theory or definition of forgiveness and is available only through a dissertation. For a shortened validated version of two subscales, the Transgression-Related Motivations Inventory (TRIM), see McCullough et al. (1998). Mauger, Perry, Freeman, Grove, and McKinney (1992) have developed a measure of forgivingness.

Much of the research on forgiveness has used single-item scales with no psychometric support (e.g., Boon & Sulsky, 1997; Darby & Schlenker, 1982; Subkoviak et al., 1995; Weiner, Graham, Peter, & Zmuidinas, 1991). Some studies of forgiveness have used unpublished instruments with little psychometric support. Efforts should be made to publish articles adducing the psychometric support for measuring instruments. Studies that purport to study forgiveness require use of validated instruments or should validate the instrument within their conduct of the study.

To date, all quantitative studies of forgiveness have involved self-reports (single items or instruments). The field urgently needs to develop other ways to measure forgiveness—methods that are validated against self-report, behavioral tests, or the reports by others of a person's forgiveness. Development of new, non-self-report measurement methods and sound validation of self-report instruments are priorities for measurement development. For example, forgiveness could be inferred from a reduction in relationship-specific stress (e.g., using physiological measures of stress). MRI (magnetic resonance imaging), PET (positron emission tomography), or CT (computed tomography) scans could locate areas of the brain where experiences of unforgiveness may be localized. In general, standards for measurement of forgiveness should include face-validity, theoretical relevance, and psychometric support (e.g., reliability, validity, norms).

Because of the dearth of good measures of unforgiveness and forgiveness, research could measure potential correlates of unforgiveness—fear, anxiety, anger, depression, marital adjustment, or family stress—that do have valid measurements, and forgiveness could be inferred from the correlates. Self-reported measures of forgiveness could be validated against potential correlates. However, this harkens back to the lack of theoretical and conceptual clarity about (a) how emotions and stress are related to unforgiveness and forgiveness and (b) which measures co-vary with unforgiveness and forgiveness and the effects of each.

Measurement of Related Concepts. Researchers also need to develop instruments that measure concepts related to forgiveness. No psychometrically
valid and reliable instruments measure reconciliation after a hurtful
offense, willingness to confess one's own hurtfulness, acceptance of apology, willingness to seek forgiveness, remorse for hurtfulness, acceptance
of offered forgiveness, acceptance of responsibility for an offense, or
repentance. Forgiveness remains broader than the mere granting of
forgiveness, which is currently the only aspect of forgiveness that has
been empirically studied. As I discussed earlier, forgiveness happens at a
variety of levels. Only one measure of forgivingness (Mauger et al.,
1992) and no measures of relationship forgiveness or of the pervasiveness of forgiveness across time or situations have been developed.

In addition, some moderating or mediating factors are not reliably and
validly measurable. For example, gratitude for having been forgiven is
poorly understood. Humility (i.e., Means, Wilson, Sturm, Piron, & Bach,
1990) is likewise poorly operationalized. Overall, progress in the scientific study of any field cannot advance until valid, reliable, and conceptually linked measurement methods and instruments have been developed.
These areas invite research scientists who study forgiveness to make
meaningful contributions.

Applications to Populations

A Listing of Pertinent Target Groups. There is great potential for application of research findings to circumstances in which forgiveness might
affect many people in profound ways. For instance, intergroup and international conflict and injustice in places such as Israel–Palestine, South
Africa, Northern Ireland, Bosnia, Rwanda, and the United States have
produced great suffering and unforgiveness. However, studies are needed
of processes of unforgiveness and forgiveness in such real-world settings.
Interventions to those populations and other yet-to-be-seen political hot
spots should not only be developed, but also investigated to determine
their effectiveness.

Needy populations require the study of unforgiveness, forgiveness,
and interventions to promote forgiveness. These include people who

(a) are victims of crime

(b) are HIV-infected

(c) are divorced, separated, or in the process of divorcing

(d) are children in divorced or divorcing families

(e) have cardiovascular disease or are at risk for developing it

(f) have mental health problems that might be related to unforgiveness

(g) are hypertension or stroke patients

(h) have problems with substance or alcohol abuse

(i) are victims of aggressive traumas (e.g., sexual abuse, discrimination, physical abuse, domestic violence, rape)

(j) are victims of accidental traumas (e.g., car accidents, earthquakes)

(k) are elderly and are dealing with end-of-life issues

(l) are (or have been) involved in intrafamily and inter-generational conflict

(m) are married or are in a cohabiting relationship in which one partner has been (or is) sexually unfaithful

(n) are victims of failed medical treatment

(o) are victims of unethical work practices

(p) are victims of workplace aggression or discrimination

(q) have been "downsized" into unemployment

(r) have a terminal disease

(s) are children who are developing the capacity to forgive

(t) have experienced domestic violence

(u) have experienced romantic rejection

(v) have experienced cross-race unforgiveness and forgiveness

(w) belong to ethnic groups that have a history of mutual conflict and harm

(x) are self-condemning

(y) have been harmed or rejected by a deceased parent

(z) have experienced other common injustices, harms, or offenses

Target-Population Issues. Forgiveness and unforgiveness are more or less likely in different populations. On the one hand, issues of unforgiveness

and forgiveness are common to all people and can be investigated in easily accessible populations, such as college students. On the other hand,
for some target populations, because of the history of anger, revenge,
abuse, violence, and the sheer impact of the problems they face, forgiveness might involve special considerations.

Following are three examples. (1) Forgiveness within a political context involves special consideration; for example, Israel–Palestine or South
African reconciliation efforts might be promoted by social-political interventions. (2) Family reconciliation efforts often involve the complexities
of daily face-to-face continuous interaction where forgiveness and reconciliation are merely part of daily life. Instigating forgiveness within the
family or between spouses or partners will likely involve face-to-face
mutual confession and forgiveness because of the day-to-day nature of
their lives together. (3) The forgiveness of individuals who have experienced sexual or physical abuse or who have a history of poor interactions
with a deceased parent requires unique attention because the possibility of the perpetrator's apology and repentance is unlikely or has been
removed.

Forgiveness research also has nomothetic and idiographic aspects.
Specific issues might differ across specific target populations. Obviously, research designs should (a) consider the special nature of their target
population, (b) tailor studies to the unique characteristics of their participants, and (c) generalize findings circumspectly and appropriately.

Publication and Dissemination

Quality of Extant Research. The present stature of the field of studies
directly relating to forgiveness is weak, reflecting a youthful field. For
example, only a few studies have been published in journals such as the
Journal of Personality and Social Psychology (JPSP) or the *Journal of Consulting and Clinical Psychology (JCCP).* No reviews of research have been
published in *Psychological Bulletin;* no theoretical or empirical articles
have appeared in *Psychological Review.* No scientific articles on forgiveness
have been published in top scientific journals, such as *Science* or *Nature,*
or in medical journals, such as the *New England Journal of Medicine* or
Lancet. Some articles addressing topics related to forgiveness—on hostility

and health, on accounts given for interpersonal offenses, and on resolution of relationship difficulties—have been published in mainline, top-tier journals; but, in most cases, those articles have not explicitly mentioned forgiveness.

Eight Goals for Dissemination Within 10 Years. The following elements are needed if the field is to advance and, ideally, should be achieved within the next decade:

✦ Empirical research on the health (biological and medical) consequences of unforgiveness and forgiveness in major health and medicine journals such as *American Journal of Psychiatry, Journal of the American Psychiatric Association, New England Journal of Medicine, Lancet,* and *Journal of the American Medical Association.*

✦ Theoretical-empirical articles and summaries of the field on unforgiveness and forgiveness in major psychological journals such as the *American Psychologist, Psychological Review, Personality and Social Psychology Review, Review of General Psychology, Psychological Inquiry, Brain Science, Journal of Personality and Social Psychology, Journal of Consulting and Clinical Psychology,* and *Health Psychology.*

✦ Empirical studies of the social psychological, biological, or cognitive determinants of forgiveness and unforgiveness in *Science, Nature,* and other top-tier journals aimed at a broad audience.

✦ Critical review of research or meta-analyses in *Psychological Bulletin, Clinical Psychology Review,* and others (when the literature has accumulated to a critical mass), such as the *Annual Review of Psychology.*

✦ Field-building edited volumes and single-authored theoretical-empirical volumes.

✦ Federally funded grant Requests for Proposals (RFPs) that target forgiveness and related concepts reflecting a national priority that allows support of large high-impact studies.

✦ Popular dissemination in magazines such as *Scientific American,* in mass media, on network and cable television, and on public radio.

CONCLUSION

I have considered an ambitious research agenda for the development of a science of forgiveness. In Table 1, I summarize the milestones in a check-list. I hope that in a decade, a review of the literature will reveal that both new investigators and established scientists will have substantially filled in the matrix and built a field on the foundation that now exists.

Table 1. Questions to Evaluate Progress in the Scientific Study of Forgiveness in 10 Years	
CONCEPTUAL CLARITY	✦ Are there consensus definitions of major constructs?

	✦ Has forgiveness been investigated at the following levels?
	  ◆ for discrete acts of harm
	  ◆ of self
	  ◆ of and by God
	  ◆ within relationships
	  ◆ of a partner (for numerous acts)

	✦ Has forgivingness as a trait or personal characteristic been studied?
	✦ Have precursors, covariates, consequences, and sequelae of both unforgiveness and forgiveness been identified?
	✦ Have conditions that indicate when forgiveness is not warranted and not likely to be effective been identified?
THEORETICAL ADVANCES	✦ Are there heuristic theories or models of unforgiveness, naturally occurring forgiveness, and the promotion of forgiveness?
	✦ What is the adequacy of evidence for each?

METHODS & MEASUREMENTS	✦ Are there a diversity of validated methods and measures of unforgiveness, forgiveness, and concepts that are related to theory?
APPLICATIONS TO POPULATIONS	✦ To what extent have highly relevant target populations been studied and interventions tailored to promote forgiveness within those populations?
	✦ To what extent have nomothetic investigations revealed information about unforgiveness and forgiveness in general?
	✦ To what extent have idiographic investigations revealed information specific to different populations?
PUBLICATION & DISSEMINATION	✦ How high is the quality of publication outlets?
	✦ How many of the objectives for placement of publications have been achieved?
	◆ Have major publications been published in medical journals and psychological journals?
	◆ Have critical reviews been published?
	◆ Have important scholarly books been published?
	◆ Has a federally funded RFP been initiated?
	◆ Has broad dissemination occurred?

REFERENCES

Al-Mabuk, R.H., Enright, R.D., & Cardis, P.A. (1995). Forgiving education with parentally loved-deprived late adolescents. *Journal of Moral Education, 24,* 427–444.

Baumeister, R.F., Exline, J.J., & Sommer, K.L. (1998). The victim role, grudge theory, and two dimensions of forgiveness. In E.L. Worthington, Jr. (Ed.), *Dimensions of forgiveness: Psychological research & theological perspectives* (pp.79–104). Philadelphia, PA: Templeton Foundation Press.

Boon, S.D., & Sulsky, L.M. (1997). Attributions of blame and forgiveness in romantic relationships: A policy-capturing study. *Journal of Social Behavior and Personality, 12,* 19–44.

Courtright, J.A., Millar, F.E., Rogers, L.E., & Bagarozzi, D. (1990). Interaction dynamics of relational negotiation: Reconciliation versus termination of distressed relationships. *Western Journal of Speech Communication, 54,* 429–453.

Coyle, C.T., & Enright, R.D. (1997). Forgiveness intervention with post-abortion men. *Journal of Consulting and Clinical Psychology, 65,* 1042–1045.

Darby, B.W., & Schlenker, B.R. (1982). Children's reactions to apologies. *Journal of Personality and Social Psychology, 43,* 742–753.

DiBlasio, F.A. (1998). The use of a decision-based forgiveness intervention within intergenerational family therapy. *Journal of Family Therapy, 20,* 77–94.

Dorff, E.N. (1998). The elements of forgiveness: A Jewish approach. In E.L. Worthington, Jr. (Ed.), *Dimensions of forgiveness: Psychological research & theological perspectives* (pp.29–55). Philadelphia, PA: Templeton Foundation Press.

Enright, R.D., & Coyle, C.T. (1998). Researching the process model of forgiveness within psychological interventions. In E.L. Worthington, Jr. (Ed.), *Dimensions of forgiveness: Psychological research & theological perspectives* (pp.139–161). Philadelphia, PA: Templeton Foundation Press.

Enright, R.D., Eastin, D.L., Golden, S., Sarinopoulos, I., & Freedman, S. (1992). Interpersonal forgiveness within the helping professions: An attempt to resolve differences of opinion. *Counseling and Values, 36,* 84–103.

Enright, R.D., Gassin, E.A., & Wu, C. (1992). Forgiveness: A developmental view. *Journal of Moral Education, 21,* 99–114.

Enright, R.D., & the Human Development Study Group. (1991). The moral development of forgiveness. In W. Kurtines & J. Gewirtz (Eds.), *Handbook of moral behavior and development* (Vol. 1, pp. 123–152). Hillsdale, NJ: Lawrence Erlbaum.

Enright, R.D., & the Human Development Study Group. (1994). Piaget on the moral development of forgiveness: Identity or reciprocity? *Human Development, 37,* 63–80.

Enright, R.D., & the Human Development Study Group. (1996). Counseling within the forgiveness triad: On forgiving, receiving forgiveness, and self-forgiveness. *Counseling and Values, 40,* 107–126.

Enright, R.D., Santos, M.J., & Al-Mabuk, R. (1989). The adolescent as forgiver. *Journal of Adolescence, 12,* 95–110.

Enright, R.D., & Zell, R.L. (1989). Problems encountered when we forgive one another. *Journal of Psychology and Christianity, 8,* 52–60.

Freedman, S.R., & Enright, R.D. (1996). Forgiveness as an intervention goal with incest survivors. *Journal of Consulting and Clinical Psychology, 64,* 983–992.

Hargrave, T. (1994a). Families and forgiveness: A theoretical and therapeutic framework. *The Family Journal: Counseling and Therapy for Couples and Families, 2,* 339–348.

Hargrave, T. (1994b). *Families and forgiveness: Healing wounds in the intergenerational family.* New York: Brunner/Mazel.

Hargrave, T.D., & Sells, J.N. (1997). The development of a forgiveness scale. *Journal of Marital and Family Therapy, 23,* 41–63.

Hebl, J., & Enright, R.D. (1993). Forgiveness as a psychotherapeutic goal with elderly females. *Psychotherapy, 30,* 658–667.

Hodgins, H.S., Liebeskind, E., & Schwartz, W. (1996). Getting out of hot water: Facework in social predicaments. *Journal of Personality and Social Psychology, 71,* 300–314.

Jones, L.G. (1995). *Embodying forgiveness: A theological analysis.* Grand Rapids, MI: William B. Eerdmans.

Marty, M.E. (1998). The ethos of Christian forgiveness. In E.L. Worthington, Jr. (Ed.), *Dimensions of forgiveness: Psychological research & theological perspectives* (pp.9–28). Philadelphia, PA: Templeton Foundation Press.

Mauger, P.A., Perry, J.E., Freeman, T., Grove, D.C., & McKinney, K.E. (1992). The measurement of forgiveness: Preliminary research. *Journal of Psychology and Christianity, 11,* 170–180.

McCullough, M.E., Exline, J.J., & Baumeister, R.F. (1998). An annotated bibliography of research on forgiveness and related concepts. In E.L. Worthington, Jr. (Ed.), *Dimensions of forgiveness: Psychological research & theological perspectives* (pp.193–317). Philadelphia, PA: Templeton Foundation Press.

McCullough, M.E., Rachal, K.C., Sandage, S.J., Worthington, E.L., Jr., Brown, S.W., & Hight, T.L. (1998). Interpersonal forgiving in close relationships II: Theoretical elaboration and measurement. *Journal of Personality and Social Psychology* (in press).

McCullough, M.E., & Worthington, E.L., Jr. (1995). Promoting forgiveness:

The comparison of two brief psychoeducational interventions with a waiting-list control. *Counseling and Values, 40*, 55–68.

McCullough, M.E., Worthington, E.L., Jr., & Rachal, K.C. (1997). Interpersonal forgiving in close relationships. *Journal of Personality and Social Psychology, 73*, 321–336.

McCullough, M.E., & Worthington, E.L., Jr. (1994). Encouraging clients to forgive people who have hurt them: Review, critique, and research prospectus. *Journal of Psychology and Theology, 22*, 3–20.

Means, J.R., Wilson, G.L., Sturm, C., Piron, J.E., & Bach, P.J. (1990). Humility as a psychotherapeutic formulation. *Counseling Psychology Quarterly, 3*, 211–215.

Mongeau, P.A., Hale, J.L., & Alles, M. (1994). An experimental investigation of accounts and attributions following sexual infidelity. *Communication Monographs, 61*, 326–344.

Moon, G. (in press). "Forgiving" God: Initially it may be a matter of heart over head. *Marriage and Family: A Christian Journal.*

Murphy, J.G., & Hampton, J. (1988). *Forgiveness and mercy.* Cambridge, MA: Cambridge University Press.

Pargament, K.I., & Rye, M.S. Forgiveness as a method of religious coping. In E.L. Worthington, Jr. (Ed.), *Dimensions of forgiveness: Psychological research & theological perspectives* (pp. 59–78). Philadelphia, PA: Templeton Foundation Press.

Patterson, B., & O'Hair, D. (1992). Relational reconciliation: Toward a more comprehensive model of relational development. *Communication Research Reports, 9*, 119–129.

Pollard, M.W., Anderson, R.A., Anderson, W.T., & Jennings, G. (1998). The development of a family forgiveness scale. *Journal of Family Therapy, 20*, 95–110.

Rusbult, C.E., Verette, J., Whitney, G.A., Slovik, L.F., & Lipkus, I. (1991). Accommodation processes in close relationships: Theory and preliminary empirical evidence. *Journal of Personality and Social Psychology, 60*, 53–78.

Sackin, S., & Thelen, E. (1984). An ethological study of peaceful associative outcomes to conflict in preschool children. *Child Development, 55*, 1098–1102.

Silk, J.B., Cheney, D.L., & Seyfarth, R.M. (1996). The form and function of post-conflict interactions between female baboons. *Animal Behavior, 52*, 259–268.

Sitkim, S.B., & Bies, R.J. (1993). Social accounts in conflict situations: Using explanations to manage conflict. *Human Relations, 46*, 349–370.

Stillwell, A.M., & Baumeister, R.F. (1997). The construction of victim and perpetrator memories: Accuracy and distortion in role-based accounts. *Personality and Social Psychology, 23*, 1157–1172.

Subkoviak, M.J., Enright, R.D., Wu, C.R., Gassin, E. A., Freedman, S., Olson, L.M., & Sarinopoulos, I. (1995). Measuring interpersonal forgiveness in late adolescence and middle adulthood. *Journal of Adolescence, 18*, 641–655.

VanLange, P.A.M., Rusbult, C.E., Drigotas, S.M., Avriaga, X.B., Witcher, B.S., & Cox, C.L. (1997). Willingness to sacrifice in close relationships. *Journal of Personality and Social Psychology, 72*, 1373–1395.

de Waal, F. B.M. (1989). *Peacemaking among primates*. Cambridge, MA: Harvard University Press.

de Waal, F. B.M., & Johanowicz, D.L. (1993). Modification of reconciliation behavior through social experience: An experiment with two macaque species. *Child Development, 64*, 897–908.

Wade, S.H. (1989). *The development of a scale to measure forgiveness*. Unpublished doctoral dissertation, Fuller Graduate School of Psychology, Pasadena, CA.

Weiner, B., Graham, S., Peter, O., & Zmuidinas, M. (1991). Public confession and forgiveness. *Journal of Personality, 59*, 281–312.

Worthington, E.L., Jr. (1998). An empathy-humility-commitment model of forgiveness applied within family dyads. *Journal of Family Therapy, 20*, 59–76.

Worthington, E.L., Jr., & DiBlasio, F.A. (1990). Promoting mutual forgiveness within the fractured relationship. *Psychotherapy, 27*, 219–223.

Worthington, E.L., Jr., & Drinkard, D.T. (1998). *Promoting reconciliation through psychoeducational and therapeutic interventions*. Unpublished manuscript, under editorial review.

Worthington, E.L., Jr., Dupont, P.D., Berry, J.T., & Duncan, L.A. (1988). Christian therapists' and clients' perceptions of religious psychotherapy in private and agency settings. *Journal of Psychology and Theology, 16*, 282–293.

CHAPTER 10

Stations on the Journey from Forgiveness to Hope

Lewis B. Smedes

I
N HER VOLUME, *The Human Condition*, moral philosopher Hannah Arendt (1969) identified what to her are the two most persistent challenges of human existence: (1) We were created with the power to remember the past, but left powerless to change it; and (2) we were created with the power to imagine the future, but left powerless to control it. She concluded that the only effective response to the first challenge was to use the faculty of forgiveness, and the only effective response to the second challenge was the ability to make and keep promises.

I agree with Dr. Arendt's conclusion that the only way to cope with a past we cannot change is through forgiveness. I would add to what she says about promise keeping as the way of coping with a future we can imagine but cannot control. What I would add is this: HOPE. None of us could ever cope well with the good and evil things we can imagine in the future unless we faced them with hope. Besides, as I see it, forgiveness and hope are vitally linked to each other. As the symposium on forgiveness on which this book is based was, in fact, insightfully subtitled "A Journey to Hope," it seems fitting for me, then, to talk about that journey—from forgiveness to hope.

This journey has four stations:

1. Estrangement—the occasion for the journey
2. Forgiveness—the path on which to make the journey
3. Reconciliation—the ever-elusive destination of the journey
4. Hope—the energy to keep traveling

Before I go on, I must explain that I do not at all mean that we travel these stages of the journey in sequence. Life is never as logical as logic; one thing does not follow another in the neat steps that we construct in our minds. "Journey" is a metaphor, and the four "stations" we will discuss are guideposts along our sojourn rather than a four-step procedural manual.

STATION I: ESTRANGEMENT

As Paul Tillich used to say, estrangement constitutes an alienation (between people who once were united) that is caused when one party injures and wrongs another. The critical word is "wrongs." The victim experiences the injury as a moral offense, a violation; and the feeling of having been violated makes it morally impossible for the victim to continue in a relationship of trust with the offender—hence, the estrangement.

It is not hard to sense the critical difference between being estranged and being strangers, between a separation caused by a moral offense and one caused by two people discovering that they are in fact strangers to each other. Our "otherness" can be a difference of location, culture, race, custom, opinion, faith, and who knows what else. No moral fault is involved. We are strangers because we *happen* to be different from one another.

Normally, strangeness can be overcome by mutual acquaintance, understanding, imagination, generosity, respect, and a bit of magnanimity. If we are strangers, we can be united if we accept one another as we are without requiring the "other" to change and become "like" us. But estranged people can be truly reunited only if the offender changes significantly; estrangement can be truly overcome only when the offender does something to undo the effects of his or her offense.

In human history, however, the distinction between two people or groups that are strangers and people that are estranged tends to be distorted. Our tribal and personal pride lead us almost irresistibly to view the other's "otherness" as either a mark of inferiority or a signal of threat. Because we tend to view others as inferior, we feel justified in treating them as "lesser," perhaps even making slaves of them, denying them equal access to our privileges or patronizing them with our benevolence. If this otherness is felt as a threat, we feel morally justified in using whatever force we need to defend ourselves.

Thus, the accident of "otherness" becomes the occasion for titanic moral offenses against the other.

Another factor that complicates the distinction between being strangers and being estranged is the victim's sense that he or she has a right to some sort of moral recompense. The victim wants the satisfaction of seeing the offender suffer pain that is at least roughly equivalent to the suffering he or she caused. (Which makes the victim a classically dangerous person.) The word we use for this demand for parity in pain is "vengeance."

Vengeance, however, is almost inevitably frustrated. The pain one causes always feels less to the one who causes it than it does to the one who suffers it. Thus, after the first stab at balancing the pain score, the original victim becomes the offender. And the original offender now becomes the victim. The new victim then seeks moral recompense from the new offender. And so, as both parties become both offender and victim, the cycle of revenge is endless. Parity in pain forever eludes us.

This is the situation for which forgiveness exists.

STATION 2: FORGIVENESS

Forgiveness forms the second station on the journey to hope. Long considered the extra mile of mercy toward the offender that is required from a "believer," forgiveness is now being rediscovered as a creative human faculty for overcoming estrangement. Religious (in my case, Christian) believers have special motivation to forgive people who wrong them (see Marty, Chapter 1; Dorff, Chapter 2). But what I do when I forgive is not a uniquely religious act. Rather, it becomes a creative human act that can transcend the doomed demand for vengeance and open up the possibility for reconciliation.

I want to discuss forgiveness from three points of view: (1) What any person does when he or she forgives someone who wronged him or her; (2) the limits of forgiveness as a means of effecting reconciliation; and (3) a few situations of estrangement that pose special problems for forgiveness.

What A Person Does When He or She Forgives

As I see it, a person who forgives does three distinguishable, if inseparable, things that tend to mesh in no particular sequence. Each person will link them according to his or her experience. The order I use seems logical to me, and I had to put them in some sort of sequence; but I do not at all suggest that this is the order in which one *ought* to proceed.

The following seem to me to be the three elements that make up the basic experience of forgiving.

Rediscovering the Humanity of the Offender. It seems to me that victims of wrong tend to caricature their offender in terms of the wrong that he or she did: What the offender *did* becomes what the offender *is*. To the extent that this happens, the offender is subtly dehumanized, reduced to an act—and a bad act at that.

Forgiveness begins when the victim begins to see the offender not simply and wholly as the bad creature who did him or her wrong, but as a weak, flawed, fallible, sinful but nevertheless human being not all that different from himself or herself. The offender is not the devil who *is* the evil that he or she *did*, but an accountable, if flawed, human being who wronged another human being. As the victim recognizes the offender as a fellow human being, the victim's passion for vengeance is moderated by a certain respect (enough to hold the offender responsible)—and even compassion—for the offender.

On the other hand, the victim also can turn the offender into a morally handicapped being who cannot be held responsible for his or her actions. This caricature of the offender dehumanizes him or her and makes forgiving *impossible* by making it *unnecessary* in the mind of the victim. Forgiving can happen only when the victim allows that the offender has enough human dignity to be responsible for what he or she did.

Surrendering the Right to Get Even. Somewhere in the process, the victim chooses to surrender (what feels like) a basic human right to get even. Whether such a human right exists does not matter; the victim feels that it does and that he or she possesses it. For example, a victim may quite understandably feel that ignoring this moral right leads to a loss of self-respect, and therefore he or she may decide not to reunite with the offender until being satisfied that the offender has made up for the wrong.

When someone forgives, he or she chooses to live with the moral scales unbalanced, the injury not avenged, the wrong not righted. Even if there is a felt "moral right" to vengeance, the victim surrenders it.

Changing One's Feelings Toward the Offender. From a wish for the offender's hurt, the victim gradually begins to wish the offender well. From demanding revenge according to the laws of nature, the victim turns to offering redemption with grace—and the freedom that this brings to both.

We need not expect the victim to become ecstatically benevolent, to call on heaven to bless the offender with spectacular success, wealth, comfort, and happiness. But we may expect that, incrementally over time, the victim gradually moves toward benevolence and the person who injured and wronged him or her.

The Limitations of Forgiving

Insofar as the objective of forgiving is to overcome human estrangement, it is important to be aware of its limits. Forgiving is a necessary, but insufficient, condition for reconciliation. Here are some of the reasons why:

+ Forgiving is individual; reconciliation is social.
+ Forgiving takes only one person; reconciliation takes two.

✦ Forgiving is unconditional; reconciliation is conditioned by the offender's response to the forgiver.

✦ Forgiving can happen without reconciliation; reconciliation cannot happen without forgiveness (see Baumeister, Exline, and Sommer, Chapter 4).

The liberating effects of forgiving on the victim are achieved quite apart from the attitude or response of the offender. But *reconciliation* with the offender can be accomplished only when the offender responds appropriately.

And just as forgiving can fail to bring about reconciliation if the offender rejects it, *it can also be aborted if the forgiver bungles it*. The bungling of forgiveness usually involves a mingling of judgment with grace. Forgiving cannot occur without judgment; we forgive only those we blame for having wronged us. But if the victim rushes to offer forgiving grace, he or she may not be prepared to communicate it as grace, and the offender may not be prepared to hear it as such. The victim may say "I forgive," while the offender may hear "I blame." And being judged blamable, the offender hurries to his or her own defense. The victim then hears the defense as a rejection of grace—and is doubly offended.

Forgiving is also bungled when the victim exploits his or her advantage as the "forgiving victim." Forgiving gives the victim a double advantage: a moral claim against the victimizer and the potential to remain the "generous" one who forgives the offender. If the forgiving victim exploits this advantage, whatever reconciliation happens becomes fragile at best and false at worst.

Some Quandaries in Forgiving

The Quandary of Forgiving Corporations. Can a person forgive a corporation? Corporations can perhaps injure and wrong people more grievously than individuals can. And yet they are legal fictions: They are "real," but—in a sense—nonexistent. Besides, forgiveness remains a distinctly personal event; one is hard put to forgive a "thing," and harder put still to forgive something that does not really exist.

If one struggles to forgive a corporation, one struggles still more to be reconciled to it. Corporations cannot repent or be remorseful. General Motors never sheds a tear, even if its president does. (This helps explain why institutions almost always have less grace than people do.) Perhaps it would be simpler if we left estrangement—between individuals and corporations—to the legal realm of contracts and compensation and limited forgiving to people *within* the corporation.

The Quandary of Group Forgiveness. Can one group forgive another group? More specifically, can an institutionalized group, such as a nation, forgive another? Certainly, one group can wrong another. But how would a group go about forgiving another group? Could one take a poll and determine whether a majority of the individuals in the group are willing to forgive? Can a representative of one group forgive the offending group in the name of the offended group? (Donald Shriver [1995] has given wise and probing consideration to such matters in his admirable book, *An Ethics for Enemies*, which could well serve as the basis for all further discussion.)

Can a person forgive someone who has injured and wronged members of his or her group, but did not directly assault him or her? This is not a question of whether the person has enough *grace* to forgive, but whether it would be morally *appropriate* to forgive. Simon Wiesenthal, while he was a prisoner in the concentration camp at Mauthausen, refused to forgive a young, dying *Schutzstaffel* (SS) trooper named Karl who begged to be forgiven for the evil he had done to innocent Jews in a Russian town called Dnepropetrovsk. But Wiesenthal was troubled by his refusal to forgive and asked his elders at the camp about it. They told him that he did not have the *right* to forgive the SS trooper on behalf of the women and children whom the trooper had killed.

Wiesenthal still wondered. If he was so "one" with the trooper's Jewish victims that, when they were wronged, he was wronged, did not his Jewishness give him the right to forgive Karl for what he had done to other Jews?

The problem of forgiving someone for wronging a member of one's own group raises this additional and knotty problem:

If I forgive someone for wronging members of my group, although he or she has not laid a hand on me, do I forgive the offender for the wrongs he or she did to the others—or only for the wrong he or she did to me?

I once felt I had to forgive an officer who had brutalized my youngest son without cause. When my children are wronged, I know what it means to identify with them. When the officer wronged my son, I surely felt that he had wronged *me*. My son told me that I was overdoing it and that he could take care of his *own* forgiving for his *own* hurts. But is my son too much of an individualist who does not—at least yet—share my sense of being who I am, because of the people I come from and belong to?

If it is sometimes right to forgive someone who wronged a loved one, how far does the circle of identity stretch?

Does our identity extend only as far as the limits of our empathy? Or does our identity with others extend as far as the linkage between us—whether we feel it or not? It is easy for me to identify with my son. But would I forgive someone who injures a fourth cousin whom I have never met and with whom I feel no identity? God forgives us for wronging one another, even though it did not hurt God directly, because he feels the same empathy with our victims that we feel with our children. But few of us embrace the whole human family within our circle of empathy with the same intensity that we embrace our children. Perhaps this is a failing, not a norm, and perhaps if all that is human is common to us, we would be able to feel and forgive the wrongs that anybody in the world inflicts on others.

It seems to me that our private identity is gained from members of the human family in a spiral of felt relationships. At the core of the spiral is my membership in my immediate family. As the spiral swirls outward, my ties to others become thinner and thinner. And only *I* know for sure how wide the spiral of my empathy stretches. The propriety of forgiveness, then, depends not on some ontological sharing of one another's nature, but on the breadth of our love.

Another quandary of forgiving occurs when we are asked to forgive the children of those who have wronged our forebears and living relatives.

I was mesmerized by the story that Rabbi Joseph Polak told in the September 1995 issue of *Commonweal*. Polak was three years old when he was imprisoned, along with his parents, in the concentration camp at Bergen–Belsen. Toward the end of the war, the Germans packed him and his parents along with 2,500 other prisoners into the wagons of a freight train for removal from Bergen–Belsen to another camp. No food or drink was provided for the trip. But the engineer missed a switch, became confused, and lost his way. The German command was too demoralized by this time to notice, and the engineer was trained to act only under direct orders. So the train puffed on and on for days and finally ground to a halt in a small East German village called Tröbitz. Five hundred people suffocated in the wagons on the lost train.

Fifty years later, in 1995, some of the survivors gathered in Bergen–Belsen to memorialize the deadly train trip by riding the same route. Before they set out, the local authorities held a ceremony in their honor. The minister of culture spoke, and one of the things he said was that eighty-five percent of the present German population were five years old—or younger—when the horror occurred. His point, obviously, was to say that the present-day Germans should not be blamed for what their fathers did.

Joseph Polak was with the group, heard the minister's words, and wrote the following in his notebook:

> The deeds of your parents cannot be forgotten, and as long as memory stirs...you are bound to be their representative, and your hands will be stained with blood that you yourselves may not have spilled. For as long as people remember history, or hear a Jewish story, or see a Jewish child, you are destined to take responsibility for this darkness and never, ever to be forgiven for it.

The words are shocking in their moral passion and their fierce judgment, somewhat the way the words of the decalogue shock us when they quote God as saying that he will hold the iniquities of the fathers against the children unto the third and fourth generation of those who hate him.

Rabbi Polak sees us all as being who and what we are because of our relationship to our people, and therefore we cannot escape responsibility for the evil done by our forebears. Thus, German children are to be forever blamed and never forgiven.

But if the children are responsible for the horror, why can they not be forgiven for it? I suppose that the Rabbi meant to say that the present generation of Germans must go unforgiven because the evil and magnitude of the Holocaust are too horrific for forgiveness. If this is so, who knows when the measure of the evil we do spins us beyond the possibility of forgiveness? Can we depend on a kind of *sensus gentium* to recognize when we have reached the boundary beyond which there is no forgiveness?

And how many generations must pass before the children need to be, and can be, forgiven for the sins of their forebears? Must white United States citizens, for instance, forever bear the burden of guilt for what their slave-holding fathers did to African-Americans and their empire-building ancestors did to Native Americans? Must the children of the Tutsis forever seek revenge on the children of the Hutus in Rwanda?

I have said enough about the quandaries of forgiveness, I think, to justify saying as well that much thought still needs to be given to forgiveness in our world.

It seems to me that we must not try to press these taunting complications into any paradigm of forgiveness. Reality is always more prickly and awkward than our definitions of it. Perhaps no actual forgiving event ever perfectly matches our template of forgiveness. So if the victims of huge wrongs—or the children of victims of huge wrongs—can do something more or less *like* forgiving, and if doing it can bring some of the healing that forgiving can bring, why quibble? Let the healing stream flow.

STATION 3: RECONCILIATION

Just as estrangement becomes the occasion for forgiving, the reconciliation of the estranged becomes the goal. This is not to say that forgiving is of no value unless reconciliation is achieved. *Much* value lies in forgiveness, because it brings enormous benefits to the victim even if reconciliation never follows. And reconciliation will follow only if the healing of the victim occurs first. Still, the final goal of forgiveness is reconciliation with the offender.

But reconciliation takes place at many levels—and in many ways. The ideal may be the reunion of the estranged persons into the same rela-

tionship they had before the offense—that is, divorced people may re-
marry, alienated friends may reconcile, and families whose members
hate one another may rejoin the loving family circle. However, reunion
is not always possible—or even advisable.

Sometimes, cool coexistence is the warmest relationship possible—
or, for that matter, advisable. If a forgiven spouse remains addicted to
physical abuse, reunion is certainly not advisable. If a forgiven former
friend is likely to betray again, it seems advisable to forgive but remain
former friends. There can be enormous benefits when warring parties,
in the immortal words of Rodney King, can "just get along." Jacob and
Esau wisely decided to live at land's length from each other, even though
Esau forgave.

It is in the nature of the case that reconciliation is achieved in varying
stages of reunion; it is never complete, never secure, but always fragile
and, usually, tenuous, only to be broken again. But besides the inevitable
variations, quandaries in reconciliation arise when the estrangement is
between groups and between later generations of groups.

Remember: Reconciliation is always *conditional* even if forgiving is
unconditional. One of the conditions for reconciliation is remorse, which
is an affective kind of honesty. How can one generation of a group of
people—whose fathers and mothers sinned against another group—
repent on behalf of the generation who did the sinning?

For instance, what does it mean when a Parisian Archbishop repents
on behalf of the Catholic Church for the sin of silence committed by
the church of an earlier time against the Jews? Again, what are we to
make of it when President Clinton apologizes to present-day African-
Americans for the slavery endured by their ancestors? When the president apologized for the wrong done to Japanese Americans during the
Second World War, financial compensation was added to the apology. Is
similar compensation due to the great-grandchildren of slaves?

The least acceptable response to these colossal issues is to say that
they are irrelevant because they are too hard to resolve. A close second
might be to require that any movement toward reconciliation match the
template of some well-defined notion of forgiveness and repentance. It
is enough here to recognize the existence of the complexities as a reason
for further reflection—and to see that any movement toward *something*

like reconciliation that begins with *something like* forgiveness and is pushed along by *something like* repentance constitutes a reason for hope.

Let us, finally, stop at the last station.

STATION 4: HOPE

The fourth guidepost on the journey represents the connection between forgiveness and the hope for reconciliation between estranged people.

It strikes me that the hope for reconciliation is linked to forgiveness at two points: (1) Forgiveness makes hope for reconciliation possible; and (2) the elusiveness of reconciliation makes hope necessary.

Forgiveness is the key that can unshackle us from a past that will not rest in the grave of things over and done with. As long as our minds are captive to the memory of having been wronged, they are not free to wish for reconciliation with the one who wronged us. And without wishing, there is no hoping.

We *hope* when we truly desire something that we do not have. And we *hope* only when we believe that what we desire is possible—not certain, not guaranteed, only possible. Forgiveness not only leaves us with a desire for reconciliation not yet attained, but also gives us reason to believe it is possible to achieve. When forgiveness happens, hope is born.

As we have seen, forgiving the person from whom we are estranged does not by itself bring about reconciliation with him or her. And even when reconciliation is achieved, it often falls short of reunion, or restoration to the former relationship. Moreover, even a reconciliation-at-a-comfortable-distance is fragile and tentative. Thus, forgiving, while it *creates* hope, also leaves us with a *need* to hope.

Meanwhile, we will not strive for reconciliation unless we hope for it. Nor will we even wait for it unless we hope for it. Thus, hope is of the essence.

In the Christian experience, reconciliation between God and us and between ourselves and others demonstrates the crystallization of salvation. And, although we are already saved, we experience salvation in the form of hoping for it. As Saint Paul cautioned his readers, "We are saved in hope." Which could also be, and is translated as, "We are saved but what we have to show for it is the hope of being saved" (Rom. 8:23).

This is also true when it comes to achieving even the most tentative, hazardous, fragile forms of reconciliation between estranged people here and now. It is so hard to achieve, it takes so long, and the path to it is strewn with new offenses and new reasons for estrangement. Without hope, we would not have the energy to keep trying. And reconciliation, when achieved, can remain so vulnerable that, without hope of making it more secure, we would not stay with it through its trials and temptations.

Forgiveness begins reconciliation.

Hope creates the moral energy to pursue it.

On the morning of May 4, 1992, I walked with my wife, Doris, among the ashes still warm after the flaming human horror known as the Los Angeles riots. A friend whose home is near the center of the fire storm led us from charred ruin to charred ruin, from burnt-out hope to burnt-out hope, each sad scene bearing us closer to the cusp of despair. Nothing in my life had left me feeling more hopeless than those awful leftovers of that one mad night.

A few weeks later, driving away about ten o'clock at night from Parking Lot C at the Los Angeles County Airport (my mind fixed only on the magic moment when my garage door would open and swallow me back into my comfortable cocoon), I was jolted to attention by a brilliant billboard hoisted above Airport Boulevard, its mere three words in huge, arresting red letters: KEEP HOPE ALIVE.

In the months, and now years, that I have from time to time recalled it, the billboard has grown in size until now it seems to fill all the open sky above the city. I wonder sometimes whether the sign was actually there—or only in my dreams. Whether reality or fantasy, that sign has obsessed me for about five years now. And after all this wondering, I am convinced that our society today is divided more deeply between those who have hope and those who have lost hope. And I am convinced that the supreme challenge of any society so divided is to enable the hopeless to hope again.

In this workshop, we have made a small beginning in finding a new way to address the human family's ancient burden—the constant threat of estrangement between people who belong together. Now we should consider whether the study of forgiveness should be complemented by a study of hope—and how to bring hope to the hopeless.

Editor's Note: The second conference in the Laws of Life Symposia Series, *"Optimism & Hope," was held in Philadelphia on February 10, 1998. The presentations will be rewritten and collected as chapters for the second volume of this book series, which is scheduled for publication in the spring of 1999.*

REFERENCES

Arendt, H. (1969). *The human condition.* Chicago: University of Chicago Press.

Baumeister, R.F., Exline, J.J., & Sommer, K.L. (1998). The victim role, grudge theory, and two dimensions of forgiveness. In E.L. Worthington, Jr. (Ed.), *Dimensions of forgiveness: Psychological research & theological perspectives* (pp.79–104). Philadelphia, PA: Templeton Foundation Press.

Dorff, E.N. (1998). The elements of forgiveness: A Jewish approach. In E.L. Worthington, Jr. (Ed.), *Dimensions of forgiveness: Psychological research & theological perspectives* (pp.29–55). Philadelphia, PA: Templeton Foundation Press.

Marty, M.E. (1998). The ethos of Christian forgiveness. In E.L. Worthington, Jr. (Ed.), *Dimensions of forgiveness: Psychological research & theological perspectives* (pp. 9–28). Philadelphia, PA: Templeton Foundation Press.

Shriver, D. (1995). *An ethics for enemies.* New York: Oxford University Press.

Tillich, P. (1963). *Systematic theology.* Chicago: Harper and Row.

Contributors

Roy F. Baumeister, Ph.D.
Elsie Smith Professor in the Liberal Arts, Case Western Reserve
University, Cleveland, Ohio

Catherine T. Coyle, Ph.D.
Researcher, Department of Educational Psychology, University of
Wisconsin–Madison

Elliot N. Dorff, Rabbi, Ph.D.
Rector and Professor of Philosophy, University of Judaism,
Los Angeles, California

Robert D. Enright, Ph.D.
Professor, Department of Educational Psychology, University of
Wisconsin–Madison

Julie Juola Exline, Ph.D.
Postdoctoral Research Associate, Case Western Reserve University,
Cleveland, Ohio, & National Institute for Healthcare Research,
Rockville, Maryland

Alex H.S. Harris, Ph.D. Candidate
Psychological Studies, Counseling Psychology, School of Education,
Stanford University, Stanford, California

Frederic Luskin, Ph.D.
Postdoctoral Fellow, Stanford Center for Research on Disease Prevention, School of Medicine, Stanford University, Stanford, California

Martin E. Marty, Ph.D.
Director, The Public Religion Project, & Fairfax M. Cone Distinguished Service Professor Emeritus, The University of Chicago Divinity School, Chicago, Illinois

Michael E. McCullough, Ph.D.
Director of Research, National Institute for Healthcare Research, Rockville, Maryland

Kenneth I. Pargament, Ph.D.
Professor of Psychology, Bowling Green State University, Bowling Green, Ohio

Mark S. Rye, Ph.D.
Assistant Professor of Psychology, University of Dayton, Dayton, Ohio

Lewis B. Smedes, Ph.D.
Emeritus Professor of Christian Ethics, Fuller Theological Seminary, Pasadena, California

Kristin L. Sommer, Ph.D.
Assistant Professor of Psychology, Baruch College, The City University of New York, & Former Postdoctoral Fellow, Case Western Reserve University, Department of Psychology, Cleveland, Ohio

Carl E. Thoresen, Ph.D.
Professor of Education, Psychology, and Psychiatry/Behavioral Sciences, Stanford University, Stanford, California

Everett L. Worthington, Jr., Ph.D.
Professor of Psychology, Virginia Commonwealth University, & Director, Campaign for Forgiveness Research, Richmond, Virginia

Index